# TRANSFORMING MEN

**Social Policy and Social Theory Series**
David Marsland, Series Editor

*Transforming Men,* Geoff Dench

# TRANSFORMING MEN

## Changing Patterns of Dependency and Dominance in Gender Relations

**Geoff Dench**

Transaction Publishers
New Brunswick (U.S.A.) and London (U.K.)

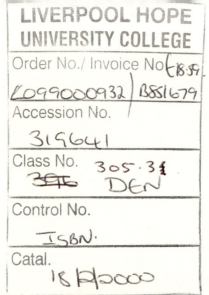
First paperback edition 1998
Copyright © 1996 by Transaction Publishers, New Brunswick, New Jersey
08903.

Library of Congress Catalog Number: 95-31409
ISBN: 1-56000-232-8 (cloth); 0-7658-0450-6 (paper)
Printed in the United States of America

Library of Congress Cataloging-in-Publication Data

Dench, Geoff.
    Transforming men : changing patterns of dependency and dominance
in gender relations / Geoff Dench.
        p.   cm. — (Social policy and social theory series)
    Includes bibliographical references and index.
    ISBN 1-56000-232-8 (cloth)  ✓
    1. Men. 2. Man-woman relationships. 3. Sex role. 4. Dependency
(Psychology) 5. Patriarchy. 6. Feminist theory. I. Title. II. Series
HQ1090.D45   1995
305.31—dc20                                                   95-31409
                                                                  CIP

*To Fan*

*whose support
made this possible*

# CONTENTS

# ACKNOWLEDGMENTS

I should record here that many facets of my thinking have been strongly influenced by George Gilder's book *Sexual Suicide*, from which I quote liberally in some chapters. That book was originally published in 1973 to warn the world about the implications of feminism, and it still has not had the full influence which it deserves, especially among academics. But times are changing fast, as they used to say. Now that, for example, the government in Denmark has had to resort to a mass advertising campaign to try to persuade men to take up the paternity leave for which a generation of feminists fought so strenuously, it begins to look as if even the much-vaunted Scandinavian model was just pious aspiration. The western world may now be ready for Gilder's message.

I am indebted to several friends and colleagues who have kindly spent time commenting on an earlier version of this book, which frequently ran strongly against the grain of their own sentiments. Not all of them would want to be mentioned here, but Kate Gavron has given me very generous help throughout the project, and I have had valuable suggestions and encouragement at various points from: Rushanara Ali, Sultana Begum, Connie Bogen, Laura Carboni, Peter Coggins, David Dewey, Mehmet Dikerdem, Lon Fleming, Julie Ford, Sharif Islam, Joanna Kennedy, Peter Loizos, David Morgan, Lena Moskalenko, Matthew Owen, Andrew Roberts, David Robins, Mike Walton, Tom Wengraf and Michael Young. More recently I have had generous help in securing publication from David Levy and Dennis O'Keeffe.

# INTRODUCTION

The broad aim of this book is to help improve our understanding of gender relations, and of their complexity, by exploring the idea that the raging sex war that has engulfed both our public and personal lives over the last few years should not be seen simply, or even mainly, as taking place between men and women. At another level, less publicly visible, it has been a struggle between different groups of *women* or, more accurately perhaps, between alternative *strategies for transforming men* into more caring partners and useful members of society.

Exploring this issue has important practical implications now that radical feminist ideas appear to be on the wane in those countries where they have exercised the greatest influence. The backlash against them currently underway is, I believe, strongly grounded in a growing appreciation by women themselves that the feminist strategy has had some unintended results, and may be contributing to many of the current social ills from which women are suffering no less than men. So reining back feminism is in reality good news for women and the community generally. But there is a danger that it will be defined as simply a reactive victory for men. This could trigger off unpleasant displays of male triumphalism, which would not lead to the constructive renegotiation of sexual contracts that our times require, but to ongoing bitterness. In the longer run, backlash is bound to be seen as a male reflex, because patriarchy regards society as a male creation. That may be unavoidable. It will however no longer be a matter for recriminations once gender relations have moved on and become eased by compromise, and the benefits for all become visible. It is in the immediate future where there is danger, and where a fuller appreciation of the complex interplay of agendas will be most valuable.

At the level of theory too it is important to look more closely at disagreements between women over gender strategies as it is probably through comparing the ideas of feminist and non-feminist women about men, and how to deal with them, that we can best determine just where we may have gone wrong lately. I myself believe that many feminists across the whole movement have made some extremely questionable assumptions about the nature of men and their place in society, and that this has weakened their broader analysis of social and economic systems, and reduced the force of their strategic decisions on how to transform them.

Before going any further, I should note that I do of course realize that the term feminism has been used to embrace a wide spectrum of approaches to improving women's lives and position in society. So in order to present a coherent argument here it is probably useful to narrow things down by indicating what I regard as the core themes marking out current feminism as a distinctive system of ideas. I would argue that the central plank in this is the proposition that women are so fundamentally disempowered by patriarchal rules that to create a just society it is necessary to do away with all of the formal institutional advantages and privileges allowed to men, and the corresponding sexual divisions of labor, and replace them with strict gender equality.

According to this definition, the current "babe" and "power" feminisms associated with names like Camille Paglia and Naomi Wolf, plus the pro-family "revisionist" arguments offered since the early eighties by the likes of Betty Friedan, Alice Rossi, Sylvia Ann Hewlett and some but by no means all of the output of Germaine Greer in her second incarnation, are not really feminist viewpoints at all. They recognize that within and behind traditional sexual divisions of labor there have been opportunities for women to exercise power, both individually through their sexuality and collectively through their influence on the morality regulating interpersonal relations and private life. To varying degrees they see women's best chances of improving their lot, in a fast-changing world, as lying in the *reform* or *refinement* of patriarchy - which some of them do explicitly acknowledge to be more of a prescriptive notion, putting pressure on men to recognize their social responsibilities, than a concrete description of how societies operate.

The term feminism is best restricted, as its champions like Susan Faludi would surely agree, to those positions towards the other end of the spectrum which reject as outmoded any conventional distinctions between public and private realms, and which advocate the use of state power (and direct state support for women) to promote the independence of women from individual partnerships with men, at least until New Men have emerged who are willing to share social roles equally with women right across the board. Feminism in this full-blooded sense, which was strongly influenced at its inception by a link with sixties Marxism (although it has tried to distance itself subsequently), allows no truck with ideas that women have access to power not available to men, and sees women as inevitably disadvantaged in all corners of social life until substantive equality has been demonstrably achieved.

It is this model of gender relations that I challenge here. Many of its defects have been evident to non-feminists all along; not least among its basic assumptions and propositions. Thus, as Michael Levin reminds us (in *Feminism and freedom,* 1987, p. 7) there are serious initial questions being begged by a doctrine that asserts dogmatically that women are socially disadvantaged while, on all of the main indices by which black Americans have been conventionally adjudged to lead less satisfying lives than whites (i.e., physical and mental health, longevity, crime, drug abuse and alcoholism ), men in both communities are substantially worse off than women. Feminists need to come clean on whether sauce for the goose really is sauce for the gander.

But beyond these original follies modern feminism, now that it is twenty-five years into its own ameliorative program of action to transform men and society, is at last being confronted with evidence, in the ways that society is now moving, that even within its own terms of reference it may be failing to achieve its desired goals and possibly even pulling in the wrong direction. The changes taking place in men's behavior are not what we were led to expect. There are far fewer New Men emerging than should be the case by now, if the concept is viable. (And many of these may be knights in disguise.) Nor can this be answered by arguing that men are resisting change because even now, when backlash is well established, the number of men angrily demanding the restoration of male roles or privileges is pitifully small.

What we *do* have in the West though are growing armies of men who are increasingly apathetic towards society, and who are retreating into private pleasures and anomic fantasies, often at considerable cost to the rest of us. They are neither reconstructed men, nor are they fighting as a gender elite to cling on to valued social positions. To non-feminists they appear suspiciously marginal in relation to society, and to have a negligible stake in the social order, with little or no incentive to obey social rules. It is their existence which feminism cannot convincingly explain now, and failed to anticipate - and so may well have unwittingly helped to cause - and which indicates that feminism itself is suffering from a bad case of theory fatigue.

## Facing up to the problem of men

There are a number of signs of incipient awareness that feminist approaches do not understand men and as a result are not delivering the promised goods. When I was writing this book, the idea of the New Man was enjoying a fresh lease on life in the UK, as the continuing recession cut deeper into women's job prospects, and stretched the welfare net underpinning them. It was becoming clear that unless men were prepared to share equally in both paid and family work, as committed and caring partners, then the objectives sought by many feminists could so easily slip away or prove illusory. And rapidly, too. The days when male prevarication could be treated with patience were gone; and several publications at the time, such as Patricia Hewitt's *About Time* and Harriet Harman's *Century Gap,* betrayed a new sense of urgency, chiding men (Hewitt) for their leisurely attitudes to change, threatening them (Harman) with the prospect of becoming beached by the tide of history.

But it was not going to happen. If it had, it would have done so a long time before then. The tone of urgency, even panic, which was creeping into feminist commentaries indicated an emerging awareness of this - though not yet an understanding of why it should be. The heightened eagerness among feminist journalists to blame everything that went wrong on male recalcitrance suggested that a debate on the failure of men to reconstruct themselves was brewing, and morale was being stoked up. The message came over clearly in dozens of articles by Polly Toynbee, Suzanne Moore, Germaine Greer and a host of others. Women's lives were no better than they ever were, and in many ways were worse. And it was men's fault for refusing to change.

The battle that appeared to be looming has not materialized though; and perhaps the noises then were just a last attempt at directly challenging men into change before a different approach was tried. But more to the point, perhaps, is that this issue has been overtaken by new worries about men which pose further difficulties for feminist theory. There are still occasional attempts to talk up New Man, as in the recent *Demos* report on feminism and the future (Siann and Wilkinson, 1995). But the main focus has shifted towards concern about the declining performance of men within their traditional domains, and more recently the media have been orchestrating a crescendo of anxiety over men's poor response to social changes occurring during the last twenty years. Educationalists ponder the collapsing morale of boys in school systems, in which girls are out-performing them in all subjects. Labor market analysts investigate trends which have displaced men from former occupational strongholds and allowed women to overtake them in many areas of work.

In spite of this new-found concern for men there is however a prudish reluctance to consider the possible role of the feminist experiment and its culture of female independence in promoting and aggravating these problems, as for example through taking away from men compelling reasons to consider seeking work that is not intrinsically interesting or of high status. This comment is perhaps less true of the emerging and vigorous public debate in Australia. But certainly in the UK explanations of men's declining public contribution are still couched almost wholly in terms of the interplay of impersonal economic forces; attempts to inject the factor of feminism into the model are seen as outrageous and deliberately provocative.

Accordingly there is still a strong feminist bias in discussions of *solutions* to the alienation of men. The principal burden is put onto the public realm and economy, where it is seen as a self-evident duty of government to provide more employment to eradicate male joblessness - though not, of course, at the cost of jobs for women. At the social and cultural level hardly any attention is given to the need to increase men's incentives to take work seriously, and a heavy emphasis is put instead on smothering them with sympathy and counselling them in order to improve their capacity to communicate their feelings and develop self-respect, *etc.* This may be done indirectly in the hope of transforming men into better domestic helpers. If this is the aim then it seems unlikely to be effective, as I will argue here and there; and if it is done to get men working again then it is certainly not constructive. Sending men who have lost access to valued and respected roles in the community along to counselling is about as helpful as telling Little

Red Riding Hood, alone in the forest and scared, to run on home to grandma. Danger lies that way too. I argue that what men need is demands on them and responsibilities to make them grow up, not the offer of eternal childhood.

So although there is increasing consciousness that men are not behaving as they should, there is remarkably little serious analysis taking place on the real nature of the problem. I cannot see that this will prove possible within the confines of current feminist discourse.

*Building an alternative model*
The general feeling which led me into writing this book is that if contemporary feminism has served women badly, as does now seem likely, then this may be because it has, in its rush for easy answers, discarded too readily the hard-won understanding of men embodied within "traditional" women's culture. If men had behaved as feminists have asked or expected, then certainly we would be living by now in a far better world. That I cannot deny. But it is not happening; and it is too simple just to see this as a failure by men. It is more to the point to ask why modern feminists should suppose that they, alone among womankind, should have suddenly lighted on how to get men to be more attentive and responsive. It is not, after all, as if men made any offers or promises. Surely it is somewhat arrogant to dismiss so quickly and comprehensively the strategies developed by previous generations for dealing with us. Men are, I suspect, always a problem, and the mistake made recently lies in the abandonment of accumulated experience about this and opting instead for a blanket assault on "patriarchy."

It is of course not possible to devise a detailed alternative model to feminism, incorporating pre-feminist ideas, at a stroke. Because so much recent research in the areas of family and gender relations has been informed by statist feminist concerns, most of the directly available evidence is organized in a way that does not readily allow those interests to be questioned. There is now a very great need for new research that systematically asks different questions; but we cannot wait until this is done before starting to build new models. There is something to be said for mapping out an area superficially before digging too deep. So my discussion is deliberately tentative and wide-ranging and touches only lightly on many important topics. Its emphasis is on clarifying where it may be most valuable to focus further thought and investigation, rather than on marshalling all existing information to execute conclusive demonstrations, though I must confess that this has not prevented me from forming and expressing firm opinions on many issues.

Condensing the argument in this way also allows me to adopt the device of hanging the main presentation onto a fairy tale. When treated as allegories on social relations such stories can hold several advantages over traditional sociology. In particular, narrative metaphors can generate a variety of different and indeed competing interpretations of events and relationships - which is precisely what most sociological theory seems to want to prohibit. It is, I would suggest, the heightened awareness of ambiguity and of different levels of meaning or action that myths and fairy tales permit, and the availability of alternative but interlocking and compatible readings that this provides, which can make them superior tools for understanding actual social arrangements and behavior and for sorting out what may be "real" from what is more superficial or merely a matter of appearances. Allegories should not be pursued too far, of course. But they do help to unlock creative thought by making complex connections very quickly, to find routes around ideological defenses, and to push debate into previously neglected terrain.

More specifically, I believe that adopting a fairy tale as framework for the discussion can bring us closer to traditional women's perspectives, which must be the logical starting point in any search for viable ways of treating the problem of men. Folk tales have been disproportionately influenced by women's concerns and definitions, and have provided vehicles for the communication of female wisdom down the generations in forms that do not explicitly contradict and challenge formal and dignified patriarchal conventions. They offer windows through orthodoxy onto real life, which then sharpen awareness of the gap between social roles and aspirations and actual human performance. Women have sustained them over millennia, and have through them imparted to children - boys as well as girls - in an earthy and often satirical way, but at the same time restrained and tolerant, a valuable sense of the possible.

Alongside, promoting healthy scepticism towards official dogma, folktales have an anti-elitist dimension, and convey a picture of society from the bottom upwards. It is emperors, not humble folk, who get stripped of their finery and artificial dignity, the inflated who get cut down to size. This facility is important in the gender arena, as modern feminist ideas often seem far less in touch with working-class lives and sentiments than with middle-class ambitions. It is their inability to comprehend working-class men in particular, and the salience of sexual divisions of labor in the successful operation of ordinary family life, which has I think allowed feminists to contribute with such clear consciences to that dismantling and impoverishment of working-class families and communities that underlies the current polarization of rich and poor. Fairy tales express and protect valuable perspectives which have lately been scorned and ignored by academic expertise.

In this instance I use the story of *The Frog Prince* as the vehicle to illuminate what I regard as a popular and still-just-about-surviving European post-chivalric tradition of gender relations and "managing men." This simple tale displays a fine recognition of the divided and ambivalent character of male identity and consciousness. And compared with most feminist accounts and academic theorizing influenced by them, it offers a sensitive instrument for comprehending male behavior. I agree with Alison Lurie (1990) that fairy tales like this are marvelous sources of insight for children about the social worlds that people actually inhabit, as opposed to those conjured up by didactic moralists, and would guess that this tale in particular has provided a subtle and realistic reference point that has helped many generations of girls and boys to learn mutual tolerance and respect.

There are superficial similarities between this story and that of *Iron John* which Robert Bly uses to launch his analysis of the condition of modern men. But that tale does not contain nearly so many resonances, is less accessible as an allegory, and is not really part of enduring popular culture in the way that *The Frog Prince* most certainly is.

I will not claim that my exposition of this story is at all original. I think that the basic reading is essentially implicit, and also that I may well have come across interpretations along the same lines as this elsewhere. But I cannot recall where; and there is no harm in repeating the exercise, for it is bound to be different in many details, and the general point needs as much reiteration as it can get at the moment.

## *Lessons from the past*

My own reaction on re-reading the old fairy tales was to realize just how much feminism has done to denigrate and drive further below the surface the consciousness, which is still powerful in non-Western cultures, that women may be closer to the heart of society than men are, and have hidden strengths within it of which men remain only partly aware. Running through many a fairy tale, whatever the story line, is a confident subtext that whoever may look and think that he is playing an important part, it is women who exercise the underlying powers and who usually ensure that social purposes are achieved or moralities upheld.

These themes are closely linked to a prioritizing of the private realm of interpersonal relations. In the story I draw on here, the prince can only realize his royal identity, and indeed achieve humanity at all, when taught some manners and accepted by the princess as her partner/friend. This is a message that we urgently need to pay attention to in the West today, before we are totally overrun by a plague of unredeemed frogs. Convinced feminists will of course discern in my endorsement of these tales yet another attempt to hoodwink women into thinking that the public realm is not where the real action, from which women are always being excluded, is at. But I don't believe that the folktales were imposed by men on women, or even developed by women just to distract or compensate themselves for their exclusion from more important matters. Also I do feel, the more that I examine the proposition, that the notion of society being a mainly female entity and even invention has much to commend it.

In this book I develop this idea by suggesting that the core institutions of society may be predominantly female in their orientation, because they arise out of any community's need to organize reproduction effectively. The activities that are most essential to the survival of a community and require most careful regulation are those that cluster around the care of children. In all societies these are overwhelmingly performed by women, and are tied culturally to the institution of motherhood. It is not too fanciful I think to hypothesize that shared motherhood is the basis of all human society. Women are the ones who bear children and so can most rationally be given main responsibility for them. This then renders them more sensitive to the needs of others and to the value of reciprocity and ideas of common interest, because their experience (or expectation) of motherhood makes them more aware of their own need for support themselves. Society is exchange, and agreement between women to help each other (provided that each accepts primary responsibility for her own offspring) could well be the original social contract.

Being central to society in this way has its drawbacks - and their greater dependence on others means that women can be more thoroughly constrained and bound by social rules, and will enjoy less personal freedom than men. Feminism has seized on this as a major injustice, for which patriarchy is roundly blamed. I find this less than convincing. No one could seriously deny that men do possess more freedom than women, and that this may allow them greater power in their personal relationships with women. But this is hardly likely to be due to patriarchy, which in most situations serves to moderate, rather than increase, differences in men's and women's lives, by extending to men the sort of social responsibilities that are hostile to individual freedom and generally bringing men into social roles like those of women.

Nor is it so obvious as to be beyond dispute that the demands of motherhood constitute such a terrible injustice. Motherhood and its attendant restraints may not, on balance, be a great *handicap* for women, because the freedoms that men enjoy are not an unmixed blessing. As shown amongst others by Durkheim, most explicitly in his analysis of the patterns of suicide, single men not shackled by patriarchal obligations to dependents tend to lead shorter and nastier lives, with higher rates of brutishness on whatever measures you care to choose. For the experience, which they lack, of being personally responsible for others is powerfully life-enhancing. It promotes self-respect, reduces brooding and introspection, and helps one to become a caring and productive member of the community, alive to the needs of others and so allowed a legitimate voice in discussions of group morality. Feminists like to trivialize motherhood and portray it as outside mainstream society. But most men see mothers and indeed women generally as in fact central to it; and "traditional" cultures pick this up and reassure women of their value and importance.

It is the civilizing influence on men of personalized responsibilities for women and children, which feminism, in the name of gender equality and social progress, has done such a great job of disrupting over the past twenty-five years. The outcome has surely been to liberate not women but men, so that now they are gravitating back nearer to the margins of society from which countless previous generations of women struggled so hard to claim them. The growing numbers of de-motivated, under-socialized and barely employable young men who figure prominently in so many of our current social problems are arguably the children of radical feminist dogma.

## The rise of radical woman

How can we have let this all happen? The answer which I offer to that question throughout the book is that this is due principally to a weakening of traditional female cultures and, above all, of the authority of older women. Modern feminists like to regard themselves as independent of men, and this is clearly an important aspect of the situation. But it is in some ways only secondary. The true guardians of patriarchal morality, who uphold the prioritizing of male rights and responsibility because they understand the value of these to women in socializing men and making them more manageable, are older women with personal experience of seeing boys turn into men, who have witnessed at firsthand the gulf between public representations of men and what the real flesh and blood is like, and who are able - perhaps assisted in this by their long familiarity with women's folklore - to interpret the interplay between these divergent and different-level phenomena. It is the declining influence of this group, and the independence of young women from *them*, which more than anything has allowed ungrounded theories about gender relations to gain such currency.

Reconstructing how this came to pass is not difficult. It is young women who, in virtually all cultures, are required to make the greatest personal sacrifices and investments in order to give men a valued place in family and community activities. For when they are at the height of their sexual power and are most desirable as partners, they are expected to make long-term commitments to and express their dependence on men who may well have far less grasp of what life is about than they do themselves, and who may moreover take them away from the family in which they already have their own place. In life many a princess is given to a frog. So it may need all of the persuasive skills of older women, and perhaps some arm-twisting as well, to get a girl to accept that she cannot expect equal freedom or rights to a man's, and that it is good for the community, and in the end for herself, to go along with it all. Slogans declaring that "It's a man's world" can be used by older women to strengthen their hand and deflect hostility by conveying gender solidarity with the young. But in the end it is I believe the judgment and personal authority of these older women that has operated and sustained the patriarchal system.

Female cultures of this sort started to receive unprecedented jolts in the sixties when accelerating medical and demographic changes came to a head. By giving young women individual control over their fertility, modern contraceptive methods reduced drastically the sharpness and immediacy of their personal dependence on their mothers and other older women. Sixties girls liberated by the pill traded in the Brothers Grimm for Karl Marx and de Beauvoir, and discovered from them that the only power that counted was control of the market and state, and that patriarchy was cheating women out of their rightful share. They dismissed old wives' tales as myths, preferring to swallow the illusions fostered by patriarchy itself.

The pill has arguably done more than anything to devalue the moral economy of interpersonal concern and support between women which is at the heart of social life, and this I think explains why moralists are so unremittingly hostile to it. Greater individual control over fertility also paved the way for women to enter the public realm on a more competitive basis with men, and this has enabled the liberation movement to define itself around the image of personal autonomy in relation to *men*. But I believe that the more fundamental liberation has been that from the constraints of the female community.

The knock-on effects of all this have been tremendous. Throughout the late sixties and most of the seventies there was a period of enormous excitement and conflict as new relationships were tried out, new ideologies patched together in which the "community" in a generalized sense was elevated at the expense of interpersonal ties and reciprocal help, and new policies for collectivized support of mothers and children were drafted. This has transformed the political economies of the West, bringing about a redefinition of *radicalism* as standing for equal opportunities and universalized provision for women and children by the state, and for a general incorporation of the private realm into the public, and on the other hand of *conservatism* as indicating patriarchy, families and the traditional sexual division of labor, and particularistic providing.

When it came to combining the management of children with commitment to paid jobs, some feminists quickly and often quietly dropped or postponed insistence on comparable individual freedom to that of men, and have even paid tributes to certain forms of family. But there remains a strong tension between the values around which pre-feminist families were organized - that is reciprocity, personalized obligations, loyalty and above all a division of labor and interdependence between young and old, male and female - and the strategy of securing women's basic rights through citizenship and legally backed formal gender equality in the public realm. It is this universalized public strategy that is now dominant and largely determines how families are defined and understood, what research is acceptable - not to mention prioritized and funded - and how public policies are framed. There was a certain black humor in 1994 to an *International Year of the Family* which was celebrated in Brussels by re-defining "family" to make men optional, and in London by declaring a "take-a-daughter-to-work-day" to familiarize girls more with the public realm. Future historians will enjoy the joke. But for us here now it is time for some hard thinking, and maybe some difficult decisions.

## The nature of backlash

My feeling while writing most of this book was that as women grew older and took on senior family roles, even the feminists among them would become more attuned to the logic of family interdependence and reciprocity, and many would return, disillusioned with statism, to their traditional folds.

This would not be so much, as Michael Levin supposed, because when confronted with a choice between domestic harmony with their partners and competition with them at work, they would opt for the former. That plays a part. But it would I thought be more a matter that as *mothers* of grown-up children they would prefer to see their sons active and making decent contributions to families, and have their daughters getting support from male providers, rather than finding that they have adult sons who are idle and self-possessed - and perhaps the absent fathers of children who barely know their grandparents - while their daughters slaved away in both social realms. Generation experience is very pertinent to these life-style choices I think, and patriarchy is a system that may well have been largely devised and promoted by primordial matriarchs in order to even out the burdens on their children. So as the Queen becomes confronted with the consequences of what has been done in the name of liberating women, she will not be amused.

A year further on I acknowledge that this prognosis was not entirely correct. There is indeed an emerging disquiet about feminism, and a growing willingness among women to express "conservative" opposition to it. But it is not only among older mothers. Quite a lot of young women, and older women without children of their own, seem very concerned too; and perhaps I underestimated the tendency of young women to rebel against their mothers (in this instance feminist ones) and of a mood to spread among women generally, not just within sectors of specific experience.

What I still see little reason to modify though is my view that backlash is not primarily a male phenomenon. I accept that there are now more men noticeably making a fuss and noise about family values, and good ol' religion. In the United States the National Coalition of Free Men and movements like Promise Keepers have increased their activities. In the United Kingdom associations like the Cheltenham Group have started to plough a similar furrow. However I would argue that these movements are mainly oriented towards specific issues of child support and custody where men have been caught out, and often penalized materially, as a result of changing public policies. They derive their energy from the sense of grievance at being exposed to mixed messages from women and state policies, and too many contradictory cues, rather than from an autonomous morality generated by men themselves.

For men are primed in all cultures to be responsive to women's needs and wishes, and to the values espoused by women. Feminism has confused this impulse considerably by introducing the notion that women would prefer to do for themselves many of the things which men were traditionally expected to do for them; and a half-hearted New Chivalry has consequently tried to articulate around the paradoxical project of helping women to be more independent of men. But now that non-feminist women are re-grouping, and providing moral support again for traditional male roles, men are perhaps even more bewildered as they find themselves frequently caught in the cross fire. It is almost impossible at the moment for men to be sure "what women want"; and this makes some of them angry.

But the main response among men to these contradictory directives has been to opt out into a narcissistic apathy. I suspect that insofar as a conservative reaction is emerging that this is in response to the re-awakening of traditional women, from whom men can derive a sense of legitimacy and purpose, and for whom they can see themselves as serving in a traditional sense as public-realm gladiators and agents. I am not convinced that more than a few of these men are operating on their own initiatives and values - though it is of course in the nature of the case extremely difficult to collect reliable evidence on this.

It is anyway now surely time for sociologists to develop new gender models that take better account of the homeostatic mechanisms available within the female community for protecting patriarchy, which are now being activated. Public opinion is moving towards recognizing that men and women do not after all inhabit the same social worlds and that if substantive equality is pursued too far, at the expense of broader equity within a more pluralist system, then it may become increasingly difficult for society to accommodate men and to harness their energies to useful purposes. For it is their role in society which is the more tenuous and problematic.

Our grandparents knew this perfectly well; and perhaps our parents still do. *Viva* Barbara Cartland. But most of us in the West seem to have forgotten it, in particular among those classes whose ideas have been most influential during the last generation. Our collective ability to understand and manage men has diminished accordingly. A vital and complex part of our culture is unravelling. But the fairy story analyzed here has not lost its inherent potency as an allegory on the importance of finding a place for men in society through their domestic provider roles, and the moment for its revival has arrived. Its interpretation does, I suspect, have a much firmer grip on the harsh realities of life than does the equal opportunities agenda. Feminists enjoy referring to traditional families as "happy families," meaning (you've got it) that very often they are not. But their own elevated visions about new men who share this and that seem to me to be kept aloft by even bigger puffs of fantasy and romanticization, not to mention energetic moral exhortation.

I am sometimes angrily accused of wanting to push women back into the kitchen. A quick perusal of chapter ten will show that this is not the case. But the real absurdity of these accusations is that anyone can suppose that more than a very few women have really escaped from domesticity anyway. Most now, as before, combine it with paid work - and are likely to go on doing so. The crucial issue is how to maximize support for them in this. That is where the options lie, and where lately we have been taken up the blind alley of state provision. In a few years time, when it has all come down to earth with a bump, statist feminism may be remembered chiefly as an ideology which simply failed to understand how to manage men. The real fairy story will turn out to be its idea that women's lot can be improved through movement towards explicit gender equality.

# 1

# THE PROBLEM OF MEN

## THE ROOT OF THE PROBLEM

*If men bore children, there would be no disguising the otherwise dubious fact that bearing a child is as much a public duty as the bearing of arms in defence of the country.* (Germaine Greer. 1993)

*There is nothing in the fact that women have the capacity to bear children which dictates that they should have children and care for them exclusively throughout childhood, still less does it imply that women, with or without children, should also feed, clean for and service men.* (Helen Peace. 1993, p. 40)

There is a rather tiresome cliché firmly embedded in popular feminist discourse which holds that if it were men who bore children then everything would be so different. Men would change their priorities. They would pull their weight in domestic chores. They would be more responsive and communicative, and take off their muddy boots at the door. Buses would run on time, and so on. It is a template which has given form and force to a thousand punch lines.

The formulation has great practical appeal because we all know exactly what it means, and could not possibly disagree with it. But in spite of this it is definitely tiresome. This is partly, I think, because it has a way of closing an argument prematurely; and in a way unfairly, because although we all must give it our assent, the way in which the idea is expressed offends against logic. The proposition in itself is foolish. If men did have the children then they wouldn't *be* men, in the sense that the rest of the expression requires. And what would women be, and be doing? It is all a bit like the games young children love to play in which we all have to say "no" for "yes" and "yes" for "no," or "left" means "right." As a contribution to a serious discussion on gender it is about as intellectually satisfying as the old schoolboy howler of suggesting that the moon is more important than the sun because it gives us light when we really need it. A little while after being offered such a cliché we are liable to feel cheated.

A second reason why this kind of expression is irritating is that it is frequently used to imply a whole lot more than it actually says - mainly along the line that if men had an ounce of decency in them they would choose to become like women are, through an act of will, even though they don't have the babies. At one level the speaker is half excusing men for being so crass; but at another level she is challenging them to outsmart their destiny, and to prove to a sceptical female observer that there is some moral fiber in them. A *real* man would surely do this or be like that *anyway*, in spite of being a man. But little of this meaning is made open and explicit; and so the expression leaves men with a distasteful sensation of having been manipulated into letting the women, yet again, have things both ways.

But the major reason why it is tiresome, and which is perhaps a corollary of the second, is that when it comes down to it most feminists are *not* willing to accept that the bearing or not bearing of children is relevant to the roles a person can expect or should be expected to play in society. They are happy to borrow the rhetorical device from pre-feminist culture, where it had some purchase, and to enjoy a certain amount of non-feminist approval when they use it. But they do it in a different spirit; and although the notion is useful to them precisely because no one can disagree with it, *they* don't really believe it themselves. Most of them are more than willing to heap scorn and abuse on anyone who brings into proper theoretical and strategic debates any notion that being the ones who bear the children or not makes any difference. Such "essentialism" is held to reveal a serious ignorance of the importance of social constructions in shaping behavior.

## Child rearing and society

This reluctance to accept the implications of childbearing is part of a wider refusal to countenance any factors with a biological basis or reference, which might put some aspect of gender relations beyond the scope of social engineering. This is what the concept of essentialism is really about. At a strategic level this is perhaps understandable. But if prior tactical considerations are allowed to limit the range of theoretical enquiries then analysis will be led by definitions of desirable outcomes, rather than interacting with these.

This is harmful to both theory and practice, and in the case of feminism is I believe a crippling handicap. For there do seem to be some non-social factors involved which are crucially important in limiting what is achievable. Strategies which deliberately screen these out are bound to be counterproductive, and probably quite damaging to women's own interests. I am not concerned here with sex-linked inborn temperament or characteristics. These may well exist, and be important. But they are outside of my own scope. Nor do they *need* to exist for my argument to hold up. For I believe that the simple fact (which is, of course, extremely complicated once you start looking at it) that women have children while men don't has more than enough immediate social consequences to render sexual equality a chimera and a delusion.

The most potent of these factors, for the purposes of my argument here at any rate, is that childbearing is universally related to the allocation by society of primary responsibility for the care of children, with men only brought into it via women. The motherhood thing. This is itself disputed by some feminists; and I will come back to it again in a later chapter, as indeed I will to all of the points sketched out in this introduction. But assuming for the moment that it is accepted that all societies have found building on the biological fact of motherhood to be the most effective and reliable strategy for ensuring that children get cared for - not, mind you, on the basis of "exclusive care" by mothers; that is just a paper tiger - then I think that a number of extremely far-reaching implications clearly arise for the relative social positions of men and women.

For the care of children must be the most fundamental and compelling stimulant to the evolution and maintenance of society itself. It is so absolutely crucial to community survival that the different ways in which groups contrive to do things will almost by definition be very quickly punished or rewarded. Where the young of a species require extended nurturing then this will obviously necessitate long-term bonding between generations; and the mother-child relationship in particular has often been portrayed, in the past admittedly more than at present, as the foundation on which all social structures ultimately are built.

In my opinion this case can be overstated. A mother and her children cannot, by themselves, be regarded as constituting society. What I think is more important for understanding the genesis of social institutions is surely that, given the very demanding nature of child care, mechanisms need to be invented for *supporting* mothers, with help both from male sexual partners and from other, experienced mothers. Without such help it would be extremely difficult for women to get through the most arduous or dangerous periods of producing and rearing children. If some help can be mobilized there are collective bonuses which follow. For when an exchange or pooling of child care takes place the labor of several mothers can be freed for valuable activities which are not easily carried out when there are children around. Rudimentary society is less likely to have been built just on lone motherhood, than on the arrangements women have made to maximize support for themselves in child rearing.

What is significant here is that this is a matter of relationships not just between an adult or adults and children, but *between adults,* in collaboration and mutual assistance. And it involves longer-term and larger associations. This in turn sets the scene for the establishment of a range of social arrangements for organizing exchanges of services more generally between members of groups, and for the emergence of self-conscious "communities" embracing and transcending their individual or even familial interests.

It cannot be emphasized too strongly, because it is now so often overlooked, that a woman's participation in such basic community structures and affairs is bound to be on a very different footing than a man's. As actual or prospective mothers, women cannot easily avoid being drawn into the network of exchanges within a community, or fail early in their lives to become aware of the "moral economy" - the system and rules of reciprocity underlying this network. They know that they will themselves need help at many points in looking after their offspring; and so it is important for them to learn to be responsive to the needs of others in return. A framework of personalized obligations to provide some care for the weak and vulnerable - the old as well as infants, and utilizing delayed as well as immediate exchanges - is more certain to prove binding on women, because they are the ones who know that they will need to draw on it for themselves, or who have done so in the past and now can be made to repay it. Reciprocity is an elaboration of self-interest.

## Marginal men

Life is just not like that for males. While young, and still thoroughly dependent on others for help in meeting their minimal survival needs, they clearly benefit from membership of a community and have every incentive to follow its rules. But as they grow older the arguments for yielding to group control become less direct and compelling. Girls have a very good reason for doing so. But as a boy reaches an age where he is able to develop some skill in satisfying his basic material needs, he is in a much better position than a girl to pursue self-sufficiency, and to grasp some freedom even if this may call for sacrifices in terms of his level of physical comfort. It is the availability of this option, surely, which makes men rather less responsive to the needs of others. Men are more likely to be able to manage by themselves; and if in the process of doing this they drift off and come to harm it is less damaging to the community. In their social relations they are correspondingly more inclined to look for short-term personal advantages, to drive hard bargains to maximize their rewards, and are less prepared to accept responsibility for the well-being of others. They can live much more for themselves.

Women rightly regard such attitudes and behavior as egocentric. But to be understood properly it does need to be seen in its context. The fundamental conditions of men's existence which allow them opportunities to remain selfish simply have not been enjoyed by women, until recently at any rate. It is not really a matter of moral choice, in which men are failing to take appropriate action. Women have formed the backbones of caring communities throughout history, but not because they were virtuous. It is the other way around. Women have been virtuous because their own needs have made it more in their own interests to attach less importance to personal freedom, and to give greater value than men to mutual support and security; and these values are defined *as* virtuous because they are more conducive to collective well-being.

This is the point of origin of the problem of men. They don't have the babies, and in normal circumstances cannot be assigned primary responsibility for them. Consequently they are not so easily drawn into the exchanges of community life, where they can learn to be nicer people. The outcome of this is a problem for women rather than for men themselves, who are by and large unaware of it, and amongst whom few would care much anyway. Between men a lack of personal responsiveness does not usually matter greatly, as relationships tend to be fairly shallow and undemanding, are often based on explicit and limited expectations, and are oriented to external goals or situations so that there is no need to practice empathy to maintain them. But for women, attuned from childhood to long-term and finely balanced give-and-take (in which it is important to have a clear sense of the current standing of one's moral account with other people in order not to give offense by relating in the wrong manner) men's offhand behavior frequently comes over as an exercise of brute male power. Men's willingness to give less than they receive, or apparent lack of interest in developing a rounder and fuller relationship, or failure to express care and commitment, and their general adoption of a take-it-or-leave-it attitude, may be experienced by women as contemptuous and hurtful. In the words of another, more trenchant cliché, men are bastards.

## DOMESTICATING MEN

*In every known human society, everywhere in the world, the young male learns that when he grows up, one of the things which he must do in order to be a full member of society is to provide food for some female and her young. Even in very simple societies, a few men may shy away from the responsibility, become tramps or ne'er-do-wells or misanthropists who live in the woods by themselves. In complex societies, a large number of men may escape the burden of feeding females and young by entering monasteries - and feeding each other - or by entering some profession that their society will classify as giving them a right to be fed, like the Army and the Navy, or the Buddhist orders of*

> *Burma. But in spite of such exceptions, every known human*
> *society rests firmly on the learned nurturing behaviour of*
> *men.* (Margaret Mead. 1949, p. 146)

The anti-social orientation of men is a burden for a community as a whole, not just for the women in it - although, of course, this phrasing is a little ingenuous because in many important respects women *are* the heart and soul of any community. If men are poorly motivated, they do not merely fail to make much input to the general cause but are liable to become a disruptive, or even dangerous element, which is a drain on collective patience and resources. Group integration suffers.

Hence it is imperative for any culture to look for ways of making men behave constructively. Ultimately what this comes down to is creating additional rewards for them. Communities always, and I believe inevitably, insist that women take primary responsibility for the care of their own children, and most of them want to do this anyway; because of which women always have a stronger disposition or even need to co-operate. Given the direct and compelling dependency of their children on them, mutual support is its own reward, as it helps to minimize their own effort and pain. The same is not true for men, who therefore need a little extra something to tempt them into relinquishing some of their freedom, and taking on a share of community work and obligations.

## Making men more like women

The vast majority of societies do this by defining men as providers for particular women and children - normally but not invariably their sexual partners and own offspring - and developing the notion that this makes men very valuable, because women could not manage without them. This is the genesis of the "breadwinner and head of family" role, which is the core element in all ideas about patriarchy.

Many feminists have vigorously contested the idea that this type of role is given to men in all societies. Their main objections are that not all societies do operate with a breadwinner or equivalent role, or that in many cases where they do, the role is a sham and men in reality contribute very little. I will look at these questions later on. But to give a short answer to them now I would reply firstly that where a culture attaches value to such a role, with the result that men receive extra rewards and do become motivated into more positive attitudes and behavior, then it is irrelevant whether or not external analysts consider them to be worthy of it. Secondly, the fact that a few societies do not exhort men to be providers or attach bonuses to this does not mean that this is a good idea. Groups make mistakes. In fact it is quite easy to show that the few societies which are out of step make quite a hash of things as a result. What the feminists omit to mention is that the exceptions to the norm illuminate very clearly the reason why the norm exists.

It is, I think, very easy to understand why this role should be so important in human society, and effectively universal. What it does is formally to incorporate men into the interpersonal support structures, the chains of dependency, which lie at the core of any human society. It domesticates them, by making them subject to the same types of pressure as experienced by women. Believing that the welfare of particular other people depends on you - and in some ways or to some extent on you alone - is a great spur to altruistic feelings and socially responsible behavior. It is the basis of a mother's devotion; and through the breadwinner role men can come to share in this too, and become lifted out of egotism. Once installed as heads of families, men have real incentives to start considering the needs of others, and can become acclimatized to the emotional hothouse of the moral economy and to learn how to behave as genuinely concerned partners.

Women should have no quarrel with this - and many would agree that it is through the continual and patient cultivation of men's domestic obligations that women are best able to improve their own lot. However, the provider role, certainly at the moment when an individual man elects to take it on, and before the alchemy of caring for others has had time to influence his sensibilities, is also the rationale for men's special privileges in society, and for the operation of an unequal exchange rate in their favor. By inflating the importance of what they do, in order to pull them in, it legitimizes their taking of more than they give in their personal dealings with women.

### Sexual divisions of labor

The patriarchal system is an incentive to men to take a more active part in community life. But there is a price which women pay for all this as individuals. For because the provider role brings men into the community on a privileged basis, as workers on a permanent bonus system, it has the effect of creating gender classes - the enduring basis of the sex war - and also leads to the formation of a more or less exclusive domain in social affairs which is always at least *mainly* a male preserve. For to the extent that men are the key providers, then those activities most closely linked to the production and distribution of the resources which have to be provided will obviously tend to be reserved for men to do.

So the provider role is both logically and historically the source of the division of social life into two main spheres: the private world of interpersonal relations governed by specific obligations and agreements, and the "public realm" of wider and more generalized relations extending throughout the whole of a political order. Under this division, women's prime duties to the community consist in carrying out particularistic obligations to *care* for other individuals, principally their children, and being active in the pool of mutual support and exchange of services which backs up these obligations. Men's main duties by contrast are defined universalistically in terms of direct contributions to the general social interest, through activity of a political or economic or possibly ritual nature. The roles available in this public realm are generally open to some competition, so that there is an explicit link between the personal effort made, or success achieved, and the reward given by the community.

Providing is clearly central to patriarchy, and so it is understandable that it should be a focus of female resentments against men. But it is a great mistake to suppose therefore that by sweeping it away we can make the world a better place for women to live in. Hold onto nurse for fear of something worse. Patriarchy is not the main danger. It is not so fundamental to their difficulties as many feminists suppose, and can itself be seen as a solution, or attempted solution, to an even greater underlying problem. If women let go of the "male main provider" role which up to the present has been a civilizing influence on men, they may succeed only in unleashing something much nastier in its place.

In the past some women have seen all or part of patriarchy as oppressive, but most have worked for improvement within it, by selective refinement and updating of those aspects of it which give them maximum control over their own situations. The emphasis has been on making men more like women, through greater involvement in domestic obligations. By contrast the mainstream contemporary feminist agenda which attempts a blanket assault on all patriarchal institutions, to make women more like men by shifting major emphasis to capturing the public realm, is an entirely different proposition. It is a bid to solve everything at a stroke and for all time. And it does not work.

## THE SYMMETRICAL FALLACY

*By half way through the next century we will see changed rules in the home, with men and women sharing responsibility for bringing in the family income and caring for children and patterns of work which recognise this.*
(Harman, 1993b)

*(Charles) Murray is a poor sociologist.*
(Hewitt, 1993c p. 18)

I believe that mainstream feminists are engaged in a highly counterproductive mission in their bid to break down the barriers between the public and private domains so that men and women can share equally in both of them. It is not, I suspect, what most women actually want, though I could be wrong on this. However I am quite sure that extremely few men are in favor of it; and even those who appear to have motives which do not presage long-term success for the project. For the ruling passion in the breast of those trying to behave as New Men seems overwhelmingly to be chivalry - a fine desire to make women happy if they can. Substantive equality is not something that they want positively, for themselves, and when it comes into conflict with more robust feelings and needs arising closer to home it gets pushed aside. Quite a number of men have tried for a while to reconstruct themselves; but very few make a career of it, and almost all of the men who are taking part in the backlash against feminism have tried and failed or retired hurt.

## In search of New Man

Certainly there is no sign of a real shift in male behavior, in Britain or anywhere else (Willetts, 1993). The annual report by SCPR (Social & Community Planning Research) on *British Social Attitudes* carries regular tabulations on gender roles which show that although women have been catching up men in their breadwinning activities, men are still nowhere near pulling their weight in domestic chores. The 1991 edition commented that some small progress had been recorded a few years earlier, but that men had been slacking off recently.

> *Undoubtedly, of course, the trend is towards greater equality and independence between men and women, and away from relationships of asymmetry and dependence. But our data suggest that a gap of attitudes and reality persists. Behaviour still seems to be lagging behind attitudes and ideals. More worryingly, the overall impression from our analyses is that, particularly since the late 1980s, there has been a flattening of the trend towards equality between the sexes both in the workplace and in the home... Still, the greater participation of women in the labour force is likely to continue to chip away at the bastions of an unequal society.* (Jowell, 1992, p. 110)

Not only are the changes which have been detected rather limited, but they also seem very likely to be overstatements anyway, because men attempt to give a good impression of themselves by talking up their behavior. This is clearly recognized in the SCPR report itself, which treats women's responses to questions as factual, and men's as needing a pinch of salt. In the report this is supplied by frequent insertion of the words "claim to" in references to them. Phrases such as "a third of fathers claim to share equally in the care of sick children" (Jowell, p. 103) are sprinkled throughout the commentary to stimulate a healthy scepticism.

The insinuations are surely correct. Nor is this very surprising. If the published version of an influential and supposedly impartial report can adopt such a high moral tone towards men's behavior, and treat their domestic performance as a sort of test of national civilization, and feminist prescriptions as collectively agreed goals, then there are bound to be tremendous pressures operating on them in the face-to-face research from which the tabulated data are generated, which will surely encourage the massaging of "public" accounts. There is indirect evidence of the sort of badgering which goes on scattered through the methodology appendices and discussions of recent research. In Brannen and Wilson's volume, for example, the researchers euphemistically offer the following remarks on the difficulty of eliciting certain types of information.

> *In the research situation, women often preferred to adopt a strategy of avoidance and silence when considering the different amounts of money to which they and their husbands had access. This enabled them to avoid confronting the contradiction between actual distribution and ideology and hence to cope with the fact of inequity. Silence constitutes an important process by which certain issues are kept "off the agenda," and so sustains the status quo.* (1987, p. 10)

It also keeps at bay intrusive researchers trying to impose their own ideologies onto informants, though the following passage makes it clear that the former do not give up that easily. By defining their own ideas as minority views, threatened by orthodoxy, they feel able to justify insinuating them into informants' silences:

> *Research in areas which are hidden needs a rather different approach from research in an area which does not challenge dominant norms and values. The first stage is to make visible the areas of experience which dominant values tend to deny or ignore. The second stage is to come to terms with the problems which arise when interviewing or asking questions in areas which women have not considered. There may be no language available to women in which to describe their experiences, let alone to make them meaningful to an interviewer or to themselves.* (Ibid., p. 12)

How much *more* malleable and vulnerable to hectoring at the hands of interviewers must men be! Bring back the fly on the wall.

So there are severe methodological flaws running through the investigations on which our picture of the slow birth of New Man is based. Given how great an impetus there is among researchers in this area to promote change, together with an eagerness to be the first to discover signs of it, and the likely consequence of all this to inflate the appearance of progress, then the small amount of shifting actually recorded must present an even bleaker prospect for feminists. There may indeed have been very little change at all - and much of that would presumably be in more visible areas, like pushing the proverbial buggy, where men can improve their image most effectively with least real effort. Also, although there are many studies which look at changes in how domestic work is divided and organized, these give very little detail (e.g. Brannen & Moss, 1990) about how this is rationalized, in particular by men.

Hewitt (1993a, p. 61) reproduces a table from Gershuny which purports to illustrate a striking increase in the amount of time spent by men in looking after children. There are some evident increases though these are negligible compared with the additional time that women, both working and non-working, record themselves as now devoting to this. While women in full-time employment record an increase from 19 minutes per day looking after preschool children in 1961 to 107 minutes in 1985, men in full-time jobs raise their contribution from 11 minutes per day to 44. Hardly Stakhanovite performances, and certainly not sufficient cause for Hewitt to draw the inference (which she echoes, without the figures, in newspaper articles) that "*the gap between men and women is closing rapidly.*" On the contrary, the gap has increased in absolute terms from 8 minutes per day to 63!

What is also striking in the figures, and not commented on at all by Hewitt, is that non-employed men have *reduced* considerably the time they spend in child care. These are the men with time on their hands, which is what she insists it is all about. But in spite of the overall rise during this period in the volume of time apparently spent in child care, and notwithstanding the fact that in 1961 (the baseline) there would have been hardly any ideological pressures on men to declare themselves as carers while now there are many, non-employed men then reported 25 minutes per average day spent looking after school children, compared with just ll minutes in 1985 (the most recent year given), with a smaller reduction (from 48 minutes per day to 37) for preschool children. Overall, unemployed men reduce their input from 73 minutes per day in 1961 to 48 in

1985. This is what is believable, and suggestive of real shifts in male behavior. Hewitt's comment (p. 62) that *"Most mothers and fathers enjoy childcare"* may be true, but it is made with her back resolutely turned to her own selected evidence, and ignores the clear signs in that data that for men this enjoyment is positively related to being the breadwinner, rather than being interchangeable with it.

These mal-interpretations of data strongly feed my reservations about taking too seriously Hewitt's assertions that men would like to change their ways - as these issues are even more amenable to dressing up. It is hard to disguise what you are actually doing; but only a real pig would come out and say that he did not intend to take on a bigger share of domestic labor if the opportunity came his way, especially of an item like child care which is regarded as a "quality" chore. So it is all the more telling that the evidence on this seems even thinner. Hewitt repeatedly asserts that men now want to have more time to spend with their children. But when it comes down to it the evidence for this seems to consist of women saying that they felt that their husbands would like the chance to do this (p. 71); dare they declare otherwise? It is surely grasping at straws to refer to the testimony of one or two older men (p. 75) who are reported at secondhand as wishing that they had been able to take more of a part in bringing up their children. This is known as Muggeridge's prayer: "Lord, please make me good, now that I am too old for it to hurt."

## Male flight from fatherhood

But perhaps the principal consideration which must lead us towards the conclusion that men are doing no more overall, and conceivably in some ways less than before the current feminist campaign, is surely the strong growth in absent fatherhood. A man who is just not around doesn't do any of that household's chores. But at the same time and by the same token, in many empirical studies he doesn't actually *count* as not doing anything, because he is not counted at all. So he does not pull down the average male partner performance indicators. He is not only absent; he is invisible. As Christine Delphy noted some years ago, divorce and separation are neat ways for a man to shed his domestic responsibilities.

Feminist responses to this are mixed. But the mainstream line, represented by Patricia Hewitt's *Mishcon Lecture* (1993c) seem to be that this is a teething problem related to New Man's infancy, and that in a while, as he matures, conjugal relationships will be renegotiated. A new sexual contract is being drawn up, in which male commitment will be back on the table in a more acceptable form.

I can find little in what is going on at the moment to offer any support for this idea. It is an aspiration which seems grounded in blind faith. The recently published results of the latest stage of the National Child Development Study, dealing with the lives of people born during a week in 1958, show that this cohort has given much more priority than previous generations to emotional satisfaction in conjugal relationships, and to notions (if not yet the practice) of greater sharing of domestic work. This is linked with a surge in living together in preference to formal marriage. Harold Newby, chairman of the sponsoring Economic and Social Research Council, has chivalrously added his weight to the view that this practice enables women to take more control of their lives.

> *The effect of family responsibilities appears to weigh depressingly heavily among females. Those living together can negotiate a position, but once a couple get married and have children, there is not a lot of evidence to show that much has changed from previous generations. Perhaps smart women should not get married.* (*Daily Mail,* 31 August 1993)

Or better still, not to have children at all. But not even this is an adequate conclusion from the research as there is an angle in it which Newby and others ignore or seriously play down. For this study shows that those relationships which do *not* convert into traditional marriages, with the consequent loss of bargaining power by women, are themselves generally very short term. After the early flush of romance fades, they break down, and growing numbers of women are being left to fend for themselves during the most arduous years of child care. The NCDS report also points out that co-habiting women, in spite of their "negotiating power," are the *least* happy with their lot, and those who are coping alone are much less content than the ones who caved in and are now living in more traditional marriages. Although most of the quality newspapers covering this report genuflected to feminist taste by failing to make the point, many tabloids drew the obvious conclusion that if women go too far in pressing for symmetry, and in trying to change the rules of the game, men will simply decide not to play. The traditional male weapons in the sex war are non-cooperation in domestic chores, and flight. The traditional female weapon is celebration of paternity and male responsibility; as it is this which is the proven key to male commitment. If women now choose to define this as patriarchal oppression and withdraw the notion that men's family role is *important,* then they are throwing away their best trick. Feminism, in dismantling patriarchy, is simply reviving the underlying greater natural freedom of men.

## Caring and providing

*Though there is a growing consensus that men should be financially responsible for their children, no one knows how to make them responsible emotionally.* (Moore, 1993a)

Perhaps the fundamental weakness of feminist analysis, from which many other mistakes flow, is to fail to see that men may need the status of the main provider role to give them a sufficient reason to become fully involved, and stay involved, in the longer-term draggy business of family life. In her Mishcon lecture Hewitt makes the almost unbelievable gaffe of declaring that the working father is the prototype absent father, because although he produces material income he is not often around (1993c, p. 9). She ridicules Charles Murray for arguing that such family responsibilities are an indispensable civilizing influence on men. Who needs an economic provider? But her own recommended alternative model, the emotionally involved father who does not set great store by giving economic support, has yet to climb off her drawing board and show us what he can do. He is a pious dream, and quite frankly a no-hoper.

A great deal of new research is needed to explore the links between material responsibility and emotional commitment to partners and children, because it is an area where so much recent work has conspired to avoid or obscure findings which might lead to unwelcome conclusions. But the indirect evidence emerging from studies like the NCDS supports very powerfully the commonsense view that caring attitudes are more likely to take root among fathers who are materially responsible, so that the breadwinner role is in reality crucial. Several recent studies (e.g. Dennis & Erdos, 1992) indicate that the erosion of patriarchal ideas of male responsibility may be giving tremendous reinforcement to men's underlying tendencies towards selfishness. Lack of dependency on them is almost certainly the key. Mothers are directly important to children in a variety of ways; so unless men are *more* important as economic providers than their partners then there is little scope for them to feel genuinely responsible.

Many women are now setting great store by the coming of New Man. Throughout history many will have had the same dream - but for most of that time they have had the commonsense to see that it was a chimera. (Men have had their fantasies about women as well, which hardly need mentioning. These too can never have any relevance to the actual lives of more than a handful.) The current attack on patriarchal conventions is surely promoting almost the exact opposite, namely a plague of feckless yobs, who leave all the real work to women and gravitate towards the margins of society where males naturally hang around unless culture gives them a reason to do otherwise. The family may be a myth, but it is a myth that works to make many men tolerably useful.

As feminist ideas become more influential the gender war takes on a more primitive aspect, with similarity and mutual antipathy replacing difference and mutual respect. Susan Faludi (1992, p. 10) roots the central discontent of women in the continuing refusal of men to share equally in domestic chores. But her prescription of more jobs for women will surely make it even worse. The increased direct competition by women with men for provider roles is harmful in two ways. On the one hand it pushes more men into becoming workaholics, in order to secure the most prestigious and interesting jobs which provide life incentives even in the absence of fatherhood. On the other hand it allows the bulk of men, who fail in this contest or don't even start the race and so need fatherhood the most, to see that there is no important role there for them, so that they might as well just enjoy being drones rather than accept the menial jobs on offer. Neither response swells the ranks of equally sharing partners.

Patricia Hewitt of all people has no excuse for not knowing this, after travelling around the country for the Labour Party Commission on Social Justice and listening to many women telling her this. Charles Murray can certainly hear them.

## MAKING MEN USEFUL

Many alterations are becoming necessary in the ways that men and women relate in the modern world. But I believe that there are also very important limits to what is possible, which need to be properly understood if change is to be effective. Contemporary feminism has raised many necessary issues; but it has also obscured some that are essential, and as a consequence it is now leading men and women down a blind alley where we seem less likely to redraw the sexual contract than to end up mugging each other.

The underlying reason why new types of relationships are needed is that advances in public health and medicine, which have produced greater control over reproduction on one hand, and real dangers of over-population on the other, have lowered the obvious value of child rearing, while at the same time freeing women to spend more time on other activities. Together, these developments have reduced women's actual dependence on male support, by enabling more of them to take on occupations which formerly were left to men. This in turn has dissolved many of the myths of male importance and centrality which protected the idea of patriarchy and bolstered men's sense of being needed. Many commentators will add to this that major shifts have occurred in the job market which have altered the balance of power between domestic partners. For example Campbell (1993, p. 202) portrays male flight from domesticity as an assertion of masculinity in the face of endemic unemployment. *"Difference is reasserted in a refusal to cooperate in the creation of a democratic domesticity."* But putting the emphasis on joblessness does not adequately draw attention to the contrast now with other periods, such as during the thirties, when unemployment did not have this effect, and I suspect that most of these market shifts are less "impersonal trends" beyond our control (e.g. Coote *et al.*, 1990) than consequences of women's readiness, indeed eagerness, to join the job market, which is mainly a cultural phenomenon.

So some serious updating of gender roles, encompassing much greater involvement of women in public activities, has become essential. But in their enthusiasm to enter the forbidden citadel many women, though by no means the majority, have not paused to consider whether patriarchal institutions served any purpose other than enslaving women for men's private benefit, or what the implications might be for the community if women just rushed in.

One very obvious implication, which flows directly from the argument in the preceding pages, is that a difficult question is bound to arise over just what men are really needed for, or even whether they are needed at all. This line of speculation may not be something which occurs readily to many women, as the idea of "not being needed" is perhaps literally beyond their experience and comprehension or, where it is grasped, represents such a paradisical state of personal freedom that it could not entail any *problems*. For a certain type of naïve feminist, breaking down the barriers means joining men in heaven.

This is an area where I think that refusal to acknowledge basic differences between the sexes' social orientations has led to great gaps in mutual comprehension. Most women know that they will be needed by others whether they welcome this or not; so that the issue for them is how to maximize their personal freedom. Men on the other hand do enjoy greater freedom. But what they may feel the lack of, or fail to become properly activated until they are given, is the sense of having a valued part to play in a community; for as so few men are actually needed to ensure reproduction of the group there is no automatic place for them. The common male angst known to us as womb envy, and recognized in most cultures but largely trivialized by western psychoanalysis as sexual inadequacy, may indicate, I believe, the desire to find some way of gaining full acceptance in society. We all need this in order to escape from the short-termism and anomie which are freedom's constant companions. This is the heart of male fragility (Greenstein, 1993).

As a Swiss general said to Napoleon, in response to the latter's jibe that the French fought only for glory, while the Swiss would fight for money, "We each fight for what we have not got." Feminists know what women have not got, and have seriously neglected the importance of anything else.

Men do not, of course, have an absolute need to feel valued. They can survive without it. I think the point is that if society is going to get the best out of men, then it is essential for them to feel that there is an important job to be done, and moreover that they personally are the only or best ones to do it. A useful occupation by itself can give that sense of value to the most scarce and skilled workers. But for most men this has to come in the same sort of way as it has traditionally come to mothers, that is through having others personally dependent on them. However they may actually earn their bread, the social value of their labor lies in the channelling of it to those other people who are reliant on them.

Again, this sense of the *personal* nature of responsibility is something which women may easily leave out of account, because they take it so much for granted in their own lives. Since the late sixties, as feminists have tried to renegotiate relations with men, many have argued (and practiced) that it is better to get support from the state than from an individual man, unless or until men are willing to agree to a better deal. Hence, amongst other things, the growing numbers of single mothers not dependent on a male breadwinner, but on the "patriarchal state" in its role as collective provider. This trend is unlikely to be sustainable for long, because by reducing reliance on personal provision, it undermines *men's* will to work, which weakens the state's fiscal base at the very time that single mothers are placing an increasing burden on it.

## The need to be needed

All this is dealt with later in the book. But the main point I want to get over here is that there is no loss of *female* personal responsibility entailed in this process. A woman who rears her children on public money rather than via private support from a male partner, or who supports them with her own wages and relies on state resources to replace her own child care or subsidize her housing costs and so on, is still very much personally responsible for the children. If she is coping alone she may well be regarded as even more responsible than if she was a dependent wife. She is the heroine of our times, and this is why it is so difficult for even the most rabid anti-statist politicians to contemplate changing the benefit rules, even though their implications are so bad in other ways.

State support does not sap a woman's sense of responsibility, and may actually enable her to look after her children more adequately than if she had a partner - so that agencies concerned with child support or welfare almost invariably mobilize in defense of the single mother when she is criticized. None of this has much effect on the lives of middle-class women, who would only find state support acceptable as a fall-back position in times of great difficulty. But for a working-class woman, where the alternatives are menial, low-paid work, or dependence on a low-paid man who would expect services to himself as well, it represents a lifeline to autonomy and peace of mind, in which she can give her children the full attention they deserve. In some ways they may lose out. But overall they may be better off than in a household racked by disputes between partners over money.

Where personal responsibility *is* lost in this process is among the men. Providing for children collectively, as workers and taxpayers, does not seem to substitute for the satisfaction and incentive of being a family breadwinner. This is partly, it must be admitted, a matter of sexual access. A man who pays housekeeping money to his partner does not see this as just a matter of child maintenance. He often thinks of it as entitling him to sex as well. If a state were to develop a scheme (a sister for *workfare,* perhaps, if someone could come up with a suitable name) whereby mothers claiming public benefits were required to carry out a certain number of hours in sexual servicing of male taxpayers, then single-parenting might actually produce a net gain for the exchequer. There are surely opportunities here for taxation and social policy experts with a Huxleyan bent.

However the main factor is I think that a man contributing to a pool of support can never enjoy the inner conviction that what he is doing is genuinely valuable. He is part of such a large army of workers, in such a vast system, that surely it would not matter if he *himself* put in a bit less effort, or even none at all. Nobody would suffer. The edge is easily removed from motivation to work. Thus the biggest problem with public dependency of women and children is, as George Gilder and Charles Murray have emphasized, that it stimulates a further rise in the number of male drones in society, many of whom become dependents of the state themselves, instead of contributors. It has led to "men's liberation" (Hacker, 1991, p. 69). This is an issue which feminists have yet to confront seriously by recognizing the actual patterning of incentives and interests involved in dependency chains. If they talk about this at all it is usually phrased in terms of men needing to make a moral choice -

as if morality operates in a vacuum, independently of personal obligations and commitments.

The extra virtue enjoyed by single mothers comes at the expense of the universally despised absent fathers. This situation is relatively new. In traditional society where women were discouraged from having children outside of marriage, they needed to establish a relation of interdependence with a man before bearing a child; and this ensured that they did not monopolize the legitimacy which having dependants imparts. Women were made a bit more like men. But now that they can easily do it by themselves, men's chances of being drawn by community pressures into parenthood have diminished significantly.

## The fragile public realm

Finally, and very briefly here, a third implication of women's greater participation in the public realm, or of a collapsing of public and private into a single domain, is that this may largely undermine many features of the public realm which made it desirable to women in the first place. They cannot enter it without changing its nature. Unlike the other implications, this is clearly a problem *for* women themselves - though not one that many seem to have considered yet. In order to concentrate the troops' minds better on incursion, feminists have portrayed the state and marketplace as a vast promised land of glittering prizes, which men have enjoyed while keeping women locked in a prison of domesticity. But this, I think, both overstates and misunderstands the importance of the public domain, which in many respects should be seen, as I hinted earlier, as primarily a device for paying men patriarchal bonuses. The great bulk of work in society is carried out, unpaid, in the private domain and women have always done most of it. The public realm, in spite of its confusing name, is not a great "out there." It is better conceptualized as a small, privileged enclave within society, which is sealed off in order to maintain a steep differential between men's and women's economic power, and to prop up the position of the family man.

If women storm this bunker in the hope of earning the sort of rewards and independence that men have enjoyed, they will be disappointed. The market cannot afford to pay everyone at the level of remuneration which men had when they monopolized it. A man's "family wage" was designed to keep a family, and was in effect inflated to allow for work done in the moral economy. To the extent that women, and their caring work, are moving into the market itself, and expect equal treatment there, wage levels are bound to be sinking, because the family wage is effectively being broken up into its individual components. The growing dependency of families on multiple pay packets marks a beginning of this process of adjustment, though it is not of course the only factor. But there is still a long way for it to go. Moreover, and insofar as this process involves a loss of male capacity to provide, even where men are main earners, then it is reinforcing massively the slide towards male fecklessness. Before too long, many women could end up doing just about everything, including looking after male drones like unattached, unemployed sons. Women will have the jobs. But they will have much greater burdens - at least the lion's share of their own households' domestic chores - without enjoying high salaries or finding independence. Men on the other hand will in some ways be even more free, because their freedom does not after all derive from control of the public domain, but comes to them naturally, whether working and providing or not.

The changes which feminism is now bringing about do not look like improving women's lives; and the movement will be repudiated by more of them as they come to see this. Backlash, I would argue, is mainly a response to feminism among women, not men, and is gaining in strength as more of them come to see that far from increasing men's responsiveness to women's needs, contemporary feminism has liberated men's natural power of choice and made it easier for them to abdicate from responsibility and leave women to do an even greater share of the work. Before realistic progress can be made towards writing a new sexual contract, it is imperative to look more closely than hitherto at the true position of men, and in particular at the importance of making them personally responsible for the well-being of others. This is far better understood in traditional divisions of labor; and there may be a case for trying to re-balance the realms of main influence, rather than further integrating them. Equity looks a better bet at the moment than equality; and pre-feminist worldviews involving pluralistic equilibrium, and which appreciate both male vulnerability and female centrality, may yet have much to teach us.

# 2

# FAIRY TALE RESOLUTION

## USES OF ALLEGORY

Sexually pluralist worldviews, which were dominant everywhere before the advent of feminism, and still are outside of the West, recognize that men and women, by nature perhaps, but also (and more decisively) by virtue of their different articulation with the community, have different paths open to them, with different possible life-styles, expectations and rewards. They accept that the sexes cannot regard themselves as direct competitors, as they will not always understand and assess situations in ways which fully make sense to each other. So agreement on fundamental issues may never be possible. There will be men's philosophy and women's; male gods and female. In place of similarity there is interdependence and amicable co-existence, with toleration of alternative priorities and perspectives, which are treated as complementary rather than in conflict.

Popular art has been central in holding this together, because its job is to encompass complexity and express it in simple ways. Although some art forms or genres appeal more to one sex than another, the reliance of all art on symbolic structures which are open to a variety of interpretations makes them accessible, albeit in different ways, to both sexes simultaneously. The more popular the form, the more likely this is to be the case. Hence folktales, or fairy stories, which serve with some variations as common currency for large tracts of humanity, and across many generations, are likely to contain representations about gender which are capable of bearing a host of interlocking readings.

I have chosen *The Frog Prince* here to be an illustrative anchor for the analysis, because its available readings quite obviously include the traditional problem of men - that is, what is their true nature and how they can be fitted into society - and because it meets

so well the criterion of pluralism; that is, it offers complementary
diets for different interest groups.

Within this reading, the main thrust of the story is I think to
orient boys towards marriage and acceptance of family
responsibilities. It portrays the life of freedom as squalid, and makes
the suggestion - which can find an echo in many boys' experiences
- that it is not something they would choose, but are having thrust
on them, as a form of banishment. It plants the idea that they have
something noble waiting inside them which a female partner can
bring out, and which will make them happy and useful and
successful. Fears of marginality in freedom are played on, and the
rewards of commitment are exaggerated. This is the patriarchal
resolution of the problem.

It is a message which is very relevant to boys, but also to girls
who are trying to understand and manage them. A boy's entry to
adult life is more uncertain and problematic than a girl's, and the
story expresses this graphically through the image of the divided self
- an ambiguous consciousness which looks in opposite directions, to
a pre-socialized world of nature and to a refined life within
civilization. These alternatives may never become resolved or fully
reconciled, because many men's hold on membership of society
remains conditional and precarious. Not all men pass the tests which
patriarchy sets them. Thus the story embraces an awareness of that
undercurrent of male vulnerability, especially of young men, which
flows from their relatively marginal status in the community.

The story manages these issues relating to masculinity in a way
which allows readers of either sex points of positive identification
with central characters. So its symbolic treatment of the problem
helps boys and girls to learn behavior towards one another which is
positive and constructive. The ways in which this is achieved will
be looked at again towards the end of the chapter.

There are of course many possible dimensions of meaning that
can be given to this tale. Some analysts like to read it mainly as an
allegory on class relations, for example, and there is clearly some
mileage in this. But most interpretations refer to sex. Bettelheim's
classic Freudian study of fairy tales (1976) is probably the best
known. In Bettelheim's schema the story figures as an example of
an "animal groom" sequence, in which a beast when treated with
trust and affection eventually reveals a sensitive, usually human,

hidden self. Bettelheim suggests that such tales help children to cope with the emotional turmoils of growing up. He proposes that girls are the main beneficiaries of this genre; for through identifying with the princess and her initial feelings of loathing, they can begin to understand, as the princess becomes aware of affection and releases the prince, that men and sex may not be so bad as they feared once they are seen in the context of a devoted and committed relationship.

Bettelheim's exegesis has little to offer male readers though; and yet surely it is this aspect of the story which makes it so interesting. For it does seem to have so much to say about male nature and behavior; and it is the frog, rather than the princess, who appears better placed to lead a young reader through emotional turmoil. The meaning for *boys,* I would argue, must carry great weight; and part of the aim of this book is to help produce a reading of the story which shows how it helps to illuminate the male condition.

The first step in developing this interpretation is to outline the key elements in the symbolization. The story itself has been recorded in countless variations over the centuries; but the essence, which runs as follows, is remarkable consistent.

*A young princess, still very much a child, who spends all of her time playing, ventures outside the palace grounds and enters the wild forest beyond. Her golden ball, which she values more than anything else, falls into a pool (or well) and sinks from view, leaving her heartbroken.*

*To her surprise a frog appears and speaks to her, offering to retrieve her ball for her if she promises to be his friend. In her childish grief for the lost ball, and carelessly disregarding the future, she agrees. So the frog restores her ball to her.*

*The princess returns to the palace, where she is later embarrassed by the frog who has followed her, and who now insists on her keeping the promise of friendship. She is reluctant, but her father, the King, insists that she honor her commitment.*

*So the frog is allowed to participate in the civilized activities of the palace, such as eating at the table and sharing the princess's food. After contact has become more intimate, variously expressed as the princess kissing the frog, or allowing him to sleep on her pillow (with the result, in some versions, that she begins to feel more friendly towards him), the frog turns into a prince.*

*He declares that this is in fact his original and true form, and that by befriending him the princess has removed him from the spell of an evil witch. They marry - for the princess has now matured - and go off in a gold coach to live at the prince's own castle.*

## UNPICKING THE METAPHOR

### Level One: The Scene

All readings of this story would probably accept a clear and fundamental dichotomy between the palace and the forest, with the palace standing for culture, and the forest for the untamed world of nature outside. In the context of the reading offered here, this can be expanded by suggesting that the palace is also comfortable and protective. It symbolizes an orderly construction of common interests wherein people can exercise mutual concern and develop long-term commitments to each other. Although it is designed around a family, the royal household, it can accommodate many more.

The forest is the antithesis, a wild, dangerous and dirty place, where chaos rules. The animals which inhabit it compete mercilessly for survival and have lives which are brief and unpredictable and appear to be almost entirely determined by material factors. If moral considerations do inform their actions, then it is not a morality which is friendly to humankind, nor even accessible to human consciousness. So people enter at their peril.

At the same time, as in so many other stories like *Sleeping Beauty,* the forest represents a perpetual threat. Whereas the palace is both artificial and fragile, and needs constant effort and vigilance to prevent it from crumbling or being destroyed, the forest is regenerating relentlessly, and is poised to invade and recolonize the palace grounds should the opportunity arise.

## Level Two: The Actors

There are two principal actors, the Princess and the Frog Prince, and two minor figures, the King and, by indirect reference only, a Witch.

The **Frog Prince** manifests very clearly the split condition of the human male. He was, significantly, born a prince. But then he was banished from civilized existence into life in a murky pond beyond the pale, in the form of a loathsome amphibian - one of the lowest orders in the scheme of things. There he might, one is invited to suppose, have languished indefinitely had that princess not turned up. Or he might have been eaten by a fox or a bigger frog. This is not spelled out for us, but we do not need to be told it to know that he was an extremely fortunate frog to have been rescued when he was, so that he could regain his other, suspended identity as an acceptable member of refined society. He might have remained trapped in an unfulfilled state for ever.

The **Princess** by contrast stands for the more unitary and secure condition of female consciousness. She is generally portrayed as extremely beautiful - that is, a perfect being who does not need to actually do anything in order to be valued by others. There is never any question about her destiny. She is born a princess in a palace, and goes on to live in another as woman/wife/queen. If she had not stumbled across and released that frog prince, then presumably some other prince would have sought her hand; or she could just have stayed a princess anyway, assured of some comfort and company and dignity in the palace of mutual care.

The **Witch**, although only referred to at third hand and in retrospect, is the prime mover for the whole sequence. It is her original enchantment of the prince which springs the drama. So who or what does she represent? I suggest that in this context she symbolizes an aspect of womankind of which men and boys may be more aware, and in awe, than are women themselves. She is a generalized mother-aunt-grandmother figure, an aspect of the "female community" or moral and moralizing majority incarnate. It is this group which men experience as having the power to define them as worthy of admission to the caring community, or as requiring exclusion.

This group may also be seen by men as harboring resentment towards them and therefore as potentially hostile and dangerous.

Although men feel that women are powerful, this is not in ways that are immediately obvious; so it is an important aspect of the story (and, see Lurie (1990) and the Opies' study (1982), of most fairy stories) that both of the female characters possess a mysterious force, to damn and redeem men, which presumably draws on some hidden collective female strength. The witch makes the spell and a princess can undo it. In this respect it is I think interesting that the witch is not active within the story, and only influences events from outside its temporal span, as this is suggestive of how the figure may be seen as representing a powerful communality.

The **King** on the other hand is the visible and official power in the land; the nominal leader of the community, and its upfront on-stage agent. He possesses the formal authority to tell the princess what her moral duty is - that is, to keep her promise. For her part she feels obliged to take his advice. But it is the rules that she is obeying, not him personally. He is the superego and voice of the group. His power is impersonal and rational, and does not extend far beyond just reminding the princess of what she ought to do.

## Level Three: The Action

### a. The original spell

The first important event in the sequence is the turning of the young prince into the frog. This I believe corresponds quite closely to the experience of adolescent boys as their position becomes more tenuous. A young man who is no longer himself a dependant, but who has not yet acquired dependants of his own, is anomalous. He is neither child nor adult, and fits with difficulty into the life of the community, where his failure to participate fully in the moral economy may earn him increasing disapproval. Eventually many boys come to feel themselves to be a lesser species, too disgusting to be seen and tolerated in polite circles, and fit only for the wilderness.

The enchanted frog knows that to return to his previous state he must win the friendship of a princess. This refers, perhaps, to the fact that although it is the community which is rejecting him, because he has no personal dependants, by the same token they cannot *as a group* reinstate him. That will turn on his ability to find an individual woman and make her want him. Only *personalized* obligations are powerful enough magic to overcome his selfishness and transform him into a valuable member of the community. For a boy, being born into the group is not enough to secure entry to the adult community. The story carries the formal patriarchal notion that a boy has much to do and prove before he is welcome.

## b. The first gift

The significance of this part of the narrative relates I think to the importance of reciprocity, and primes a boy who may still be a novice in the arts of the moral economy on the strategic use of a pre-emptive strike. The frog presumably knows that in order to reclaim the human aspect of his destiny and personality he has to become acceptable to a princess. But an adolescent boy reader is also probably very conscious that he is not worthy of girls' attention and favor. The story reassures him however by showing that if he can just get her to be his friend he is halfway there.

The visit of the princess to the forest might not have worked out well for the frog if she had not lost her precious ball. For it was that which gave him the chance to offer her some assistance. Her acceptance of help was crucial, because the rules of the moral economy insist that a service must be reciprocated. Civilization and order depend on exchange. If the princess had been older she would have been wary. But even though she was a child, once she had given her word she was bound by it; and the frog, by using his initiative, was thus able to enter the palace. Boys can learn from this the value of being responsive to girls' needs, and of not being shy in proffering gifts. A good lesson in life skills.

## c. Metamorphosis

Once the frog is her friend, the princess needs to teach him some nice manners before he can fit in properly. So a process of socialization is embarked upon, which culminates eventually in a kiss or whatever, which in turn triggers off the transmogrification of the slimy amphibian into a resplendent and fully house-trained prince. However this is not a quick process, and the story carries the implication that the end result is not certain, and that it is the princess who ultimately holds the key to what the frog becomes. Men must do their best to be acceptable to women; but in the end it is a woman's choice. The princess repaid the original gift by becoming the frog's friend. This was a necessary condition of his transformation. But it was not sufficient. Only when her feelings had developed beyond friendship, could she see him as other than a repellent beast. So a boy has to be patient, and can never expect fulfilment as a right.

In some versions of the story the princess has not been compliant through all of this, though, and some moral pressure has been applied by the King, who perhaps remembers going through a similar grooming himself. Thus, as Robert Bly goes on telling us, the aid of men already established in society is a valuable support for callow youth, which often despairs of ever gaining admission.

### d. Maturation of the princess

The princess undergoes some changes herself, though not so visibly that a male reader would notice; and not dramatically. The girl who plays innocently in the wood is still a child - with her self-absorption signified by the obsession with her golden ball. But by accepting the gift from a stranger, she becomes subject to the logic of reciprocation and is forced to concern herself with the frog's desires; and this precipitates her maturation into an adult.

Thus give and take between strangers sets in motion a relationship which may lead to marriage. As may be a woman's lot, the princess then has to leave her own palace and go to live in a distant and unfamiliar one, where she may presumably come up against the witch who put a spell on her husband. This aspect of the drama is not given much attention in any version of the story that I have seen - although Zipes' analysis of the tale (1986, p. 15) does explore the rough justice whereby women are rewarded for virtue by being taken over by a dominant male. The limited development of this theme in the story rather reinforces the view that its main reference is male anxieties and identities. Nevertheless the implications of the princess's own changes are interesting, and are considered later.

### e. Royal marriage

The transformation of the frog and the celebration of engagement are virtually coterminous in the tale. The kiss which releases the prince stands for the female approval and acceptance of dependence which in real life brings and binds men into polite society. By passing this test a man is able to take his place in the community as a husband and potential father. It is these roles and their fulfillment which offer men their most reliable chance of a rewarding life, by instilling in them the long-term motivation for orderly participation in useful and productive activities. Being responsible for a family gives every man the opportunity to be a king.

## READING DIFFERENT MESSAGES

*Maidens, treat all frogs with care!*
*One may be the king's heir.*
(Naomi Lewis)

The most obvious reading of this story, especially in the context of modern gender relations, would probably be that it is concerned, as in the animal-groom interpretation, with preparing girls for marriage; or, more strictly perhaps, for a more sympathetic appraisal of the partners realistically available. It probably does help to orient girls in this direction.

However, I would urge that the story is probably much more important in giving *boys* incentives and inducements to marriage, by revealing it as a key to the successful management of their divergent identities. The frog image, which is painfully apt for adolescent boys, draws vivid attention to their shortcomings, and raises questions about whether they will make the grade. But if there is another self locked inside, just waiting to be released by the friendship, tutelage and then partnership of a suitable girl, then all is not lost. So the tale manages, I suggest, to incline both sexes towards marriage at the same time.

This is no mean feat, given that each sex will have reservations to overcome, and that there is obviously a danger, in an area of endless and shifting tensions and suspicions, that reassuring one interest group may alarm the other. But because the issues are handled at a symbolic level, both boys and girls can each extract the message they need, without paying too much attention to others embedded in it - and this can be done quite easily as their own major anxieties are clearly addressed.

For boys the main anxieties raised by marriage relate to the curtailment of freedom, followed perhaps by the question of whether they will be able to cope with the responsibilities entailed. The story deals with these firstly by portraying freedom as a dirty, undignified existence far away from courtly pleasures. The idea of transformation into a glorious prince, accompanied by seductive illusions of patriarchal privilege, combines a powerful inducement to give up some freedom with a reassuring vision of a miraculous acquisition of adult male competence. By getting boys to identify with frogs, and *then* showing that it is possible to escape from this if they are smart and lucky, the tale predisposes them more towards high valuation of patriarchal constructions, and to responsive behavior towards the girls who might redeem them. At the same time it prompts them to develop a healthy contempt for those feelings within themselves which resist the idea of commitment. Thus, although they do have a divided self, the *real* one is manifestly the prince.

For girls the key problem in patriarchal marriage is probably having to accept male authority, including perhaps-feared sexual demands. This tale reassures them by hinting that in spite of patriarchal appearances the central position in society really belongs to women - and that men are capable of being shaped by them. Women play the active and powerful roles in the plot, expelling, re-admitting and remolding men. An important part of a girl's destiny is to make men fit to play a constructive part in society; and if there is any submitting to be done it will be to a prince of her own making, who ought to know, since he has read or been told the story too, how much he owes her. Confident in the knowledge of her own essential superiority, she can relax and look forward to exercising power from behind his throne.

Although these messages are very different, they are also complementary, and could be expected to encourage mutual dependence and tolerance. Girls recognize the portrait of adolescent boys, and their need to become more cultivated; but also that once transformed the boys can actually be helpful to them. Boys are taught that there is something special inside them waiting to be released, and that for this to happen they must accept some female management. The allegory improves on nature, male nature to be exact, and leaves the sexes better disposed than before to each other's needs.

It can only do this at all, though, because the allegory is able to complement formal patriarchal models by being grounded in a very realistic appreciation of gender relations, and in particular of the central position and *informal* power of women. In this it is pre-Freudian. There is much that Freud has to answer for; not least his reification of the notion of patriarchy. For this has helped to erode traditional belief in the strength of women, and thus to upset the gender pluralism and equilibrium which this tale embodies. He has effectively inhibited some of the readings previously available.

## Getting past Freud

What Freud's work does is to take the idea of patriarchy far too seriously, and turn it from a set of prescriptive ideas designed to get more out of men, into a theoretical proposition about inherent male dominance. It is I believe necessary to talk up male importance, in order to give men a sense of having a stake in the community, and patriarchal notions may sometimes be not much more than conventions, insubstantial mirages hovering above the surface. As Gilmore puts it, *"True manhood is a hortatory image that men and boys aspire to and that their culture demands of them as a measure of belonging"* (1990, p. 17). Freud's mischief lay in formulating a model of the soul out of the fantasies of assorted neurotics who lacked the confidence and insight to separate out illusion from reality. The resulting account has convinced many people, including feminists who disagree with most other aspects of his work, that patriarchy is the creation of fierce and deep urges issuing from inside men themselves - a primeval and passionate demon which can furnish the raw energy for building civilizations, but which can also damage and destroy. This reified monster - an all-powerful enemy, which modern women have decided they must slay before the world will be safe for them to live in - was fathered by Freud.

Building straw patriarchs or chasing shadows like this does not advance the understanding of men's position, because it is blind to the mythical aspects of patriarchy and to the social influence of women, especially women acting in concert. A Freudian interpretation of the *Frog Prince* story manages to obscure a number of self-evident references to the centrality of women. Take

Bettelheim's analysis of the witch. You might imagine that it would be hard to see the witch as a manifestation of patriarchal force. But Bettelheim rises to it. The witch, he argues, is an embodiment of the maternal repression of children's sexual interests:

> *In animal groom stories ... mothers are outwardly absent;*
> *they are present, however, in the guise of the sorceress who*
> *has caused the child to view sex as animal-like.*
> (1976, p. 284)

Fair enough, you may think, so far so good, even if a little narrowly conceived. The model I have been putting forward can encompass that. But then the real power is unsheathed. For although this repression is to be seen as carried out by mothers, Bettelheim points out that this is of course done on behalf of fathers. The patriarch cannot allow girls to regard themselves as being in control of their sexuality; while it goes without saying that if boys are required to reject their mothers (and cast them as witches) this is from fear of castration by a jealous father. Patriarchy rules after all.

There may be some untutored readers of the tale whose psyches are drawn to this exegesis. But many twentieth-century western intellectuals, who have taken in Freud with their mothers' milk, swallow it whole as a matter of reflex. This is not all bad. Fairy tales can be read in any number of ways, which may all carry a resonance for some people, and which may often play against one another to increase a reader's sensibilities. But I do feel that rigid Freudian orthodoxy has imposed a rather over-sophisticated analysis here which, by reflecting exhortations as realities, and fantasies as routines, inverts rather than reveals the feelings of most people. Surely it is more straightforward and satisfactory to see the banishment of adolescent boys as rooted in the community's evaluations of them which, given the female character and complexion of much of community life, is experienced as judgment *by* women. This I am sure is much closer to the ordinary lives of young non-neurotic males, in whom Freud had little clinical interest, and offers a more illuminating model for grappling with everyday problems of male identity and consciousness, and the gender roles which these relate to and help to reproduce.

# 3

# A FROG'S LIFE

## THE WITCH'S CURSE

*What everybody has to do at some time, 18 or 22, 25, is to
make up his mind how much of what he's doing is to express
himself and how much is to annoy his mother. The
fundamental question is; if there was no praise and no
blame, who would you be then?*
(Quentin Crisp, 1990)

*Boys and men find through their gender difference, through
taking up masculine behaviours and activities, and through
foisting on women the power that they experienced in
infancy, a way to assuage the helplessness they may have felt
in their original encounter with the feminine.*
(Susie Orbach, 1993)

The forest inhabited by the frog is not a place apart. It is a state of
mind which arises in any of us to the extent that we become morally
detached from our community, essentially the "private world" of our
interpersonal relations, and move towards a solitary consciousness
where we are concerned only with our personal interests. It is
typically a male experience, certainly in its fullest development;
though with the onward march of individualism more girls and
women are trying it too.

The usual time for entering this state is during adolescence, when
a boy may start to pick up some crumbs in the public realm and
begin to feel less dependent on others. Nowadays the process is
often analyzed, and as in Crisp's case may actually be experienced,
in neo-Freudian or Kleinian terms as a breaking away from maternal
control, as part of a bid to create a secure sexual identity. In fact a
veritable industry has grown up which is devoted to psychologizing
men's problems by rooting them in boys' supposed difficulties in

detaching from their mothers and constructing satisfactory gender roles for themselves. Nancy Chodorow (e.g., 1978) has been a major supplier in this business, by fashioning the proposal that women grow up more easily and with less psychic damage than men into a very useful strategic device for banishing earlier Freudian concepts of women as a weaker, envious sex, and replacing these with a stereotype of warped, infantile men. This is all valuable and very saleable grist for feminist mills.

The device has a number of interesting features. Firstly, of course, it allows women's modes (responsive, sharing, intimate) to be seen as normal, and men's (withdrawn, secretive, selfish) as weak and pathological. Secondly the obvious solution for men's problems, which lies in greater sharing by men in the parenting process, to break the cycle of alienated male identities, also just happens to present women with some handy extra support in child care. Thirdly it enables feminists to trivialize any hostility towards women or resistance to feminist ideas as irrational and infantile misogyny, betraying an unrecognized emotional dependence on mummy, and not worth paying any heed. This in turn means that any men who, like Adam Jukes (1993), have a fear of being dubbed as women haters cannot afford to dispute the word, and become recruited as apostles in the mission. So it is a theoretical offering which cannot be refused. The anti-feminist exposes himself as a man who has transferred his rejection of his mother onto her, and is now blaming her for it.

> *The baby boy, without the intellectual knowledge to understand what is going on, believes the mother is rejecting him. In his eyes she stops being simply the "princess," who made him feel totally and unconditionally loved, and becomes a "witch," making him suffer.* (Jukes, quoted by Neustatter, 1993b)

This general model has been widely popularized (e.g. Skynner & Cleese, 1983) and rejigged (e.g. Olivier, 1989) in a variety of ways. The danger in it all is that by focusing on sexual identity in psychological terms it draws attention away from the real and growing problems of men in society, and in particular their loss of roles within the public domain which formerly privileged them. This is not something which feminism wants to consider. But it should.

For if men hate women (which I don't think many do - although some may resent what they think women are doing to them) then in all honesty I cannot believe that it has much to do with parenting experiences. However it may have a lot to do with the fact that boys are told constantly that it is a man's world and they are its princes and so should be grateful, etc., but then find as they grow up that they are in fact seen as louts and brutes and judged by rules which seem to have been drawn up with someone else in mind. Society is hostile and unexpectedly female; and if there is a witch out there then she is the secret force which is keeping them from their birthright. If men do hate women more now, this is because the contradiction is becoming sharper, as equal opportunities policies intensify the sense of exclusion. The growing aggression of young men is not, *pace* Angela Phillips (1993b), to do with issues of sexual identity in abstract, but is a reaction to objectively changing gender situations in the marketplace.

Thus although relations with a mother may be pertinent in some cases, in general the feeling of disapproval experienced by boys needs to be looked at in a more down-to-earth context, as a movement involving mutual rejection between them as individuals and the controlling mechanisms of the wider community. This may indeed be perceived, by an adolescent, as alienation from a generalized mother. But it is not I think about particular relations with actual mothers at all - which may stay strong even when the rest of society turns against a lad. It is, essentially, about general attitudes to moral transactions, and reflects the ambivalence which boys of this age have towards the demands being made on them, and which communities feel towards *them*.

### Helping men to belong

> *Before he can return to a woman, he must assert his manhood in action. The Zulu warrior had to kill a man, the Mandara youth had to endure torture, the Irish peasant had to build a house, the American man must find a job. This is the classic myth and the mundane reality of masculinity.*
> (Gilder, 1973, p. 16)

Life in a community is about give and take; and this is regulated by its moral economy which rewards giving with status and respect and a legitimate return call on other people. As a child, it is permissible just to receive, and be supported by others. But it is not possible to become a full adult until one has become committed to giving, and has some long-term dependents.

Boys and girls have very different incentives to discover and practice this. A girl "matures" quickly because she knows that she may have to ask for a lot of help herself before too long, so that it is imperative for her to develop her skills in being sensitive to people's needs and giving appropriate support. It helps to build up her credit in the moral economy.

Boys on the other hand, especially in less patriarchal cultures, where there is a weaker pressure on them to anticipate a destiny as an involved family man, can afford to be more offhand towards a process of give and take. This attitude interacts with their more marginal position. For as they themselves may not feel much need for society, in its private aspect of community at any rate, they are consequently less amenable to the rules, and actually *become* less useful in it anyway. More effort would have to be expended in getting them to take on commitments than would be generated as a result.

All men are potentially feckless drones; and this feeds the common portrayal of them as morally inferior to women. The bad-mouthing which Neil Lyndon made such an extended fuss over (1990 & 1992) is not exactly new. Women have long felt this way - as millennia of fairy tales make abundantly clear. What is novel is expressing these ideas so openly; and I believe this indicates a significant recent shift in female strategy. Formal flattery has been replaced by direct challenge, with major implications for men's manageability. But the underlying views are the same.

The wild beast which Robert Bly detects at the bottom of men's psyches (1991), whether it be ancient hairy man or slimy frog, is not a lost father to be pulled out and hugged. He is a construct or refraction of community judgment and disdain. He should be thrown back in and repressed right away if men are going to regain a respected place in society.

Fortunately there are tactics which a group can develop for minimizing adolescent male withdrawal and ambivalence, or even turning it to some purpose. If men respond differently than women to the demands of the community, then the community can learn to treat them differently. It cannot entirely stop boys from wandering off in pursuit of freedom. However it can, via its culture, play on the anxieties which inevitably go with freedom, and raise the stakes by promoting the idea that boys have not chosen this path for themselves, but have been banished in some way or set some tests. Furthermore it can arrange things so that it is not actually up to the boys themselves to decide how or even whether they rejoin the fold.

Thus in all societies the productive roles created for men in the public realm are far from guaranteed. Even though the more confident young men may have few doubts about their own capacity and destiny to succeed, the potentiality of failure produces a generalized insecurity among men which helps to make them manageable. Their immanent marginality means that they are available on a more flexible basis as a different sort of work force, which can be drawn on to meet needs outside the central social business of reproduction and mutual care. This treatment of men divides society into two classes; those in the core who get on with the essential tasks, and those at the edge who can be called on to help out, but may not be. Men are the original reserve army. Segal (1990, p. 80) has mocked male rivalry as *"functional for success in capitalist competition."* But it is not only Fordist systems that we don't like which use men in this way; most societies do it.

## Manhood as reward

Withholding automatic membership introduces a competitive element into the process of male social maturation, so that some men are bound to fail to achieve full adult status, and the community can keep some initiative. This prompts boys to perform great deeds, and undergo high risks, in order to win respect and adult status. What different societies may ask of men varies a good deal. In some, like the Samburu of East Africa, a boy faces a series of painful initiations which have to be undergone without any appearance of pain. Among Jewish communities, where other skills are more important to group survival and prosperity, a Bar Mitzvah initiate will have to memorize sacred texts from the Torah and recite them in Hebrew in front of the synagogue congregation and Rabbi. Some such setting of tests and ordeals is however virtually universal; and in all of them boys risk failure and ridicule.

Thus as a spur to achievement and service, men are morally excluded and made to feel unworthy or redundant and that they have to prove their case before being admitted to the group. This is the curse. Some will then perform heroically and become champions admired by the whole community; though their fame may be short-lived. Most men will prove themselves to be reasonably valuable; and this is usually a prelude to their taking on the status, via marriage, of provider to women and children.

Gilmore shows that although marriage can be seen as a reward for passing a manhood test, that is not the end of the matter, and marriage itself becomes the arena for further public tests of competence. The modern Jewish man, a category which includes Gilmore himself and makes his commentary all the more telling, is subject to continual evaluation of his manhood:

> *A wife who is satisfied with her husband will say that he is a "Mensch," which in both Yiddish and its parent tongue, German, means a real man; and her mother, the ultimate judge of manly virtue, might even agree. Being a Mensch means being competent, dependable, economically secure, and most of all helpful and considerate to dependants. In modern middle-class Jewish culture, the Mensch is a take-charge kind of personality, a firm, dependable pillar of support. He has fathered presentable children, provided economic support for his family, and given his wife what she needs (or, rather, wants).*
>
> *The opposite of the Mensch is the bungler, the failure who lets others take advantage of him. He is alternately called, in all the richness of Yiddish, a schlemiel (jerk), a schnook (dope), a nudnik (nincompoop), a schmendrick (nitwit), a shnorrer (toady), or most commonly a schmuck ('prick," but literally a useless bauble, used to mean bumbling or incompetent).* (p. 127)

So the adult male role generally combines the reward of privileges in the public realm with ongoing tests; and the prior ordeals of adolescence turn out to be merely qualifying rounds, or perhaps even just devices for making the real work of being a husband and father *look* like a reward. Often the ostensible "tests" are very brief, or in themselves only make a nominal contribution to society. This is certainly the case with most ceremonial activities. Robert Bly has been causing men to appear very foolish by getting them to beat drums in assertion of the importance of their role. This is ritualism gone crazy. Very few ceremonies have much value *per se* in modern contexts. Men who are genuinely productive do not have time now for that sort of thing. In most cultures it is possible for men following certain specially honored occupations to avoid the provider role and make direct inputs to the community as a whole. Religious orders for example; or military leaders. But even for men in high status positions marriage can be a useful adjunct and motivator. By giving him a firm location in the private realm, the providing role anchors his incentive to compete and succeed in the public one, and leads to a more secure integration of his life as a whole. This is of course most important where a man's occupation is dreary or low in status and cannot by itself get him up in the morning.

A few men will fail altogether. Some have to, in order to maintain the credibility of the test and value of the prizes. Some of those who do are likely to be the ones who started with some handicap, and who find the ordeals too demanding or daunting. Others may simply find the enchanted life in the forest so appealing that they reject the patriarchal propaganda calling them out, and instead penetrate deeper. This can be dangerous. The forest implies rejection of community regulation, and those who refuse to come out if they are offered a chance may become increasingly anti-social, to the point where they have to be forcibly regulated for the public good.

Western society is sliding away from patriarchy and from the control over men which it gave. The more important that family status is made for a man as a prerequisite for having his own needs met, and the more formalized the qualifying tests are to this end, then the more compliant men are likely to be. For most of the time in earlier centuries the frog image was probably somewhat of an exaggeration. It indicated a tendency, but helped to deter it from happening. Life avoided imitating art. But in recent decades the metaphor has become closer to real life, and it seems ever less able to play a deterrent, self-negating part. Princes are *passé* and the frog is now inheriting the world. Male adolescents are as heavily burdened with feelings of guilt and isolation as ever (Lee, 1991);

but they are no longer being shown a way out.

So youthful rebelliousness, interacting with fear and awareness of not being needed or wanted, may be hardening in western cultures into something more violent and disruptive than hitherto. Young males may objectively be becoming repulsive to other people, and genuinely spurned or condemned by the wider community. The metaphor of the frog as a slimy, selfish, amoral, lazy and libidinous creature, capable of blithely devouring its own offspring, has become flesh in the contemporary yob. Many now belong body and soul to the atomistic, individualistic jungle, where the most typically male experiences are to be found; the crucible of egoistic masculinity. The curse is upon them.

## IN THE FOREST

*Whenever a friend succeeds,*
*a little something in me dies.*
(Gore Vidal)

The forest is partly a refuge from unwanted demands, and partly, if the community manages things properly, an arena where men may prove themselves worthy to be re-admitted as adults. The character traits which this experience elicits in men, which remain with them long after their rehabilitation and influence both the roles that they take on and the way in which they meet them, vary somewhat between cultures. Masculinity takes a variety of forms, depending on how the detachment is defined. Different emphasis can be given to coping and surviving in marginality, escaping from it through successful competition, and even to refining skills or orientations developed while away which may prove useful on return to society.

There is a crucial common element running through all of the resulting forms of masculinity, and this is competitiveness. This is obviously to some extent natural, and arises out of men's sexual rivalry. But women are sexually competitive too; so even if this is a root of the male character, it does not fully explain why it develops in this way for them. The crucial difference may lie, I suspect, in the implications of competition for the cohesion of a community. Women are required to interact in the moral economy with great sensitivity to each others' needs. Over time this *could* arguably have led to the natural selection of sex-linked predispositions to be co-operative. But what seems more likely, because it is more flexible and does not interfere with selection at the level of individuals, is that it has promoted conventions in most cultures which reward women for showing solidarity. Competition between them is therefore more discreet and indirect. This point is taken further in chapter five.

## Stimulating competition

This consideration does not apply for men though, and given the different basis on which societies draw on men's energy, it may well be advantageous for them to stoke up men's natural rivalrous instincts instead in order to maximize their efforts and inputs. In this respect it is significant that men's competitiveness is highly generalized, even pervasive. This is perhaps partly an adaptation for survival in chaos; but is more likely to be related to the conditions in which they are tested. To be certain of winning approval, and thereby getting out of the forest, it is important to be the best at whatever it is which is being valued and judged. The candidate may never be quite sure exactly what he is being tested for. The boys or men in the forest are not the ones who set the rules, or who decide what society will reward. They just respond competitively whenever they can, taking whatever cues are available, to maximize their changes. The sexual roots of male rivalry are not displaced in this, because the prizes are partly sexual and the operative community values (*pace* Orbach) which govern approval and define what life is for are widely felt by men to be female. Women help set the tests, and the highest flying drone catches the queen.

The rules governing competition are minimal. Men are not hindered by moral obligations. In the forest there are no dependants needing care or other social bonds to confuse motivations and calculations. The forest is just a tangle of unregulated desires and impulses, of which each person has to make sense as best he can. It is like a game with no objective beyond itself; and men are free to work out, single-mindedly and ruthlessly, how to maximize their lives, both in terms of emerging at last into the best possible position in society, and of looking after themselves and maybe having some fun in the meantime. Impersonal, universalistic rationality becomes in many ways the defining feature of masculinity (Seidler, 1991, p. 65).

This in turn then strongly determines the nature of specifically male forms of behavior and action. These can be characterized as a number of overlapping themes: namely a closeness to nature and things rather than people; a pervasive quality of "play" in activities, in that these are carried out for personal improvement or gratification rather than to help others; and a mechanistic aspect to the rules and organizations constructed around play and shared play.

## Men and nature

Closeness to nature is fundamental here. The lone frog is first of all a material being ruled by the imperatives of his own flesh. So he relates very directly to the natural world where objects for satisfying desires, and instruments for facilitating this, can be found. I am aware that women often complain that they are designated as more "natural," and men as more "social," in the conventions of many cultures. The western patriarchal religions of Christianity, Islam and Judaism are undeniably offenders here, and some analysts like Sherry Ortner (1974) have detected in this a massive cultural conspiracy against women, to denigrate them and deprive them of due dignity. I think this is one of the great canards of gender theory. It does not take into due account the different levels of formality which all cultures comprise, and the illusions which they conjure up to help redress or improve on nature. I would argue that all but the most ideologically blinkered or naïve members of the cultures in question would recognize that deceptions and inversions are involved in these representations.

For example, although Islam formally portrays women in this way, if you talk to even fairly unsophisticated Muslim men and women in private many will readily volunteer the observation that women are more social and spiritual than men - and even that this is why religion is more *for* men. Religious dogma does not prevent them from articulating this for themselves. What seems to be happening here is that men are "talked up" by religion, and by patriarchy generally, in order to compensate for the fact that their general dispositions are usually less social - and of course to justify their privileges in the public domain. That is, men need it most. It is part of the theater of patriarchy which I look at in the next chapter. But few people, I believe, are wholly taken in by it.

In fact, if you look carefully at specific statements made by people about women's being more "natural," then it soon becomes clear that what most of them have in mind is exactly the opposite; that is, that women are "naturally social" by comparison with the more artificial social identity of men. They know vaguely that women are supposed to be natural, and then interpret this in ways which actually make sense to them in their own lives. Most people in most cultures, including all branches of feminists in our own (who may think that they are out of step in this but are not), in reality see women as more closely involved in society and as belonging more to it. Everything else is patriarchal illusion and verbal confusion.

Women's lives are much more fully and genuinely described by the sum of their social relations, whereas men are more detached, so that their "social" aspect, even where it may be very powerful, is also much more superficial and possibly fragile. Specifically male groupings and associations often have the inorganic mass quality of gangs - which seem almost designed to permit the avoidance of intimacy and maintenance of personal privacy, even in the heart of collective action. The solidarity which they have is of the sort Durkheim would have called mechanical - arising out of physical juxtaposition rather than in any linkages of close interdependence; and as noted below there are situations in which this can be an advantage.

A woman's relations with natural objects are more often than a man's secondary to, or mediated by, relations with other people; and these humanize her objectives and perceptions. Bryan Magee noted a few years ago that:

> *In every organisation I have ever worked in or with, I have found that when I discuss its affairs with one of my women colleagues she tends to talk first and foremost about the human beings in the organisation and the relationships between them, and then to approach questions about work via these considerations. If I discuss the same questions with a male colleague, he is more likely to talk in terms of abstract aims, policies, organisation, planning, budgets, figures.* (1989, p. 4)

Men on the other hand tend to minimize personal relations and seek an almost mystical communion with nature itself, or its essence, and with the hidden rules that hold the secret to the order behind the apparent chaos. Men's strongest religious experiences, of the noumenous, usually occur alone with nature. Most of the great religions have been powerfully influenced by jungle hermits or men in other types of wilderness whose formative situations have allowed them to contemplate direct bonds between themselves as individuals and a central deity, life force, or universal principle. Moses went to the top of a mountain to talk to God; John the Baptist heard voices in the desert; Buddha withdrew for a decade into the forest; and Mohammed, while Khadiya took full responsibility for their family, meditated for years in a cave. Men's relations with other people are mediated via this external focus, so that even in groups, as David Mamet notes (1989), their bonding with the universe is dominant.

> *And the true nature of the world, as between men, is I think community of effort directed towards the outside world, directed to subdue, to understand, or to wonder or withstand together, the truth of the world.*

When beset by problems, men will often try to find solutions entailing the use of objects or systems, rather than communicating with other people. Relatively detached from moral pressures and evaluations, and people's everyday needs, the forest dweller has no ready-made meaning in the world, and tries to create it by learning to control the physical universe and constructing mechanistic rules which promote this physical domination. There is an avoidance here of personal interaction, with its risks of moral hassle, deals or debts, and whims or changes of mood, and a clear preference instead for a direct approach involving knowledge and manipulation of invariant rules.

## Things to play with

After men have achieved adult status and admission to society, nature still retains value as a refuge from other people. To some extent, though this should not be taken too far, male "playing" with nature, whether by splitting atoms, going fishing, following a hobby which involves collecting and organizing and learning about material things, scaling mountains or messing about in the garden shed, can all be seen as ways of escaping the demands of domesticity and avoiding too much direct competition with other men. Has anyone yet been able to devise a pastime quite so harmless and peaceful as train-spotting? Even pursuits like shooting, so often reviled as the essence of naked masculine aggression by women who would like to bring the natural world into their protective moral community, seem to be valued by most men less out of a desire to destroy or dominate than as a way to become part of, and merge with, nature on its own terms.

There is a distinction here which needs to be made between understanding nature and dominating it. Pure scientists, who are mostly men and whose frequently withdrawn personality, even gaucheness, are certainly male features, seem often rather uninterested in the practical application of their ideas. They may even be hostile. What they are absorbed by is the mental quest to discover how things work. So long as they are permitted to carry on with their work, and are not pressed to publish articles and account for themselves before they are ready, they often care little about its possible implications for the community, or even indeed about what their colleagues may be up to unless they are close or direct competitors. This is precisely what many women find alien in science, and are seeking to change (Walby, 1990, p. 117; Kirkup & Smith, 1992).

As things stand, however, the scientific community is hardly a group in any real sense, but primarily a gang involved in parallel play. Interpersonal communication between members may be very limited, even off-duty. Women, including, I guess, female scientists, are said to talk to each other about their personal problems. But men, and that most certainly includes scientists, are more prone to openly regard each other as competitors and say little, since to expose your thoughts and anxieties is to risk giving an advantage to your rivals. The prevailing wisdom, following the Chodorow line discussed above, argues that men communicate less and are afraid of sharing and intimacy because of the way that they have been socialized, and related as children to their parents. But I am more impressed by the approach of Deborah Tannen (1991) who links this difference to the recognition by women of the importance to themselves of maintaining a strong community. I would take this a little further and suggest that men avoid expressing feelings partly because they know that they have a weaker articulation and entry to the world where these are relevant. They have to fight for a position first. When I see Susie Orbach arguing that men should take emotional responsibility for themselves and find a masculinity that is more fulfilling and less precarious it looks like royalty telling the masses to eat cake. It is just not relevant to men's objective situation, which *is* much more insecure than women's.

## Talking without communicating

Thus communication seems to play a rather different part in the lives of men and women; and this can lead to serious misunderstandings between them, and different evaluations of behavior. To borrow a Tannen technique, let us imagine a conversation in which Jane, who is still clawing her way back up from a bout of depression, goes to a meal with her friends Sally and Dave, and spends most of the evening talking about her problems. Sally and Dave are quite likely to respond to this in very different ways. Sally almost certainly will feel obliged to refer at some length to her own breakdown a few years earlier (even though Jane has heard about it before) because she sees this as the best way of expressing sympathy and solidarity, and of making Jane feel that she has not been selfish and boring in unburdening herself at such length.

Dave, listening to all of this (yet again) may well feel that Sally has ridden insensitively on the back of Jane's comparatively minor difficulties, and succeeded in trumping them with her own much greater crisis which (unlike Jane, so far) she has heroically surmounted. This interpretation (which he assumes Jane will share) is based on, and reinforces, his own gut feeling that when people bring up their problems the decent thing to do is to express some sympathy (giving support by showing that you care) and then slide reasonably quickly onto another subject (giving Jane a chance to escape from her obsession). He regards this as good both for Jane, as he will not then be competing with her in any way for sympathy, and good for him, because as he is not demanding attention for himself he is not incurring debts for himself. So this is what he eventually does; and he feels rather pleased with himself when the conversation settles down on Maastricht.

Sally, we may surmise, feels on the contrary that Dave has offered purely nominal support to Jane, thereby belittling her problems, and only did it anyway in order to get credit for himself as a sympathetic ear. He had been patronizing and made her feel even worse. If he had really cared he would have talked about the difficulties he is having with his mother, so that Jane could see that he is not above such things himself. The scene is set for a further round of misunderstandings after Jane has left to go home.

Situations like this arise constantly because for men there is an inherently competitive and calculating aspect to relations, and hence to communications. Women use language to spin a warm web of mutual care and affection. But men are much more afraid of giving anything away. This male reticence has an image problem these days; but it is organically bound up with the underlying conditions of male existence. I would argue that there is nothing inherently wrong with it. It assists in survival, because often the only way to reduce tension and competition, which are there and cannot be willed away, is to say nothing.

Not long ago the press had a field day mocking the alleged inability of a teenage hacker to express his emotions. Paul Bedworth, in court on charges of breaking into dozens of computer systems, was described variously, and "in spite of extremely impressive A-level results," as a lonely and vulnerable loser, a computer nerd, and hopelessly addicted to the intellectual game of trying to outwit computer security. But what really seemed to damn him was the psychologist's evidence that *"He became profoundly embarrassed when asked to talk about his own feelings. He simply couldn't cope when asked what sort of person he was."* (Watts, 1993).

But why should he have to talk about his emotions? They're his after all; if he did come out with them other people might well find them unacceptable, or use them *against* him in some way. Men's silence may well have something to do with the fact that male feelings are much more likely to prove unacceptable than those of women, which is why men say ask me no questions and I'll tell you no lies. So let him button up. Emotional espionage has to be resisted. He knows what he feels and he can talk about it if and when he wants to. Keep right on, son. Don't let them grind you down. Do not, moreover, forget Jill Tweedie's confession that she likes taciturn men anyway: she may not be alone.

> *...it has lately dawned on me that certain traits more common
> in men than women may or may not be a burden to them but
> are surer than eggs an asset to me. The shameful truth is:
> I'm pleased that men are out of touch with their emotions.
> For one thing, they aren't always rabbiting on about theirs
> when I want to rabbit on about mine. Someone has to give
> ground and other women mostly don't. ... As for those who
> urge men to display their vulnerability, the very thought
> sends me into a flat panic. Putting on a good show of
> invulnerability is surely what men are* for. (Tweedie, 1990)

## Playing together

Staying buttoned-up may well be what is required in order to engage
in parallel play, as opposed to open fighting. This is perhaps
illustrated by some recent revelations about the world of arduous
expeditions - those trials of endurance where men pit themselves
against nature at its most indomitable. Social bonding between
players appears to be kept to an absolute minimum; and for some
time now I have felt that a medal in this field should be struck for
the legendary Ranulph Fiennes and his collaborators in various
attempts, most of which appear to have been unsuccessful, to walk
to the North or South Poles. For by Sir Ranulph's own account, he
and his companion would often spend several days walking along
side by side, quietly wondering at the changing scenery, traversing
crevasses, and generally pitting themselves against the elements,
before one of those rare moments occurred when they might have
a conversation.

New light has been shed on all this by the recent publication,
separately, of accounts by Sir Ranulph and his companion on a
number of recent adventures, Mike Strand, of their recent crossing
of Antarctica. For it seems that behind the noble silences dwelt
fierce rivalries and resentments, and that for long periods they were
driven by mutual antipathy. *"Fiennes and Strand tottered, mostly in
silence, across a 1,350 mile plateau, hating each other."* (Lennon,
1993). Hence the separate memoirs. Yet they are apparently
planning to do something else together soon. So silence may have
its value. This is how to share fierce and crazy competition, without

actually doing each other any mischief.

Rather a lot of what men appear to do together is really done alone. The crowds who assemble each week to follow the fortunes of a football team do not know each other, nor do they bear feelings of mutual interdependence; and they wouldn't want to. But the sharing of hope, elation and despair which their team brings to them unites them briefly and transcends their individualism in a very male sort of way. What holds them together is the common purpose; the idea. Men do not thrill to a particularistic voice summoning a personal response, but to the calls of solidarity or honor in an impersonal group. The chant of the Kop; a bugle sounding the last post; beer hall shouts; a mullah's wail.

From common purpose it is only a short step to collaboration and association, which are the characteristically masculine modes of bonding that operate in the marketplace and state - those arenas for male activity which have been partially regulated and incorporated by the community, but which are still sealed off sufficiently - or were until recently - to allow men to become part of society without having to submit fully to the rigors of the moral economy. Female groupings tend to be built around personalized relationships, where each participant has a unique and in many ways irreplaceable position and function. This is the essence of particularism. But male competitiveness finds that too irksome, and prefers looser linkages between associates - which can very often include alliances between men who are rivals, certainly in other spheres. Collaboration and cooperation do not signal the end of competition. Usually they are its continuation by other means, whereby rivals agree to pursue common or compatible goals in that context. They can manage to play together. And the fact that they can multiplies the possibilities of finding games which are useful to society.

## USEFUL PLAY

The distinctive orientations which men acquire in the forest equip them to make contributions to the community which can be complementary to those made by women. Some masculine traits, notwithstanding their egoistic roots, which often import problems into society along with men (e.g. Bokun, 1990), become defined and utilized as social virtues.

## Dangerous games

> *There is no discourse (in feminism) of ordinary male sacrifice. Where were the women when the Titanic went down? In the lifeboats, that's where.*
> (Alex Pilling, *The Times*, 28 Sept. 1992)

A common feature running through most definitions of useful masculinity is the relative detachment and consequent expendability of men - which fits in conveniently with the polarization between core community work, which is continuous, committed and personalized, and marginal work, which is irregular, more risky, and located in the public domain. The simple fact that men don't have other people so directly dependent on them gives them more freedom to undertake distant and hazardous enterprises - conquering nature or defending the realm - which have relevance to the community as a whole. This applies whether they actually feel like doing it or not; and Gilmore repeatedly makes the point that exhortation to manhood, and its celebration as a public duty, is emphasized most when dangerous roles need to be performed, because boys have to be prodded hard before they will take them on.

A predilection for play is also an advantage, as it helps men to get through assignments with uncertain outcomes without being worn down by the idea that time is being wasted. The job is fun in itself, as a challenge. The motto of the male reserve army is that they also serve who only play.

Military service epitomizes these characteristics to the full, and is an obvious focus for masculine roles in most cultures. Men in general, single men in particular, are dispensable; and it is through war that men are able to make their distinctive sacrifices to the common good. This situation is much misunderstood or misrepresented nowadays. Men have been regarded traditionally, at least since the days of chivalry, as the main combatants in war; and this is, I think, basically because their sacrifice causes least damage to the moral heart of society. It is *not* that men are emotionally incapable of resolving issues peacefully (Bosely, 1992) or are compulsively drawn to mindless violence; most will only fight when a battle is presented to them as the defense of friends and loved ones. Nor is it just that women are normally excluded because war is somehow "too important" for them, or in order to justify male monopolies of political power, as is often claimed (Coward, 1990). This may be a part of it; but it is not the key. It is mainly that war gives men a chance to display and exercise their commitment, with minimal damage to the fabric of society.

The utility of military service and in particular the national conscription of young men, which is periodically held out as a means of regulating the troublesome male lout, lies I believe not so much in the "discipline" which it is held to impart, as in the notion of useful "service" itself, to the community, which gives a context and rationale for the acceptance of that discipline. The authority of senior officers, which young men can learn to respect, would not exist if the job being done were not seen as a valuable social contribution. Women can and do bear arms. But in the military domain they are the reservists. Israel has had female conscription for half a century now. But it still prefers to keep women away from front line duty; not because they can't do it, but because they can do *other* things that men can't, as Ben-Gurion emphasized (Almog, 1993). They make many sacrifices for the community, in a thousand routine ways. For men, fighting is the best chance to identify and serve.

Another standard objection to women fighters, which has surfaced recently in the United States as a reason for not tolerating gay soldiers, is that military efficiency is at risk unless front line units consist only of identical and instantly replaceable comrades. Quickly forged, fairly superficial, mechanical bonding is what is best. The possible presence in a fighting situation of sexual partners, with deeper relationships, may not frighten feminists, but it certainly terrifies the chiefs-of-staff. I think this is, however, a secondary consideration, which usually only arises when the question of female soldiers is introduced. Normally a front line role for women is not considered at all because the amount of risk-taking they would be exposed to is regarded as too damaging to the community which the army is supposed to be protecting.

It was noteworthy during the Gulf War, in which American servicewomen were allowed for the first time to take an active fighting role, that several of them were reported as saying that the worst thing about combat was that it made you think all the more about your children back home (Swain, 1990 and Tisdall, 1990; but disputed by Muir, 1992). They had broken through the barrier which proclaimed that women were not capable of fighting, only to find that it was not questions about their skill or ability, but their own concern for their dependants, which raised problems for them. This anguish undoubtedly exists for men too, and is difficult enough for them. But as women are generally so much closer to children, and feel more responsible for them, it is in their case all the more arduous, for the children no less than their mothers.

## Lonely games

Physical adventures are not the only ones to which masculinity is better fitted. Greater detachment from daily caring also enables men to indulge more fully in intellectual fantasy, and in those obsessional feats of imaginative creation which produce original science and art. Nabokov saw his art as a "divine game" (Boyd, 1992); and Anthony Trollope's novels arose out of a lifelong habit of daydreaming (Glendinning, 1992). Most inner adventures are also driven by compulsion to express or understand something which has not been formulated before. Truly original work is a journey, very much alone, into an unexplored corner of the natural world or a mental universe, to bring back some artifact or insight unlike any which has been witnessed before.

Some work lately (e.g., Chadwick and de Courtevron, 1993) has challenged the stereotype of a lonely genius - usually meaning a solitary man or one sustained by an invisible and self-effacing wife - by looking at the influence of partnerships on creativity, as for example between Vanessa Bell and Duncan Grant. Clearly the stereotype does not have absolute validity, and has obscured many cases in which people create together and spark each other off. But the idea does seem to contain a general truth, all the same. This is surely because creativity is so much easier for someone alone, or who is able at least to shut other people out when desired. We are often told that genius is ninety nine percent application; and solitude is usually a precondition for that.

Often intense concentration is called for. Followers of the Frederick Forsyth divorce hearings will recall his wife's statement that it was his tremendous bouts of concentration while weaving elaborate plots which destroyed their marriage.

*He would get an idea and then he just wasn't there as far
as his family and his wife were concerned. He was in a
complete world of his own. He had incredible powers of
concentration. I just had to get on with keeping the children
out of his way and the house run. For periods of up to a year
he would think of nothing else but his latest book.* (Ambrose,
1990)

Similarly P.G. Wodehouse, creator of Bertie Wooster's *Drones
Club,* was a loner and emotional hermit, in spite of a jocular and
sociable exterior, and chose to belong to a quiet club where nobody
knew him, so that he could work without interruptions (Usborne,
1991).

Presumably artists who are not successful are no less obsessional.
And most surely are unsuccessful. Only a limited number of fruits
of this sort of work can be taken up by the community and absorbed
into its culture with appropriate rewards and honor given to the
progenitors. Most products of intellectual labor are doomed to
remain undiscovered, sunk without trace, of value only to their
begetters. They are, in the words of an old Roy Harper album title,
if I recall it correctly, just *Footnotes in the Archives of Oblivion.*
Most seed that is scattered is lost. Richard Wagner lived despairing
of failure even in the flush of success (Vulliamy, 1989). It is a very
high risk area, which you might not want to enter if your real life
was more satisfying and creative.

Until recent decades most women, in spite of artistic and literary
capacities which are certainly no less than men's, and in some
areas such as narrative fiction, which are less abstract and closer to
daily life and experience, probably much greater than men's, simply
have not had the time to spare for creative ventures. But it is not
just "about time." Just before her death Jill Tweedie lamented the
way in which girls fail to *do* things, because they get diverted into
relating to people instead, and she indicated that this was a real
problem for women, which she was not confident that they would
overcome (Tweedie, 1993). Even where women do manage to
pursue literary or other artistic careers, they may be nagged by
doubts or guilt, like Kathleen Raine who said in a recent interview:

*In doing what I have done as a writer, I suffer from a sense*

> *of guilt and betrayal of a much more profound nature than*
> *that of merely betraying my parents and my children - it's*
> *a betrayal of woman. I have not fulfilled the true tasks of*
> *woman, either as a daughter, a spouse or a mother, and that*
> *is the price of being Kathleen Raine.* (Raine, 1993)

So the choices for men and women are not the same. Camille Paglia
has contrived to get up the noses of many feminists by arguing that
life usually *is* more absorbing for women, and that it is damaged
psyches which perform the greatest miracles in art. Certainly
Virginia Woolf was never quite sure that she had made the right
choice by leaving it to her sister Vanessa Bell to have the children
- which is perhaps also germane to the question of what Bell might
have produced as a lonely genius (Dunn, 1990). Also Mount (1982,
p. 227) refers to a fourteenth-century French feminist who, although
being artistically creative, for which she was renowned, saw her
widowhood as slavery:

> *The most famous feminist of the time was Christine de Pisan*
> *(c.1364-c.1430), the daughter of an Italian physician in the*
> *service of Charles V. She was brought up in Paris, became*
> *a keen French patriot, married and was left widowed at the*
> *age of twenty-five. Widowhood, she said, had made her fall*
> *"from freedom into slavery"; she was "a turtle dove without*
> *a mate," "a sheep without a shepherd," "a ship without a*
> *skipper," "languishing in orphanhood." She took on what*
> *she called a manly role with energy, writing poems and*
> *treatises on popular subjects from the education of women to*
> *the laws of chivalry, although she continued to claim that she*
> *would rather have been a wife again.*

It may be difficult to decide which is the cause of what, but
amongst writers and artists there are indeed many who express great
antipathy to family life - as the bane of all creative souls. Beneath
Philip Larkin's misogyny lay a fear that giving himself to another
person, especially a woman, would be the end of his creativity
(Thwaite, 1992). Mount, although himself a eulogist of family life,
points out (p. 157) that many of the greatest English writers were
unhappy in marriage - including Shakespeare, Milton, Dr. Johnson,

Byron, Thackeray, Dickens and T.S. Eliot - while a great many women writers did not marry at all, or only very late. Also, among philosophers many of the greatest have been unhampered by family ties - i.e. Newton, Descartes, Locke, Pascal, Spinoza, Kant, Leibniz, Schopenhauer, Nietzsche, Keirkegaard and Wittgenstein.

## Abstract virtues

Not only does male detachment from interpersonal obligations provide marvellous opportunities to indulge in obsessional adventures. It also, I believe, has a profound bearing on the nature of the product. It is men freed from personalized demands, like the motionless thinker hewn by Rodin (himself supported in his labors by the self-abnegating Claudel) who have played the major part in putting together the abstract systems of thought and philosophical constructions which can go beyond familial and parochial loyalties, and which inform generalized codes able to stand above, and hence unite, opposed and disparate communities. Einstein, a scientist and great humanitarian who devoted much of his life to the cause of peace, was, like many great men, a rotter to his nearest and dearest (Highfield & Carter, 1993).

But we should expect this to be the case, almost as a matter of definition, because what such men are pursuing is so very different to the moral precepts by which they are now, increasingly it seems, being condemned. Anyway, what they did was still valuable and perhaps necessary. As I have shown in some detail elsewhere (1985, chapter 10), universalistic values run counter to most of the principles generated by everyday life, by which people order most of their routine activities, in which priority is inevitably given to the people who are closest to us. Universal schemas do not arise from within caring communities. However once they have been invented they can be useful to such groups as formulae for handling external relations with others, or for coming together with them into larger associations. Male universalist speculation and idealism has been a considerable virtue in assisting the emergence of political civilization, although this may have been overstated by male philosophers, who have frequently cited male abstraction as proof of real impartiality - by the same logic as the ancient world loved a eunuch - and justification for the exclusion of women from public affairs. Hegel for example (quoted by Pateman, 1989, p. 177) insisted that women were overly particularistic:

> *Womankind ... changes by intrigue the universal end of government into a private end, transforms its universal activity into a work of some particular individual, and perverts the universal property of the state into a possession and ornament for the Family.*

This proposition begs many questions about how universalistic men are in practice. It ignores the ways in which the public realm often provides a masquerade for purposes informed by the private, or a charter for hypocrisy as I note in chapter eight. Possibly when women operate the public domain, its masking of the private realm becomes more transparent; but I am sceptical. It is, after all, male politicians who are currently the focus of corruption scandals and black holes of public confidence in a number of contemporary states, from Japan to Italy.

What seems more likely to be the governing principle here, which underlies the public realm generally, and has already been spelled out earlier in relation to military roles, is that where there is some valuable activity which men are half good at then it makes sense to treat this as their work, in order to give them something to do. Men need philosophy more than women do because they have to create a place for themselves in the world. It would seem likely on Kant's principle that the foundation of morality is the distinction between treating a human being as a person rather than as a thing, that much inspiration for philosophy comes from women, and then perhaps gets its codification and elaboration and disputation at the hands of (celibate) males. Letting them take it on makes them more useful to society than they would be without it.

## Chivalrous impulses

The various male virtues stemming from their greater freedom from social obligations combine very harmoniously in the figure of the knight, the samurai or the lone ranger in western terms. He is the archetypal male hero. The knight is sworn to uphold a universal idea or cause, and will help any who invoke it - especially the weak who have no other recourse.

The knight is a warrior, and highly competitive. But he competes only for honor; in everything else he is generous, giving all he has, and taking nothing more for himself than he needs in order to perform his task. Being a warrior means that he is expendable; and he achieves greatest honor for himself by sacrificing his life to a cause. The knight has no roots, belongs nowhere but everywhere, and wanders endlessly in search of just encounters through which he must continually prove himself. This is a quest which can never be completed. It is bounded only by the necessity of combat and the certainty of succumbing eventually to a stronger opponent.

This role lends itself rather nicely to the idea of mechanization; for robots encapsulate marvellously the negation of self and the programmed dedication of a male avenger or champion. Terminator, the futurist polymorph through which Arnold Schwarzenegger has chosen to express himself, is *more* than just a neat fighting machine, and is arguably the latest in a very long line of altruistic knights. As the peerless body, in the final scene of *Terminator II,* sinks bubbling into the vat of industrial acid, it dawns on us that this time he is not being recycled. He is deliberately sacrificing himself for the sake of the woman and her child. Arnie is a real man, after all.

The idea of the knight captures the idealistic enthusiasm of young men before they settle down to becoming committed members of real communities. The trouble with it of course is that the unattached life-style of wandering hero is so appealing to them anyway that it requires no marketing. Societies don't need any more wannabe Don Quixotes, or even Cyranos - however great the panache with which they may expire at the end of their brief and largely parasitic lives. This is getting worse too. As feminist discourse erodes the family man role model, there is not much else for a lad to aspire to. Who can blame young boys if all that they are interested in these days are books and films about superheroes? And whom should we blame if they actually turn into something else?

There is no need to glamorize the single state; and what *The Frog Prince* and its ilk have done in the past is to sell the path of matrimony and responsible fatherhood. Patriarchal cultures teach boys that their nature is evil and that they must rebuild themselves around a sense of duty (Seidler, 1991, p. 77-8). In practice only a few frogs could ever hope to become great and useful knight heroes. The realistic choice for the majority of boys is between opting for marriage, or facing a bleak and undignified life alone in the forest.

## DRONES AND DRIFTERS

If masculinity is about being competitive, then it is also necessarily about the fear of being a loser. A few males can go a long way, so it is not unreasonable for most to feel surplus. This is something which traditional women do experience but usually I believe to a lesser degree. They are expected to have children, and in some cultures failure to do so is seen as a disaster, and may occasion disgrace or divorce and even suicide. But this is comparatively rare. Even in some of the societies where children are valued most, as around the Mediterranean, the shame of being unable to reproduce attaches mainly to the husband, as the provider of the seed. In most societies a barren woman can still fulfill part of her destiny by helping to care for the children of others. It may entail a lower status, but it does not involve loss of membership of the community. There is a place for her.

Among men, the consequences of failure are generally greater. Until recently in the west, men who do not marry by a certain age, or who cannot cope with the responsibility of fatherhood, and who do not make up for this by eminent achievement in a prestigious profession or occupation through which they directly contribute to the life of the community, do not receive respect in it and may have an extremely tenuous place in that community. There are great cultural variations in this, I accept, but it is generally true that a man who does not become a provider in one way or another fails to become a proper adult, and faces reduced life chances in almost every dimension. The community cares little about such men, because they make little input to it; and in turn this renders them prone to self-neglect. Warren Farrell would argue that men are neglected by the community itself (1994). I am doubtful about this though, as it seems well established that men who are locked into caring families fare better than those who are not (e.g. Bernard, 1973). The income, career development, physical and mental health and general life expectancy, suicide rate, and range of social contacts and activities of single men are all significantly worse than for married men. It is mainly from their ranks that vagrants are drawn, prisons are filled, and the demons of drink and despair harvest their victims.

## The option of withdrawal

But it is not all loss; not just failure and rejection. Men have mixed feelings anyway about being drawn into community life, for drones do at least retain their freedom. If you can't win a respected position in society, then this freedom becomes all the more valuable and may serve as an alternative basis for self-respect. The exaggerated dignity and prickly pride commonly found among dropouts and vagrants is not entirely self-deluding, for although it may be hazardous their life-style does embody much which is seductive to men: the closeness to nature, absence of demands and restrictions, time to sit in the wilderness seeking inspiration or regeneration. The pride appears exaggerated because it is all that he has left. However, he does still have it. A woman on the road, the bag lady, invariably appears a sad and odd figure, pathetically trying to carry too much of a previous domestic world with her, and thereby evoking a breakdown of the moral community somewhere. By contrast the male tramp is sometimes a figure of fun but he does not seem out of place. He is much more continuous with ordinary male roles in society. He is not remarkable.

He may in certain respects even stand out as something of a hero (Tressell, 1955; Orwell, 1949). For the vagrant's image as "king of the road," free to choose where he lays his head and the direction in which he sets off the next morning, is a potent reminder that a man's pride and independence may be greater than his need for domestication. This underlines men's original power, very different from and far older than patriarchy, of being freer than women to walk away from relationships and situations that don't suit them. The tramp never lets women forget that men may only stay around for as long as they are compensated for the freedom that they have foregone, because they do have an alternative.

I believe very strongly that it is this raw power of men to care less than women which brings about patriarchy, rather than vice-versa, because it is this which sets initial exchange rates in gender relations so firmly in men's favor. According to the principle of indifference or "least interest" (Willard, 1938), the party to a relationship who values it less is most able to impose (his) will on it. Patriarchy may appear to be the problem, and may *be* a problem, but it surely originates in cultural efforts to cut the primordial freebooting male down to size, partly by loading him with some responsibilities too, but above all by making him feel that the role is in fact valuable to him. So while one aspect of this cultural response to male offhandedness is to denigrate irresponsibility as childish, or a place of banishment and eventual failure - the forest - this probably will not be enough to convince all men. Some carrot is needed as well, some pull factors as well as push. Hence the substantial material privileges which are on offer for the successful patriarchal prince. These are a rich prize indeed. The boy reading the story feels immediately that he does not want to stay a frog in the dismal forest, and that the surest way of escaping is to find a princess and claim his kingdom.

# 4

# THE ROYAL FIX

The crucial event in the whole drama is the transformation of the odious frog into a handsome prince. The symbolic importance of this is tremendous as it tells boys that marriage is desirable. Acceptance by a woman will turn them into little princes; from yob to nob at a stroke. Surely worth sacrificing some freedom for.

## THE TRANSFORMATION

A man entering marriage is trading a life of independence for a position of responsibility with dependants - that is a wife now and the assumption of children to follow - in the structure of personalized supports which makes up the fabric of community life. Many of them might regard this as a poor exchange; and this is why it is significant that men are seen to be brought into chains of personal dependency above their wives, as authorized providers for the family. The act of marriage imparts a patriarchal bonus to the husband.

The image of prince is accurate here as the idea of domestic monarchy is frequently used in discussions of patriarchy - just as, since Filmer at least, political analysts have pictured monarchs as fathers of their people. At an obvious level, the notion clearly expresses the status given to men in relation to their wives in the kingdom of a family. But it also, more subtly - but I think very persuasively - makes a reference to the territorial fix which marriage symbolically entails. The frog, or knight, is free to wander following his fancy, and needs to recognize no frontiers. But a prince belongs to the land and his subjects. They will only honor him so long as he serves them. No authority without responsibility. *Noblesse oblige.* A prince always has a territorial designation; that is his identity. The single man is free; but a married man is tied to his family and has overriding obligations.

Thus the imagery helps to clarify the nature of the transformation by showing the price which has to be paid for the title. A husband cannot expect to go on pursuing grand universalist plans. You can't be a prophet in your own country; and the buggy in the hall is a notorious enemy of creative promise. This does not mean giving up all ambition or idealism, so much as finding ways to pursue them which fit in with domestic commitments. I saw a delicious cartoon a few months ago in a daily newspaper (I forget which now) depicting a man standing rather stiffly over a distraught woman with children, and saying something like "I'm leaving you so that I can devote more time to promoting family values."

The transformation of the frog represents movement in the opposite direction. Sometimes the man's vision may help to pull a kingdom into a universe of general values, and overcome a possible tendency towards parochialism. But more often it is he who changes. A political activist who at first just drags his infants along on protest marches and demos may eventually realize that they have problems at their school which need some principled input. It makes good sense to give this priority. A kingdom which does not protect its own people and interests will not be very effective in supporting any values at all; so it is essential to put the realm first sometimes.

The reformulation of ideals into achievable goals may also make them more satisfying. You can't operationalize a universal principle everywhere; you have to act, or at any rate start to act, in a particular place. Men often have a strong tendency to see their obligations in abstract terms. Several contributions to Sean French's recent collection on fatherhood (1993) betrayed that their authors still saw their children as imagined, even generalized ideas, rather than flesh and blood. Some fathers may go through married life without changing these perceptions much. But the experience of fatherhood is the best chance most men will have to humanize and actualize their idealism, by giving them a concrete reason and location for operating - in the kingdom of dependants. Martin Amis has described how having children gave him a stake in the world's future, and caused him to become concerned about the bomb:

> "*I am sick of nuclear weapons,*" *he wrote in the introduction to Einstein's Monsters (which is dedicated to Louis and Jacob). "They make me feel as if a child of mine has been*

*out too long, much too long, and already it is getting dark."*
(Toby Young, 1993)

What actually transforms men is not marriage itself, in an abstract sense, so much as the commitments to real people which flow from it, and the experience of being responsible in other people's eyes for their wellbeing. Just like women, in the "original social contract" which I envisage occurs in relation to looking after children, men enter into an undertaking which they know they will be held to. So it is in their interest to take it seriously. This is how men start to learn how to become like women.

## Man the provider

The first stage in this process involves making men useful by defining them as *material* providers. Although many people would like to think that it is largely a legacy of Victorian industrialism (e.g. Davidoff & Hall, 1986; Hearn, 1992), which can be cleared out like old lumber, this is effectively universal. In a few cultures, outside of the European tradition, men are made responsible for the support of sisters and their children, as well as or sometimes rather than wives and their own offspring, and there are variations in how support is provided. But the underlying principle is the same. This was posited by Margaret Mead as the essential distinction between human society and groupings among other animals.

> *(Man's) nurturing behaviour, this fending for females and children instead of leaving them to fend for themselves, as the primates do, may take many different forms. ... The division of labour may be made in a thousand ways, so that the men of a given society are very idle, or the women left disproportionately free of effort, as in the childless American urban home. But the core remains. Man, the heir of tradition, provides for women and children. We have no indication that man the animal, man unpatterned by social learning, would do anything of the sort. (1949, p. 146)*

Margaret Mead occupies a curious position in relation to postwar feminism. In the interwar years Mead herself was regarded as a feminist by most people who read her books. She wrote extensively on the plasticity of human behavior; and her work on a number of non-European societies was key reference material for debates on the limits of variability in gender roles, and on different patterns of sex and culture. Her books were important influences in post-war America, in promoting interest in women's issues, and the emergency of a popular feminist movement.

And yet, perhaps ironically, current feminism did not get properly underway until it had distanced itself from her. One of the founding enterprises of second wave feminism, Betty Friedan's *Feminine Mystique* (1963) was in part organized around a matricidal rubbishing of Mead's main thesis. This is partly explained by Mead's tendency, notwithstanding her emphasis on the formative power of culture, towards admitting some biological determinism. This went down badly when the US moved into the post-McCarthy era, where socio-biological arguments were increasingly being interpreted as fascist. But the *main* thing I suspect was what Mead saw as the *content* of this biological programming.

> *The mother's nurturing tie is apparently so deeply rooted in the actual biological conditions of conception and gestation, birth and suckling, that only fairly complicated social arrangements can break it down entirely. ... But the evidence suggests that we should phrase the matter differently for men and women - that men have to learn to want to provide for others, and this behaviour, being learned, is fragile and can disappear rather easily under social conditions that no longer teach it effectively. Women may be said to be mothers unless they are taught to deny their child-bearing qualities. Society must distort their sense of themselves, pervert their inherent growth-patterns, perpetuate a series of learning outrages on them, before they will cease to want to provide, at least for a few years, for the child they have already nourished for nine months within the safe circle of their own bodies.* (Ibid., pp. 147/8)

Motherhood is biological, fatherhood is social; "learning outrages," "perverted growth-patterns"! A committee convened to devise ways of winding up feminists would have a job to improve on *Male and Female*. If Mead the revered authority on cultural elasticity believed that women were nurturers by instinct while men contained none of this (though she softened the latter part of this later on, in response to fierce criticisms), then what hope was there of renegotiating domestic contracts? She had to be discredited. It was important for feminists to believe that social justice could be achieved through institutional reforms. Mead stood in the way; and although this book continued to be popular for some time after Friedan's attack, opinion leaders rapidly moved in to close off the area, which has been out of bounds since to all those who know what is good for them.

George Gilder, who knew but did not care, later ventured in with his lively books, starting with *Sexual Suicide* (1973), which reiterated man's need for a main provider role. But feminists suspected that he just wanted them to get back into the kitchen, and detected traces of Mead's biologism, and so refused to treat the argument seriously. In spite of popular sales he has had little impact on academic work. More recently Charles Murray (1984), echoed in the United Kingdom by Digby Anderson and others, has helped to recycle some parts of Gilder's message; but broad models of gender relations built around recognition that men find their place in the community via women have barely had any consideration.

What there has been instead is much scholarly quibbling about providers which avoids the central issue. Some writers for example have taken the idea of men providing *food* very literally and argued (surprise, surprise) that men in some societies are not providers because the food produced by women has greater nutritional value than that brought in to households by men, that where men are hunters the meat they catch satisfies only a small fraction of a family's needs, and so on. These arguments miss the main point of male providing, which is that regardless of protein values or calorie intakes these cultures are attaching importance to men's contributions, and thereby encouraging them to *do something*. If that valuation is hyped or puffed up, this may just go to show the importance of its psychological aspect - to which feminism as a whole, I suggest below, is steadfastly resistant.

Other scholars have tackled the universality angle, and have laboriously delved to find societies in which there is little or no importance attached to male providing. A few can be found. They are however very small fragments of evidence indeed. And insofar as so few cases can show anything they damage the anti-provider case seriously, because they indicate unambiguously that where men are not obliged to provide, they become utterly feckless. Gilmore comments (p. 218) that *"perhaps without a typical manhood ideology, men are permitted the luxury of remaining passive and dependant, rather like stone-age Peter Pans."* Thus among the Semai of Malaya, the clearest instance of a culture untainted by sexism, and which he examines in some detail, men have no concept of manhood and don't compete for anything, nor show any sexual jealousies. But nor do they seem to actually do much child care or domestic labor either. They sit around quietly, running away if challenged by anyone, and their territory and society are fast disappearing as pushier neighboring groups move in, and take over Semai women. However, even Gilmore, well armed as he is with comparative evidence on the importance of the male provider role, is reluctant to provoke feminist wrath by openly drawing the obvious conclusion that you can do what you like culturally, but you will then have to pay the price. Instead, he suggests very limply that it is a question for philosophers whether a society more complex than the Semai could eschew manhood and simply run away from problems (p. 231). This is eloquent testimony (or is it dumb witness?) to the continuing muzzle on free speech.

### Learning to care

The issue of how the role of main family provider interacts with male characteristics and wider social performance is crucial to gender relations, and urgently needs thorough and impartial research. Now is an excellent time to commission it, moreover, as the number of men liberated from pressure to be breadwinners is greater in the West than we have known it before. This is not just a matter of recession. During the thirties there were more men who were out of work. But they still retained the notion of being a provider, to help them through without going off the rails. But now there are virtually whole communities of young men, especially on the sink estates, who not only have no work, but have no particular reason to want it or expect it. These are the ones that Patricia Hewitt and her colleagues at the Institute for Public Policy Research (IPPR) seem to expect to become caring fathers; but the truth is surely that this is the last thing they will do.

Many feminists would resist any research which threatened to attach a positive value to male providing, as the movement is still collectively wedded to the belief, which Susan Faludi expresses several times, that this is the mainspring of the male "urge to power." It is the sisters who have challenged this nostrum, like Sylvia Ann Hewlett, who are being subjected to the anti-backlash purge. This is perhaps why several prominent feminists seem so incapable of talking sensibly about the problem of male fecklessness. At one level they are aware that men are often ineffectual and lazy, but they don't know how to square this with their political objectives, and so repress or compartmentalize the knowledge. They are simply afraid of admitting to themselves that breadwinning might be important for men, and that their capacity to be caring, rather than violent and troublesome, may be related to this.

This sort of mindset can lead to absurdities. In an interview reported in the *Evening Standard* a while ago (24 March 1992) Marilyn French was quoted as saying how men are all bullies and tyrants and in many instances rapists too. But when asked a little later about her own father, she carried on in exactly the same dismissive vein to deplore him as a hopelessly weak and ineffectual man, Gilmore's total schmuck, who was always being bossed around by Marilyn's mother. Heads she wins, tails you lose. If we are talking about real people, ah yes, men are feeble. When we are engaged in collective strategy, then different data and arguments apply. The treatment given by Germaine Greer to her parents is remarkably similar (1989).

Neil Lyndon has a good chapter, his best, in which many similar discrepancies are revealed. There is a whole dark continent of women's experience of weak, hopeless men, which all feminists of course know about, but which they have signally failed to enter and explore, and which even the most cursory reading of George Gilder would illuminate for them. They are in a sense right to ignore this, because they would find it much harder to retain faith in their current strategies. But if they seriously want to know what makes men tick, they have to risk examining the real implications of the male provider role. Maybe it is absence of it which leads both to male fecklessness and also brutality, and its presence which helps to civilize men.

Bringing in men as material breadwinners leads them into a world of meaning of which most would otherwise remain innocent. It does this gradually, by accepting that in the first instance men will operate best mainly in the material world to which they are accustomed, and where they can also play. But commitment to dependants is an entry point to concern for others, and a more collectivist way of being. In the frog stage, self can be everything. But the prince who accepts responsibility for his people learns to experience new pleasures and pains with them and via them, and comes to feel a direct personal interest in their well-being. The surest road to community lies, I shall argue below, through acceptance of highly personal obligations. By taking on dependants, the prince moves into the domain where self becomes merged into the wider community.

As he becomes domesticated, he matures and mellows and is increasingly capable of interacting responsibly in the moral economy. This is highly germane to current assertions about New Men, in particular Hewitt's claim that providing inhibits caring. Common sense suggests that the opposite is the case, and that men who are secure in their breadwinning status are more concerned and affectionate to their children, because their lives are far more committed to them. This is what most ordinary people assume. They know that it is precisely the stake in their children which comes from being responsible which lifts men beyond mere chivalry - where abstract morality is the only spur to virtue - into a position where it becomes in their own interests to care.

And I think that the most crucial aspect of all this is the highly personalized focus of an individual's responsibilities to the community. It is this which gives other people leverage over him to maintain his level of commitment. The essence of the royal fix is that it concentrates everything on one individual - the prince. He has to continue to earn his title and lifestyle by delivering the goods. *Noblesse oblige,* with a vengeance. And a crucial analytic mistake on the Left, which has misled feminist thought for the last generation, is to overlook that collectivism cannot just operate in a soup of romanticized consensuality, but does actually need to be grounded in a firm recognition and acceptance of individual obligations. From the community's point of view, this is the key feature of patriarchy.

# THE SEED OF PATRIARCHY

## Biology and politics

*In a society where contraception was readily available, where medical technology was geared towards minimizing the rigours of childbirth, where the breast-feeding of infants in public was not regarded as a social solecism, and where children were cared for equally by men and women - and where responsibility for children was not used systematically to block women's employment prospects - the material conditions of women's dependence on men would not exist. The fact that we do not live in such a society is not to be laid at the door of biology: it is a political question.*
(Barrett & McIntosh, 1982, p 36)

Attacks on patriarchy usually contain some element of hostility towards the family. There are strands of attachment to family within feminism; but these are often so hedged around by qualifications about the form it should take, and ideas on the way that state help is necessary to promote this, that they come near to rejection. The central plank in this approach is the notion that the family stands for biological nature, and that the whole point and drift of social evolution is to move beyond this. Progress requires it. Politics enables it.

But this common line misunderstands both the nature of families and equally importantly, I think, what politics is about. To take the latter part first, much of what passes for political commentary among feminists is really just the expression of political values, or an assertion of correct moral force. The community should provide this; men should do more; the state can do that. It is making a noise in a good cause - in an aping of the most idealistic male dreamers. But it ignores most of the difficult questions about how an idea can be realized. It brings to my mind an early Peter Cook and Dudley Moore sketch. Dudley asks, "Why are you looking so pleased with yourself today?" And Peter replies that he has just invented a machine for turning old cars into platinum (or something along these lines). "How does it work, Peter?" "Well, I haven't got round to thinking about that yet, but it is a good idea, isn't it!" Much of feminist commentary, likewise, is just pious aspiration.

Real politics needs to concern itself with how to achieve something, and this means looking closely at the personal interests which are involved in a situation, to see what stake people have in different systems or outcomes and how their behavior can be influenced. It is extremely easy to think of things that ought to be done, services which should be provided. What is hard is generating the will and the resources to do it. In the end, what this comes down to is finding ways to mobilize people's support, because any community, whatever the octane-rating of the ideology it is running on, can only deploy for the benefit of its members that which people are putting into it. If group members are not giving as much as they take out, then services cannot be sustained.

Later on in this book I will be looking at the recent shift in the West away from an emphasis on individuals' obligations to the state to a view which prioritizes their rights and claims on it as citizens, and at the relation of feminism to all this. But here all I want to stress is firstly that the state (loosely conceived as any arm of the community in the public political domain) is ultimately fuelled by a system of obligations and responsibilities, which make it possible to provide rights, and secondly that the obligations on individuals are very closely bound up with their personal interdependence with other members of their families. Citizenship cannot, as in some contemporary idealist models, be based only metaphorically on the family. It also and necessarily entails taking actual family obligations seriously, and this was well understood by the fathers of Enlightenment:

> *Can devotion to the state exist apart from the love of those near and dear to us? Can patriotism thrive except in the soil of that miniature fatherland, the home? Is it not the good son, the good husband, the good father, who makes the good citizen?* (Rousseau, 1911, p. 326)

Thus a fundamental public duty of any able-bodied citizen is to minimize calls on community resources both by being self-reliant where he or she can, and through helping out family members too, in order to limit the use made of state help. Communities would soon get overdrawn without families.

In a very real but frequently overlooked sense, the community and state depend on family obligations, as the basic means of ensuring that the most important work in society does get done. The most fundamental ideological apparatus of any viable group is that concerned with making people take family responsibilities very seriously. This is no less true in socialist societies, whether on the Chinese-Albanian model, or Soviet-Cuban. In fact, to the embarrassment of our own libertarian brothers and sisters, it is usually far more true. Although romanticized socialist metaphors refer to siblingship as their model, socialist systems in reality rely heavily on parents.

Family relationships are highly political. They may appear to some people just to be a biological tie, but they are always much more than this. They are those biological links - out of a range of possible relations - which have become endorsed and amplified by a society into bonds which the community then insists on people accepting as foci of mutual concern and responsibility. The community does this because it recognizes that its own coherence and capacity to organize human effort requires it.

The conceptualization of family ties as being natural may have something to do with instinct. But this is largely latent until fostered; and what makes the ties useful to society as a basis for key relationships is not any instinctual content as such, but the fact that such links are not voluntarily breakable. Whatever we feel about our parents, children and siblings, we are related to them - and also, though indirectly, through children, to our sexual partners - in a way which we are powerless to change. We are not able to opt out or legitimately escape. Family offers a firm foundation, which all cultures build and rely on, for constructing long-term relationships of personal interdependency, and through this a system of obligations to the community for maintaining mutual support. This is real politics.

It also brings us back to the original social contract I posited earlier on, between women and other adults, whereby women secure the promise of back-up support for child care by agreeing to be primarily responsible for the routine care of children. This ensures that the most arduous and essential work gets done, by mobilizing mutual help in moments of greatest need. In many ways this is the source and inspiration of all citizenship - as perhaps acknowledged in the way that most cultures celebrate the female spirit, Marianne, Mother Russia, Britannia and so on, as a symbol of their collective strength and sense of community. This contract is at the same time the primordial invocation of motherhood. It is politics at its most grittily realistic; and it works not by looking around to see what would be nice, or identifying someone who is available to do something; it takes the person who is closest to a fundamental human need, that of children for care, and who is least able to say no, and loads her with a responsibility to the community to get on and do it. This is the social basis of gender differences:

> *Whether "instinctive" or not, the maternal role in the sexual constitution originates in the fact that only the women is necessarily present at birth. Only the woman has a dependable and easily identifiable connection to the child - a tie which society can rely on.* (Gilder, 1973, p. 93)

## The primacy of maternity

> *i am a dancer archy*
> *and my only prayer*
> *is to be allowed*
> *to give my best to my art*
> *but just as i feel*
> *that i am succeeding*
> *in my life work*
> *along comes another batch*
> *of these damned kittens*
>
> (*archy and mehitabel,* don marquis)

Communities which are concerned about children, and this means all of those which successfully reproduce themselves through time, know that the only reliable way to ensure that children get looked after properly is by making a particular individual responsible for this in the first instance, and then organizing support systems for that person so long as the original commitment is honored. The natural mother is by far the easiest person to pin down in this way - for considerations which are partly biological. She is the one who, by virtue of proximity, first witnesses the utter dependency of a baby, and whose emotional reaction to this can be so strong that the child's own pain will be almost equally distressing to herself. But the allocation by others to her of social responsibility for the child is a political matter, and adds a further level of interests to her natural desire to care.

There are some who refuse to accept that this allocation of primary responsibility to mothers is universal; Julian Hafner (1993) for example:

> *In western society, the pressure on married women to take primary responsibility for raising their own children, ideally as full-time mothers, is very strong indeed. It comes as a complete surprise to most western women that other societies have a different view of child-raising. This difference is most marked in developing countries, where married women are far too valuable as an economic resource to devote much of their time to child-raising. In the industrial nations women grapple with varying degrees of guilt and conflict about the idea of not raising their own young children on a day-to-day basis.*

Several points are noteworthy here. Firstly Hafner, like so many other insurgents against patriarchy, fails to draw a crucial distinction between responsibility and actual caring. No one who asserts the universality of primary maternal responsibility has ever, to my knowledge (even the redoubtable John Bowlby) suggested that this means that mothers do all of the actual looking after of children. But it is a standard feminist response to conflate responsibility with caring - which makes it easy to then shoot the proposal down. This is deceptive and slippery. Henrietta Moore should know better than to wheel out the middle-class nanny as evidence that women don't always care for their children all of the time (1988, p. 26). We understand that. Having primary responsibility means being the one who makes decisions about care, exchanges personal services with other people to make sure that it takes place, and so on. It does not mean doing it. This really should not need spelling out.

Secondly, and less directly, Hafner manages a fashionable nod towards the idea that men would like to look after children by implying that in these non-western societies men do a larger share of caring. He is himself too cautious to say quite this, because it would easily be shown to be rubbish. The truth is that if children are not being looked after by their mothers in non-western cultures, then it is almost certainly being done either by slightly older sisters (imagine the reactions of educationalists in the West to this!) or by grandmothers or sometimes aunts, in return for other services from the children's mothers. There are cultures in which men have more direct responsibility for their children than in the West. The most obvious examples are the more fundamentalist Islamic societies in which fathers can assert sole control over their children and dispense with their mother if they can justify this as in the child's interest. But this is ultimate rather than primary responsibility. It happens very rarely (and a mother can often mobilize local opinion to resist it), and represents interaction from higher up in the chain of personal responsibility, when care is unacceptable or breaking down. At no point does it involve men doing the caring itself. Hafner and his ilk know all this but keep it quiet as it does not help their case.

Finally, and subtly again, statements like Hafner's manage to convey the message that other societies do not give as much priority to children as we do, and that in doing so we are not fair to mothers. As an angry woman shouted at me not long ago, during a meeting discussing these issues, British society must be the most child-centred in the world. All of which is even higher grade rubbish. It is difficult to think of a culture which values children less than ours does at the moment, and which puts less automatic pressure on women to have them and to mother them. It is probably because children are valued so little by us that the idea of motherhood appears to many as so outrageous. This may all be related to our long-standing national anxieties about over-population, which mark us off sharply from neighbors like the French, whose strategic concerns and attitudes to motherhood are very different to our own. But whatever their final cause, these valuations are surely part of what has created the crisis for women which feminism is an attempt to resolve.

Anyway, giving primary responsibility to mothers makes good sense in all known types of human society, for the very practical reason that this maximizes the probability that proper care will take place. In spite of what some feminists have declared, though less strongly of late, most women do want to have children and then to look after them (e.g. Epstein, 1988). Also, as Mead insisted, carrying a child through a long gestation, followed by a demanding birth, normally results in strong attachment. But most importantly I think, the mother is very easily identified as having produced the child, and is the individual who is least able to avoid having responsibility to care for it thrust upon her. Even if the father is known or, more to the point, a social father named to the satisfaction of the local community, he may not be around to play much of a part when a birth occurs. So attachment of a father to children is almost invariably mediated by his relationship with the mother.

## Hierarchies of dependence

In any viable community - which I have to say must exclude large tracts of the contemporary western world, which would regard the the following proposition as paradoxical - membership of the group and enjoyment of its benefits necessarily entails acceptance of highly individualized duties to other people. This operates very differently for men and women. For women these responsibilities are assumed almost automatically in the concept of womanhood, which elides with motherhood, whereas for men the whole matter can be much more uncertain and contingent, and when it does occur is invariably indirect, linking them to children, the ultimate dependants, via the women who are their mothers. The only circumstance in which men have a *de facto* direct responsibility for children is where the mother has died or disappeared or is otherwise unable to take a part herself. It is a residual case. But even then she is still there as a logical link in the chain of obligations and dependency, without whom there would be no relationship. There are almost always women in between men and children.

There are two types of relationship between men and women which are used to structure men's obligations to children. On one hand there are ties between women and men who are already biologically related. In matrilineal cultures, for example, although men do have important roles as fathers, they also play a significant part as uncles to their sisters' children. These cultures often contain beliefs in strong spiritual bonds between children and their uncles - sometimes with the spirits of the latter playing a part in sparking off procreation - in order to compensate for the less direct nature of the biological connection between them, and perhaps to provide some explanation of why a particular uncle (out of several available) takes on a special role (see Malinowski 1929, & p. 178 below).

In addition to this there are frequently conventions within patriarchal societies whereby the children of an unmarried woman can become treated formally as the legal children of her father, their grandfather. Within patriarchy a woman's father retains responsibilities towards her (and by extension to her own dependants) until he has been relieved of these through her marriage. Although the biological link here is weaker than for a father, it still exists and is strong enough for the community to hang social obligations on. We have perhaps seen some steps towards the reformalization of this lately in the United Kingdom, with the kite-flying report in which Peter Lilley has suggested to the cabinet ways of making the parents of single mothers responsible for their grandchildren. In both of these situations the duties of men towards children are added to an existing set of rights and obligations, and are largely patterned by them.

The other category of relations between a man and children occurs where he and the children's mother are sexual partners, and where he is likely to be their natural father. In these circumstances the tie between men and women is much more closely linked to their joint responsibility for the children, and is more shaped by this shared experience. In all cultures sexual relations are regulated in ways which protect the interests of children who may result from them, and this generates an important element within the social contract - i.e., the sexual contract between men and women as conjugal partners. Also, in this case the matter of a biological link is altogether more crucial. Men who don't believe themselves to be the father of a woman's children - such as the proverbial stepfather - are notoriously less committed to caring for them.

Physiological paternity is widely regarded as an important factor in ideas about true fatherhood, and there are theories (e.g., Kraemer, 1991), which I touch on in the following chapter, which see it as central to the whole development of patriarchy. Socio-biologists would phrase this in terms of genes struggling to reproduce themselves, and this may have some validity. But I think that it may be less a matter of man's instinctual desire to spread his maker's image, than to do with the fact that the community can put a lot more pressure on men to be responsible and responsive fathers where they are causally responsible for their existence. Just as pressure can be put on mothers to look after children because they produced them, so too the group can lean on the men who provided the seed. Fatherhood is a political fact of the same type as motherhood.

They are not, I fear, of the same order though, since fatherhood obligations are inevitably secondary. This is true logically, in that you cannot easily determine who a father is until you have identified the mother, and even genetic testing requires information about the mother before it can examine hypotheses about possible fathers. It is also true at moral and legal levels, in that unless a mother renounces all ties with a child, which is not feasible in many cultures, then fatherhood is mediated by motherhood, and hence by the nature of the relationship between a woman and her partner.

## Equal parenting

The derivative and less direct character of men's obligations to children means that it is extremely difficult to institutionalize conjugal partnerships around the idea of equal parenting. The relationships are just *not* the same. In theory, there are I suppose three general ways in which the dependency relationships of couples and their children could be organized. Firstly, fathers could be defined as taking direct and primary responsibility for their children, and enter the dependency chain immediately above them. The father would occupy an inferior or ancillary role *vis-à-vis* the mother, as a helpmate. He would be like an *au pair* in status perhaps, and formally dependent on his mate for representation in wider society. Secondly both partners could pool their parental identities into a strictly co-eval responsibility for their children, in a dependency triangle. In this case both could enjoy equal citizenship outside the family; the New Man vision. Finally, women can have direct charge of their children, with men formally dominant and providing for them, as in the patriarchal model.

This last is overwhelmingly the most common cultural definition of how things should be done, and is, I suspect, the only one which is workable and sustainable in practice. To take the more attractive of its alternatives first, men have little incentive to become fully sharing partners, because although it is possible for a woman to achieve an equal position as a provider, even if it means working harder than a man, it seems far less feasible for a man to get equal control of his children. If the mother is not around it can be done. But while she is, there are problems. Over the last twenty years or so quite a few couples, though I suspect rather fewer than commonly supposed, have attempted to move towards more equal division of domestic labor. But I have heard or know of extremely few where the mother did not, sometimes in spite of conscious efforts to restrain herself, continue to see herself as the better judge of her children's needs, so that the father sooner or later realizes that he could not be an equal parent, merely a helper, who had to follow instructions carefully. Neil Lyndon refers to several friends who became disillusioned with the calling of New Man after of this sort of experience (1992, ch. 4).

More specifically, a number of valiant attempts no doubt fell victim to the Marietta Higgs affair, which revealed to a lot of men for the first time just what their partners really felt about equal parenting. Women's suspicion about predatory man's ability to control his lust is quite clearly a factor which inclines them to keep a watchful eye on their helpers. Anna Coote discusses this as a problem with men without any apparent awareness that her attitudes justify the reluctance of many men to take on the full caring role which she is herself ostensibly advocating (1990), and Patricia Hewitt has delivered a similar message about the need for surveillance of men.

> *But if we want fathers to play a full role in their children's lives, ... then we need to bring men in to the playgroups and the nurseries and the schools. And here, of course, we hit the immediate difficulty of whether we can trust men with children. ... Unfortunately, the experience of many of those working with children is that the men who abuse often seek out jobs with children. So we need safeguards. .... Distasteful though it may seem, it may well be necessary to follow the practice already established in some schools of not leaving men on their own with groups of children. (1993b, pp. 24-7)*

All this is surely more than enough to scare off men toying with the idea of being carers, because it is clear that they are only there on probation, and easily shunted on and dispensed with. And if it isn't, there are other ways to turn men off the idea. In several places lately, Hewitt has suggested that the shift of skills in favor of women in the labor market adds weight to the argument that some of them should become breadwinners while their partners look after their children.

> *The failure of a modern economy to employ large numbers of women with children - particularly women who have already acquired a high level of education - suggests profound structural inefficiences as well as social inadequacies. There are many reasons why women's employment cannot always* (sic) *be substituted for men's. But an economy which appears to be successful in other ways may be operating below its productive capacity if it is employing (some) men with less education or potential than (some) women who are caring for children.* (1993a, p. 168)

The underlying attitude that performing child care is a suitable punishment for failure in the job market, or, to read Hewitt even more bluntly, requires less intelligence, further explains not just why men resist the idea of being a probationary helper, but why more women are rejecting motherhood themselves. How soft a sell can you make?

A constant barrage of persuasive articles in the quality newspapers about the joys of fathering (e.g., Kahn, 1993; Roberts, 1994) has failed so far to conceal these underlying hazards, and there is no sign yet of men rushing to help out. While it may be true that some men are doing a little more child care now to enable their wives to hold down proper jobs, few of them regard it as a long-term thing, even fewer go on looking after the children when their partners get home from work, almost none do as much of it altogether as their working partners, and, as the NCDS findings have underlined, such arrangements and relationships formed around them do not seem to be very durable.

What do work, and do last, are conventional partnerships which re-affirm the original social contract whereby a woman can expect a certain amount of help from a man if she accepts the main responsibility for caring activities while he is defined as pursuing material supports within the male-oriented public realm located on the margins of the moral community. Within the ideology of patriarchy, this division of labor assigns higher status to the male role, and as such is increasingly unacceptable. But, as I shall explore in chapter six, there are a number of devices available to women for countering or even reversing this evaluation. These have become less easy to use in an age devoted to explicit and formalized equality in the public sphere, and where the business of reproduction has become less central. But they can still be resuscitated; and when they were operable, they ensured that for most women the overall benefits to be gained from acceptance of conventional marriage were broadly equal to the costs incurred. Patriarchal dependency-chains work.

For their part men never have had, nor can I assume are ever likely to have, the same level of incentives to submit to dependency on a partner. The frog, knowing no dependants, is largely self-sufficient in his pool, and can find little reason to abandon freedom and precious playing time just to become a domestic help. To be tempted from the pleasures of the forest, men need to be flattered by an important sounding title, and by the hint - which becomes absurd as soon as it is examined closely - that all of this business of child rearing and reproducing society is in some way being done for them, and takes place under their indispensable management. Want to be my helper? Well, maybe; I'll let you know. How about head of household, domestic monarch? Now that's more like it!

## ROYAL CLOTHES

This title is however a fabrication, certainly in relation to domestic activities themselves, where men's contribution and importance are often puny. They may be valuable as providers, boosting family resources, but at home many are useless. Tasks which couples claim to share are mainly done by women. And the more time-consuming business like relentless child care is explicitly defined as women's work. Even matters like the administration of family property, nominally vested in the male partner, are often handled by women behind the scenes, who carry out the negotiations to secure, mobilize and transmit it (Finch, 1989, p. 15-16). The male head of family is often little more than a figurehead or non-executive director.

This is not to say that figureheads do not have their uses. A father who is not closely involved but is visibly present can be helpful in conjuring up a threat of punishment. Sometimes a head who is a bit withdrawn can bring impartiality into deliberations, which may assist in integrating the family by bringing greater moral certainty into its affairs. But this potentiality by itself seems insufficient to uphold the domestic monarch idea. Surely a prince needs to offer more active and substantial leadership than that.

The unavoidable truth seems to be that the idea of a husband/partner as a prince/patriarch is less an accurate job description than an effort to dignify him and dress him up. This cultural fix is a great improvement on nature. In many ways it almost exactly reverses nature. The theater of family life frequently presents us with a mirror image of reality. It is father who is seen to have the job of Santa at Christmas, and who puts on a gown to place the stockings at the end of beds. But the hard work of knowing who will want what, or won't mind someone else having it, of shopping around to find it, and then remembering which cupboard to look for the costume in on Christmas Eve, is not done by him. Growing up is a bit like watching *The Wizard of Oz*. As the plot unfolds, it slowly becomes clear to the children that the wizard is all front, and can do nothing by himself. All the real power to get things done is held by the witches.

## Portraits by Daly

This general point has been developed brilliantly by Mary Daly in her various works, which draw on a number of discourses from religion to science fiction in order to help re-create the female universe which she feels has been stolen from women by patriarchal images and fantasies. Through her marvellous command of language, which includes the liberal coining of expressive new words, she is able to convey how patriarchal terminology has woven complex illusions which can turn reality inside out in order to make men appear competent, moral and hardworking, and which allow them to appropriate the credit for the fruits of female labor. The first and greatest of her "deadly sins of the fathers" is deception, which she defines as patriarchal processions which are mirror images of real processes (1979, p. 30/31).

Daly is herself sometimes portrayed as a crazy word-spinner who is out of touch with realities. But I find her a remarkably perceptive analyst of the hollowness of many patriarchal claims, and of the ways in which illusions are upheld. The idea of women's dependence on men, for example, is revealed as such an exact opposite of the true situation, in which men's labors are underpinned on all sides by much harder work on the part of women, that the falsity of the implicit proposition is easily overlooked. Because it shadows the truth, it is the same shape and can pass easily for it. There is no lie like a direct inversion. The title of her latest book, dealing with women's escape from the patriarchal planet, is *Outercourse;* a characteristically neat verbal trick which speaks volumes in a single word.

In the end Daly disappoints. Although she demonstrates marvellously how the mirror images operate and are sustained, at no point does she ask whether there is any reason in it beyond the simple and selfish maintenance of male privileges. She does not examine the consequences of patriarchal illusions for how society works, nor does she consider the implications of their being swept away. It is as if she believes that holes will appear conveniently in the ground to swallow up all those men she is declaring redundant. So her books, great fun though they are, fail to explain why women, many of whom must have had insights like hers throughout history, have overwhelmingly collaborated in the deceptions on which patriarchy rests. It suggests that although many veils have been drawn back on patriarchy, more still may be waiting to be discovered.

In a way she may be leading us on to this. Daly's deconstruction is a powerful weapon but it cuts both ways. By highlighting the idea that men are not as important and competent as they seem, she inadvertently provokes the questions of whether they are as *powerful* as they are portrayed, or if the upholding of all these illusions may not perhaps suit women - not necessarily as individuals, but certainly as core members of the community - more than might be obvious superficially.

To get at other sides of the story we would need to pursue the interpretations of women like Camille Paglia, who represent a strand of female self-respect which is quite comfortable with patriarchy, which it also sees as extremely shallow but, more to the point, as rendering men open to control and manipulation by women.

According to Paglia, men are uncomplicated machines which run well on female flattery and pack up very quickly when deflated. This model, equally one-sided of course, would see women not as collaborators in deception, but as its authors.

Most women, I imagine, even at the moment, would stand somewhere between Daly and Paglia, and combine some resentment towards patriarchal notions, and scepticism about their validity, with a willingness to play along with them up to a point. Mothers are so important, and their children know it, that they can afford to try to bolster their partner's ego and motivation. By dressing them up a little, they can flatter them into performing a few domestic functions; and something is better than nothing. Also it keeps men out of trouble, which is good for the whole community. Thinking about a domestic kingdom, even if that is all it amounts to, stops men from being negative, anti-social beings. It stops them from drifting and droning. So a little deception and perhaps even self-deception is energy well spent.

## A picture of omnipotence

Inflating the importance of what individual men do has probably had the effect of making the whole so-called public realm, where they do most of it, appear more important and influential too. The women who, exceptionally, have entered these preserves have until recently respected the male conventions governing them. But equal opportunities legislation has enabled ever more women to penetrate the public realm, and some are discovering just how little real work is done there - and how easy and rewarding the living can be compared with running a family and a home. Some of what goes on clearly isn't necessary - rather marginal to the life and central concerns of the community. Given the opportunity, many feel that a woman could make a better job of things. Women who have broken in and succeeded are convinced of male inferiority. If you want something done, ask a woman. The cock may crow, but it's the hen that lays the eggs, and so on.

Now many women are very ambivalent about the public domain. They want to get "out there" and take part. But they are very ready to denigrate it at the same time. The talking up of male activities, to flatter men, had caused women to develop an exaggerated idea of what goes on out there. The real world is taking some getting used to. And the more involved they become, the more directly women are confronted with the heavy over-evaluation of male activities and the uncomfortable issue that to avoid having men as drones, and to get anything out of them at all, it may be necessary to give them extra rewards.

After the prodigal son we need a new faith-testing parable, of the ineffectual and uncaring husband, who nevertheless has to be humored. The ideal provider is supposed to be generous and give more than he receives, and produce more than he consumes (Gilmore, pp. 226-9); but this is surely far from the actual case, and may only be a sustainable precept in a context where men appear to have much to give because they are relatively over-rewarded by society for what they do contribute. Having a man around may impart some benefits to women's life-styles (Walby, p. 76), but again this is most likely to be true if women are excluded from the public realm, and men monopolize access to the most valuable resources. This problem is more basic than patriarchy itself, and rests on the fact that men's underlying levels of commitment are low, so that unless they are given an easy ride many would remain marginal or even choose not to take on any responsibilities at all. However, at the end of the day, these are the people who are fêted as princes, and who can adopt a take-it-or-leave-it attitude to personal criticism. It is they who, within the home, can indulge their private interests the most. The incentive ennobles; but sometimes the reward corrupts.

## The dual economy

There is an under-recognized but very significant difference between the sexes here. Women will readily labor, both domestically and in public spheres when they are permitted, while men appear to need all manner of inducements:

> *Manhood ideals force men to overcome their inherent inertia and fearfulness and to "work," both in the sense of expending energy and in the sense of being efficient or "serviceable" in doing so.* (Gilmore, p. 227)

But Gilmore fails to address this difference seriously. He asks himself why it should be that women do not need the equivalent of "manhood" tests, and comes up with the suggestion (p. 221) that because women are usually under the control of men they have someone leaning on them to do things anyway. Come on David, this looks like a defensive nod to feminism, and does not tally with the rest of the argument. The difference is far more likely to be linked to relative positions in dependency chains. Women, I think, work hard because their children and other dependants need them to, and the community strongly expects them to care. Men experience weaker pressures on them, expecially within a culture which accepts that women can cope without them if it comes to it. The dependency of a woman on a man is secondary and less fierce than that of children on her. So men don't have to push themselves so hard. The outcome of this will clearly be unfair if we try to judge men and women by the same standards because, as we all know, within patriarchy they receive larger formal rewards for less overall effort. The marginal value of the marginal man is greater than the core value of the central woman; and while the committed and public-spirited will serve as volunteers, the mercenaries have to be hired.

## OVER THE WALL

The end of the fairy tale sees the royal pair riding off to their new life together, to be happy ever after. Marriage has made a real man out of the adolescent frog, and the cycle of magic is complete.

What the tale cannot afford to spell out is that this is by no means the end of the story. The integration of men into dependency chains above women and their children is fraught with difficulties, for the resulting conjugal relationship may fail to meet anyone's needs adequately. Most wives at some level resent being cast as dependants, and will typically experience a partner to whom they submit less than wholeheartedly as being insufficiently responsive to their personal feelings and needs. For his part, when accused of trampling all over his wife's desire to be more valued and cared for, a husband may well feel that her dependency is so demanding emotionally that it is actually putting her in control of *him*. Instead of just gratefully accepting his efforts to provide, she is trying to possess him, body and soul.

The average prince is still, especially in the early years, very much a frog inside; reconstructed and nicely dressed up, but frog all the same, and ill-suited to flourish in the moral hothouse of the caring community. If too much is expected of him, in particular beyond material duties, he may not be able to take it. Or on the other hand if the princess, aware of his limitations, protects him too obviously from the demands of his office, then he may see through the whole pantomime and realize that he is not genuinely needed after all. Or she may herself become disillusioned and emotionally castrate him, by declaring that she can manage very well by herself, better probably, and doesn't need his support.

Whichever way the strain shows itself, one day he may start to brood over the pleasures he is forgoing on the far side of the palace wall. And it is only a small step from listening to the call of the wild, to stripping off clothes and, like John Updike's anti-hero Rabbit, disappearing to freedom in a white flash.

> *His hands lift of their own and he feels the wind on his ears*
> *even before, his heels hitting heavily on the pavement at first*
> *but with an effortless gathering out of a kind of sweet panic*
> *growing lighter and quicker and quieter, he runs. Ah: runs.*
> *Runs.* (Updike, 1964, p. 249)

This abdication may not be complete or permanent. Sometimes it is just a matter of the occasional adventure, or refuge in a *garçonnière*, or even nothing more than a regular stand at the pub. Often it may be only a threat, linked to the notion of take-it-or-leave-it which runs through many men's attitudes to their domestic commitments, and which many women experience as a tangible manifestation of patriarchal power. Men do not in most situations feel domestically powerful; however, the fact that it is usually easier for them to leave and survive by themselves or set up another life predisposes them to put up with less frustration. So they are more inclined to hold out for their own interests (see Cline & Spender, 1987). Also men's looser and in some respects more voluntary binding into dependency chains, plus the fact that as unreformed universalists some may still be seeking the ideal partner (Seidler, p. 83) and so have correspondingly less personal investment in any particular relationship, make it more likely that in difficult times they are the ones who will walk out. The threat of male flight is endemic in marriage, and is man's primary and primeval weapon.

And so, unfair as it may be, it is largely the level of men's satisfaction in marriage which determines its success and durability. (This is not the same, I hope I do not need to point out, as saying that it is mainly men who file for divorce, as they do not.) I suspect that this level of satisfaction is itself largely determined by the demands made on men. Some amount of male supporting is a necessary ingredient of the relationship. This is the central argument of this book; and it is a very rare man who does not like the idea of helping a women out. The damsel in distress is a most powerful image, very flattering to a man, almost erotic - and where women are not prepared to play along with it to some degree, marriage may not materialize, as Jane Austen never forgot (Weldon, 1993), and its stability is much lower, as Maria Scherer has belatedly acknowledged (Saunders, 1989).

## Asking too much of men

However, dependency which is too great or lasts for too long is suffocating, and liable to provoke escape attempts. Over-dependency is usually over sooner (Friedan, 1963, p. 354). Durkheim had a little-explored category of suicide which he called fatalistic, which he applied to slaves and men drawn too young or unready into marriage commitments, and, one could now add, with the benefit of much subsequent ethnography, of similar relevance to women in any number of strongly patriarchal cultures where girls are pressed early into becoming wives and mothers. As a staunch advocate of the family, Durkheim could not elaborate the concept very far; so theoretically it has had less influence than the rest of his typology. In the real world, though, it has a good deal of purchase. The issue of over-dependence is avoided altogether in the fairy tale, as a certain turnoff to men. In it the princess acquires her husband almost by accident, before she even started thinking that she might want one, so that the marriage occurs as a result of male volition. I suspect that this convention of male subjectivity and proposal is again partly a device to help flatter young men into feeling sovereign, and not trapped.

In real life possessiveness undermines many relationships, prompting both infidelity, whereby some (usually) male independence can be restored, as well as full escape moves (Friedan, *op. cit.,* p. 273). A woman may often be more successful in holding onto a restive man by telling him that he is always free to go if he must, rather than by trying to imprison him with demands for exclusivity. I don't know of any research on this, but introspection and art, not to be dismissed too easily, support it - as when Angela, the narrator's sick wife in Melvyn Bragg's *A Time to Dance* (1990, p. 160) swept all thoughts of leaving from her husband's mind by saying simply: *"So if you want to have another go - I won't stand in your way. You've been very very good to me and that's all I will remember. I could not bear it if I weighted you down now and stopped you enjoying some happiness."* What could a man say after that? *"I knew that I could never leave her."* Exactly!

Children play a very important part in these equations. No children, no dependency chain. They are the main subjects the prince is supposed to rule over, and without them the princess has much less call on his loyalty. The dependency of a woman who does not produce children is much harder for both parties to bear, and feminists know that the surest way to avoid dependency on a man is not to have any kids. Similarly it is likely, though not easy to show, that a woman who is so emotionally reliant on her husband that she gives second place to her children may be liable to forfeit her own importance in the support chain originating with them. A good father might be expected to give priority to children's needs, and in the end bypass a wife who refuses to do the same herself.

As children grow up and families mature, the character of dependencies within them alters. When children are small a man relies heavily on his wife to look after them - thereby enabling him to fulfill his princely obligations. If a wife is not happy to do this without a lot of help, then her husband may be all the more tied to her and less able to leave. As children get older, all members of the family become more independent of each other, and the moral chains binding them together loosen (although as parents age they may need support themselves, but rarely so intensively as young children, unless serious illness or incapacity strikes). Basically, as children make fewer demands on their mother, so she may resent more her own dependency on her husband. A damsel's distress wanes as her children grow up. I argue later that this loss of female dependency becomes endemic once a state provides alternative support systems; but historically this only really occurred as chidren grew up and became responsible adults themselves.

## Dissolving chains

So in middle age there is in many cultures a shift towards more companionate relationships, entailing a cessation of flattery towards men, and a general adoption of "unisex" roles. As a woman's independence grows and her partner becomes more schooled in the ways of the moral economy, earlier inbalances in their relationship may fade. This means different things in different cultures. In strongly patriarchal societies it takes the form of older women becoming honorary men. In the contemporary West it means that older men become honorary women. This process may however weaken the tie. Some men, now liberated from the illusion of importance, and at some increasing risk of becoming properly defined at last as domestic appendages (Friedan, 1963, p. 47), may feel free to go at last.

Hence in more traditional cultures the dissolving of the child-based dependency chain is a signal for men to move on, their reproductive-support task completed. In the old world many would have entered monasteries or, as in the Hindu paths of Vanaprastha, or more especially Sannyasin, buried their social personalities and distanced themselves from daily cares by going into the wilderness and becoming hermits. Or those with enough energy left could set out at last like Odysseus on voyages to explore the world or, like Gauguin, take up that new life as artist in a tropical paradise.

This re-opening of horizons is an important factor in bringing on the male mid-life crisis, aptly likened by Danté to a journey through a deep wood, in which men experience a powerful sensation of having been released for a second chance, an opportunity to put their life right. The reproductive process is far less wearing for men than women, so that it remains possible for them to start again with another relationship late in life, or even, emulating the Marquess of Bath, to collect several wifelets. Believing that there should still be a reasonable amount of life ahead for them, and armed with the experience of past mistakes, many men yield to all the frustrations of the foregoing decades and decide to break free of the traces and have one last big throw.

Some just drop out and abandon patriarchal conventions in order to have a good time. My kingdom for a whore. These tend to go back after a while. But others change jobs and direction, or look for a new dominion to rule - often with a younger princess who can renew their sense of being needed. Jaded personalities become reborn and revitalized. Shelved ambitions are taken down and dusted off, and new magic may be enacted.

The most difficult part in the renewal is the first, the decision to leave. There is always a wall of guilt to clear, which may prove insurmountable to many, especially those who have taken their role as prince at all seriously. If they are still frogs inside, and perhaps did not spend long enough by the pool in their narcissistic stage first time around, there is no problem. Their legs will be strong. But if that consciousness is fading then they are perhaps ready anyway to fall back into the embrace of unisex.

# 5

# SECRETS OF THE PALACE

*Every woman should marry - and no man.*
(Disraeli, Lothair)

*If you consider the past there is no doubt at all that the whole structure of society was designed to keep women entirely in the power of men.* (Richards, 1980, p. 275)

*Monogamous sex and marriage are the ways that women catch their men and induce them to join and support families.* (Gilder, 1973, p. 107)

The palace of social life is, I believe, grounded in a basic social contract between women, mainly as sisters and mothers and daughters, which helps and constrains each of them to meet obligations to their children and other personal dependants. These ties are logically and perhaps even historically prior to any which involve adult men. But I doubt if it is possible to build more than rudimentary social structures without including men. The key to a civilized life capable of separating human society from life in the jungle lies in building on the original contract by extending it to cross-gender relations and exchanges, to include men. This means marriage. It is the domestication of men and conquest over male negativism which lifts humans above a state of nature.

These sentiments are often disputed, especially in recent years, and many now would say that marriage and family life do not form part of any palace for women - they are more a prison. But this judgment is I think superficial, too concerned with formal appearances and unwilling to explore strategic dimensions of people's behavior. Patriarchal exaggeration of men's importance obscures the deeper power of women, and behind the theatre of male dominion the palace may hold many secrets, of which most people remain partly aware, but which conflict with current public accounts and so are not seriously considered.

Feminists have given a great deal of attention to prehistory in their quest for the origins of patriarchy, and although analysis of these matters is notoriously speculative it is, I believe, important to delve there briefly myself, to illustrate the sort of assumptions that feminist thinking is based upon and show that there is an alternative. It is unlikely that the secrets of ancient social history will ever be revealed in a satisfactory way; but I strongly suspect that regardless of who may appear to control family systems, women have carried out a great deal of the construction work, not just as accomplices of men but as direct beneficiaries. Although this area may often be designated now as a less important or subordinate realm, there are important senses in which it is still the centre and source of all social life.

These propositions go straight to the heart of the backlash debate quietly raging inside the feminist movement, largely but not entirely on a generation basis. The chief sin of the older feminists attacked by Faludi for selling out on equal opportunities and for conducting what her book's subtitle represents as *the undeclared war against women* seems to be their willingness to recognize the crucial value to women of marriage and family life. This has always been a divisive issue for feminism, even in the sixties and early seventies (Barrett & McIntosh, 1982, ch. 2), and it will I think increasingly split the movement until the line adopted by radical feminists, which is still dominant, is recognized to have been a mistake.

## Changing family valuations

Only a short while ago the family was seen by many as the heartland of the domain of women's interests, not simply as a locus of interpersonal influence but also the source of any institutionalized power which they might hope to wield. In the fifties Young and Willmott, in their classic study *Family and Kinship in East London* (1957), could refer to the family as the women's trade union without any fear of ridicule or reprisals. Others too, like Madeleine Kerr in her analysis of working-class life in Lancashire (1960), were finding it to be the hub of female community organization. But soon after that it became defined, by fellow travelling male academics looking for a quiet life as much as by feminists themselves, as the prime site of man's oppression of women, where the unfair sexual division of labor is laid down, and hence a major obstacle to be overcome or severely refashioned on the road to equality (Lerner, 1986).

What keeps this anti-family stance powerful among women, while making it difficult to take seriously as an academic theory, is the way that it enables women to blame men for their problems. I am sure that many men too see themselves as highly constrained by family life (see Ehrenreich, 1983), and have only gone along with the idea that they were its authors so long as they felt generally expected to, and qualified for some special status and privileges in society by doing so. As more women repudiate it, more men will feel free to do the same. If feminists imagined - and I am guessing here - that by unveiling their own discontents they would persuade men to join them in restructuring family relations more in women's favor, then I think they will be very disappointed.

The shortage of individual freedoms in women's lives does not occur because men are shutting up women and stealing it all for themselves. Men too are more free without family obligations. Restraints on both arise from the imperatives of community life, which itself is generated as much by women's pressures on each other as anything else. Family institutions, in particular marriage, give women the power to bring men into their systems of mutual support, and they must I think be seen as having evolved as part of communities' strategies for getting the best possible value out of men. To try to introduce some reflexivity into the discussion of strategy, it seems very likely that feminist promulgation of ideas that family life mainly serves men, and that women are "doing it all *for* men," is in part, at least, a reworking of traditional devices for exerting more leverage over men. The appearance of male control and benefit is a cover which permits women considerable moral power in practice (Sanday, 1981). Hera, goddess of marriage and a jealous wife is also the power behind the throne.

Pre-feminist women took much of this for granted and, within the framework of a pluralistic value structure, did not attach too much significance to their formal designation as dependants, minors, chattels or whatever terminology current patriarchal conventions decreed. Equity was not seen as requiring formal equality. However a variety of factors, some considered in this chapter but more in those which follow, have challenged the traditional segregation of public and private realms, and disturbed the equilibrium operating in conjugal partnerships. The sexual division of labor, or sexual contract, or what you will, is now the subject of fierce disputes, and scene of alarming polarizations of views.

Much needs to be renegotiated before a new accommodation can be reached which properly reflects the conditions of modern life. Before any debate is possible, though, it is I believe essential to sort out some of the basic issues and ground rules, which apply within all types of society and political or economic circumstances, as these have become clouded over by the dust from so many recent skirmishes. Serious exchanges cannot begin until, in particular, women agree to accept more responsibility for shaping existing family and marriage systems. In this chapter I will look at some of the factors underlying marriage and the related sexual division of labor, to argue against the notion that these institutions have self-evidently been imposed by men on women. Later I shall look at the nature of the power which is available to women within the conventional division of labor, and at the asymmetry in sexual relations which women commonly take as the basis for their belief in the systemic nature of male domination.

## SEXUAL MARKETS

The search for new patterns of conjugality in the sixties and seventies triggered a strong revival of interest in the family, which in the process became redesignated as the patriarchal family, for the whole point of that exercise was to discover alternative forms where men were not dominant. In practice it has proved possible only to find different variants on the patriarchy theme - although some unrepentant ideologues appear still to count matrilineal cultures, in which property and position pass between men along the distaff line, as matriarchal. But the bulk of the movement, in all its rich complexity, basically accepts that no contemporary or clearly documented historical society has been discovered in which women are formally powerful and in control.

So the main attention shifted quite quickly to prehistoric cultures beyond the scope of rigorous method, where speculation is sovereign. Two male authorities have been relied on particularly heavily here to give added weight to the cause. One is Freud, whose analysis legitimized a departure from female commitment to the family by conveniently revealing the monogamous family as a male invention, designed by men and for men, to help them tame the beast of aggression present inside themselves. It was not something women needed for themselves. The other was Engels, who by linking family forms to types of property rights, and sexual liberation to class war, pointed a way out of domestic oppression which would integrate men and women in a new order, rather than just diverting the sex war into a different arena. Between them they fuelled a thousand flights of optimism in those intoxicating years.

In spite of the fact that Freud was not greatly concerned about women, and that much of what he did have to say about them has been objected to and discarded by many subsequent analysts, and moreover that even his view of the family does not readily lead to positive ideas about alternative forms which it could take, he has been the more fundamental influence I think. The reason for this I suspect is his brand of heavy patriarchalism. Although this is ostensibly not at all friendly to the idea of matriarchy it does in fact give it strong backdoor encouragement, by presenting an image of man which offers the perfect fall guy to women who want to blame most of present society's ills onto him. As Lyndon puts it (1992, p. 127):

> *Human society, in Freud's account, provided an external framework of constraints and taboos by which primal man was kept in check; and, internally, man converted his repressed desires into guilts and anxieties. Without those constraints, man would naturally run amok in murder, rape and incest.*

Here are strong grounds for giving *Mutterrecht* a chance.

Freud's main service to feminism then was to put misandry on a more scientific footing, by confirming the reality and power of phallocentric patriarchy. He attached his authority to the idea that the family as we know it is not natural, but a male concoction which was, in effect, imposed on women through male conquest; and this was consistent with the belief that there was both a time before it - which corresponded to myths present in very many cultures concerning pre-patriarchal eras - and, by implication at any rate, potentially after it as well. He does not attempt to map out prehistory in a precise manner, and there is no need to assume that particular events happened at certain times or places. Instead he just takes some ideas loosely from Darwin and other nineteenth-century modellers, and reworks them in the light of the tendencies he believes to be inherent in the human condition and nature, which can be drawn on to delineate the broad social context within which the family, and personality conditions linked with it, together evolved. This is not history but a statement about the continuing interaction between forces contained in human personality, and basic social institutions.

## Freud's patriarchalism

To summarize his argument very crudely, Freud speculated, most explicitly in *Totem and Taboo* (1950), that for most of prehistory humans were organized in female-centered hordes made up of women and children, with men roaming nearby and fighting each other to determine who should have sexual access. Each band of adult females would be visited by the dominant male, or patriarch, who in fighting off the competition would also give the female group some protection against male violence, and who would, during his reign, be the father of all of their children. The transition to a family-based society occurred at the point when the excluded males, some of whom would have been the sons of the current patriarch, came together fraternally to overcome this "father" - in the original act of patricide - and to institute a new regime of monogamous marriage, through which all of them could be attached to the band. Once they were drawn in, and given assured sexual outlets, their creative energies were available for harnessing to build great civilizations, instead of being dissipated in endless internecine combat.

Freud portrayed the ousting of the primeval father by an orderly union of younger men both as a Rousseauesque fraternal contract, and as the inauguration of egalitarian, one-to-one relations between men and women. But it can also be rendered from a woman's point of view, without much reinterpretation, as the termination of a period in which contact with men was restricted to the essential and probably speedy business of fertilization, and its replacement by comprehensive and organized male control. From this perspective the sexual contract of marriage is not an arrangement set up for the mutual benefit of men and women, but is the ongoing result of deals struck between men to help them to regulate their own sexual drives and rivalries, by democratizing access to women. It is not a real contract at all, as it is struck between very unequal partners (Pateman, 1988). The social order is fixed by and for men. Men agree to respect each other's rights to exclusive possession of their wives, and instead of fighting each other over women they collaborate in keeping women in their place.

This is surely why Freud is the analyst whom feminists most love to hate. Although objecting to the way in which he upholds the idea of female passivity in his clinical works, they have found it very handy to have his weighty confirmation of men's carnality, drive to control women, and specific responsibility for the family. He could almost be speaking for women, and perhaps in a way was. Freud's ideas were strongly influenced by his clinical treatment of neurotic women; and this I think led to a kind of intellectual ventriloquism, whereby Freud was acting as a mouthpiece to voice sentiments about men which, in the context of puritanical Viennese society, had no legitimate public outlet. It was an area where a conspiracy of silence reigned; and we now know, through the work of Masson and others, that Freud came under strong pressure from colleagues to tone down his public statements about male sexual urges.

Posterity has chosen to define his revelations as illuminating the dark side of patriarchy; but they could equally well be seen as the neurotically amplified and possibly attention-seeking expressions of the negative aspects of traditional female constructions of men; a restricted subculture, which hitherto had been contained among women, or had not been very interesting because it was not regarded by men as a threat. By the turn of the century, with an emerging feminist challenge to patriarchal privileges, a new public appetite for misandric views was building up, generating male sensitivity (H. Anderson, 1993). What Freud did, very much like the editor of a modern tabloid, was to spice up some normally unspoken but nevertheless conventional juicy stereotypes of men as sexual predators violating pure women, and to lob them into the public's eager mouth.

## Inverting Freud

But however tasty the prospect, Freud's offering of male volition and subjectivity is extremely difficult to swallow, and cannot really feed the implications which many have drawn from it - namely that family and the social structures built around it grow out of men's need to contain male libido. Controlling male urges is obviously an important factor, but it is a long jump from that to proposing that men could get together by themselves to agree and organize self-regulation. The weakness of the model (and contrarily its attraction for a certain masochistic strand of feminism) lies in the way it rules out women as important players in the drama. Women cannot really be seen just as passive participants in the sexual marketplace, with little incentive of their own to regulate sexual competition. Any argument on this is necessarily very speculative; but I think that common sense insists that women had both credible motives as well as great opportunities to help invent the marriage systems which bring men into patriarchal families and that, whatever the historical processes might have been, they must be regarded as having played a deliberate and significant part in doing so. Several considerations point to this.

Firstly Freud requires us to accept that the major sexual rivalries take place between men, and not least fathers and sons. There can be no denying that men are subject to very powerful sexual feelings, which can make them extremely jealous of each other. But being prey to strong feelings is not at all the same thing as being able to set up a regulatory system, even one which holds possible advantages. The power to define and control a relationship is not necessarily held, as Freud implies, by the party which is moved by the stronger emotions. On the contrary, men are constantly fearful of becoming putty in women's hands. The Mike Tyson prospect. That is perhaps why so many otherwise resolute men seem so weak-kneed and tongue-tied in female company. They are suppressing their emotions in the hope of staying in charge of themselves.

Passion may provide a motive for men to exercise control over women; but it surely does not make it any easier to do so. The object of desire is sovereign. Numerous Greek myths recount the struggles of heroes to escape from female seduction - like Adonis fighting with his desire for Aphrodite, or Hercules becoming emasculated by Omphale. Equally Samson was no match for

Delilah; and man's fall from grace is depicted in Genesis as having been caused by his submission to lust. The gothic vampire, who drains men of their bodily juices, and whose appetite never dies, still lives on all around us in the modern West, stalking the catwalks or draped languorously across flickering screens. Cecil Parkinson's old sergeant-major knew a thing or two as well. *"If you want it, you'll find it. If you find it, you'll get it. And if you get it, you've had it."* (Parkinson, 1992)

William Willard's principle of "least interest" is applicable here (1938); that is, the person with least interest in an association is the one best placed to dictate its conditions. The more powerful men's sexual impulses are, the stronger the bargaining position of women, and the smaller men's chances of coming together in a mutually regulatory system at the expense of women. Freud envisages a fraternal alliance being hatched against the primeval patriarch, who symbolically represents the enduring triumph of individual passion over group regulation; but he fails to demonstrate how the idea of monogamous control over women would provide enough incentive for men's adoption of this radical departure. If it was rational yesterday to prefer the chance of winning all for oneself, over sharing with everyone else, why should it cease to be rational tomorrow?

If on the other hand we start to treat female interests and actions as having a bearing on the matter then things fall into place, as it is clear that women too have problems of sexual competition which *do* provide good reasons, and always have, for the regulation of sex. Freud assumes women to be both sexually and socially passive, and assigns overriding importance to conflict between males. But this seems to be based on a quick reading of Darwin and the adoption of questionable analogies with mammals among whom female sexual interest is limited and whose receptivity is concentrated into certain periods of the year. In such conditions female passivity is more convincing, and male competition for access would be especially intense.

These assumptions mesh less well with the particular biological characteristics of humanity. If we consider the virtually continuous availability of human females and the fact that most can enjoy very frequent orgasm, even during pregnancy, and set this against the rather smaller performance capacity of males, then it is difficult to

believe with Freud that male sexual over-excitement or frustration
is the only problem. There is little danger of men flooding an
unresponsive market, as a small number of women can satisfy a
large number of men if it comes to it, but not vice-versa. If there
were any tendency towards severe competition, this could also arise
between women, more specifically between older and younger
women, and that means mothers and daughters. This has far greater
implications for core social structures than does rivalry between
men.

## Women in the market

In a free sexual marketplace all young people would have an
advantage over older. It is not easy to gauge just how big this would
be for men living in a state of nature, because in social contexts
women judge men according to a variety of criteria, not least
responsiveness to their personal needs and demands, in which older
men may sometimes be able to win. Male status and wealth, both
linked to patriarchy, are factors here. But even these don't hold in
all circumstances, as Dai Llewellyn recently pointed out (1992).

> *Young women are dangerously powerful. They are able to
> make men publicly ridiculous. This power is lost in later
> years. In smart discotheques, even in London's top club,
> Tramp, I have observed many successful men with much
> younger girls. Over two and a half decades I have seldom
> seen it work out well. The man arrives proud of his young
> conquest and spends the rest of the evening in fear of losing
> her.*

So a free market would certainly, as Freud assumes, be the scene of
considerable male conflict, including between generations. But given
men's limited sexual capacity this would be finite. Furthermore the
implications of such rivalries would not be great so long as the men
concerned remained, as the *Totem and Taboo* model portrays them,
outside of society and with no vital relationships or shared interests
requiring them to associate peacefully with each other. So it doesn't
matter that much.

The position of women is infinitely more delicate. To start with,
if even men within organized and highly regulated societies judge

their partners more on the basis of physical attributes, then in a free market younger women would surely have many more suitors dancing attendance on them, to be favored or not at their pleasure. And this might apply even to young girls. Civilized communities try to conceal and contain any tendency of men to fancy very young women by making it a taboo area which men have to pretend does not exist. Vladimir Nabokov was only able to write *Lolita,* which revolves around this phenomenon, because he was living abroad and was beyond the moral reach of his friends and community. Many westerners condemned it and were glad that it was written by a Russian, while Russians everywhere held their heads in shame when the book was published, and told each other that it must be the looser American environment not his Russian upbringing which had caused such a disgraceful lapse (Glendinning, 1992).

But more crucially than this, it is very difficult to imagine a state of nature at all in which there could be a free sexual market embracing all women. For not only is a steep gradient of advantage likely to occur between women on an age basis, but the conflicts which resulted would cause very serious problems between sisters and mothers and daughters. Although feminist sensitivity has prevented much delving into this, as it raises awkward questions about solidarity (Engel, 1980), there seems to be considerable conflict between women over men and jealousy concerning sexual relations - as I discovered quite by chance when doing some research on extended families (Dench, 1992). Several single mothers whom I was interviewing about child-care arrangements, who had very close relations of mutual support with sisters, told me that they could always find someone to help out when needed, *unless* it was to free them to go to a party or out with a man. Helping one another through hard times is one thing; letting someone else have a good time is another. This is what keeps the morality in the moral economy.

Because of the centrality of relations between women, which surely are important threads within any community and regardless of whether and how men may be brought into it, sexual competition creates much greater danger of damage to the fabric of social life. The relative power of a young woman in the sexual arena severely threatens the position of older women, and is liable to upset the power relations of matriarchs over their daughters. It does seem to be the case that even within societies where sexual behavior is highly restricted some fathers do have incestuous relations with daughters, but very few mothers with sons; and this suggests that Freud was way off mark when analyzing sexual jealousies. Although it may be quite rare, some women do lose men to their daughters, and when this happens their authority is totally broken. For women this is a reality. For men, the equivalent contest is not worth thinking about.

## Competition and community

Which brings us to the instructive case of Woody Allen. If a civilized society is uncomfortable with the idea of an older man desiring a younger woman or girl, this attitude is magnified into utter disgust when the girl in question is a daughter - even a step or adopted daughter. This I believe is largely because it is recognized to be so damaging to the self-esteem and place of the mother. Woody Allen's fall from grace is more than usually interesting in this respect, for he is a man whom younger women cheerfully admit to finding very attractive - perhaps, ironically, because he is seen as highly sensitive and not at all predatory. By a curious twist, only the day before British newspapers first carried stories of his involvement with Soon-Yi, the adopted student-daughter of his partner Mia Farrow, several had reported (17th August 1993) that a survey carried out by *Cosmopolitan* (the magazine which tells modern woman how to get what she wants) found Woody to be the preferred fantasy sexual partner of female British students; 33 per cent for Woody compared with 31 per cent for Sylvester Stallone (though the range and parameters of choice were not made clear in the reports). Just a few hours later he was being vilified in the same columns for confessing that an actual relationship of this sort had in fact taken place; although it was of course his baseness in rejecting a woman in favor of her daughter which made the difference.

Meanwhile Mia Farrow was said to be devastated; and it is clear that in spite of the fact that her career was built on playing the young girl to older men's fantasies, feelings like hers are the ones that a caring community needs to consider. Young women's choices would prevail in a free sexual arena, and it is accordingly older women's interests and attitudes which require most protection by society. Some control of sexuality is I suspect a basic requirement of female moral solidarity, and the community could not survive perpetual internal rivalries, especially as the sexual pecking order would severely contradict the generation hierarchy and lines of authority. Young women with the highest sexual value are in all societies regarded as the greatest moral danger and have to be regulated for the sake of group cohesion, as well as in their own longer-term interests. And this is why some inversion of Freud's model of sexual competition is called for. It is older women who have the greater structural need for rules to reduce sexual freedom. They also have the experience to understand this, and hold enough social power in the community to be able to back up such rules. Self-interest, lines of interpersonal influence and group morality come together in an irresistible combination, whereby it is older women who formulate the general interests of the group.

So it is extremely hard to accept the Freudian line that it was men who dreamt up sexual regulation and marriage. There are material advantages, to men as well as women, which follow from the development of marriage and family systems; some of these I am just about to consider. But if we are concerned with marriage as a means of limiting competition in the sexual market, then the picture only makes sense when we bring in women as full participants and include the need of older women to keep ambitious or rebellious girls in their place. Men obviously played a part in devising marriage; but I imagine that this was more a matter of responding to bids or initiatives offered by women, than of making their own suggestions. For women have a much stronger incentive to establish a framework for mutual control, and men could not achieve much without this anyway.

Without patriarchy there may be a tendency towards a sort of matriarchy in which men are marginal and social power is concentrated in the hands of older women. Don't forget that the princess did not know that she was going to transform the frog. She was the conduit for enchantment, but she did not yet know the spell, or even that there was one. The whole plot existed first in the mind of the witch. It was, I suspect, the mothers who conjured up the prince in their efforts to turn men into more reliable helpers; and it is the arrangements they invented which feminism now seeks to blame on men.

# PATRIARCHAL PHALLACIES

## Big bang theories

Taking female initiative and action seriously does not simply upset Freud; it also has profound implications for those feminist theories which depend on visions of male conquest to help explain to the troops how women come to be in a society which they represent as unequal. I can understand the dilemma. It is important for them to believe that there have been non-patriarchal societies in the past - as this keeps up hope for something analogous in the future (Eisler, 1988). But since societies all around *are* patriarchal, something must have gone wrong. Womankind has fallen. This cannot however have occurred by continuous creation whereby patriarchal societies evolved gradually, as this would mean that women had collaborated in their own downfall and actually signed away the privileges which men now enjoy. This is too horrendous to contemplate. Prehistoric woman surely did not jump; she must have been pushed. Men must have risen up in some way. Male violence is at the bottom of it all. Chevillard and Leconte, for example, find evidence for this in the near-universal myths of past conflict between male and female principles:

> *Though analysis of mythology should be undertaken with the utmost caution, two major facts can be accepted:*
> *- the great female divinities predate the male gods;*
> *- an opposition between gods/goddesses (or male/female ancestors)... that ended with the females' defeat. ...*
> *If women had never held the slightest power, it would be hard to understand why such myths existed. It would seem more reasonable to assume that they reflect a very old and very unpleasant memory of humankind, a memory that had to be forgotten insofar as women themselves internalised their status. ...*
> *To conclude, we do not believe that patrilocal societies emerged through continuous evolution but rather through a violent upheaval that took place within a small number of groups, which were efficient enough to transmit their*

*experience to others. Men, who were the actors in such a
transformation, formed a ruling class, access to which was
subject to extremely strict rules. We have already noted that
women were regarded as an exploitable labour force, and
that all women in lineage societies could be regarded as an
"alienated social class." Such societies are indeed the first
class societies known to humankind.* (1986, pp. 103,104,107)

Even moderate feminist theorists have assumed that systemic
violence must be involved; for example Coontz and Henderson
(1986), developing on the work of Leacock (1981).

*(We) do not believe that patrilocality, where it occurred,
developed out of any confrontation between men and women
or was necessarily instituted in order to oppress women and
appropriate their labour. However, (we) list a number of
features of patrilocality which allowed the potential
inequalities of the kin corporate mode of production to
develop ... And (we) argue that the resultant worsening of
women's position was forcibly maintained, first by lineage
heads and later by the state. .....The subordination of women
as a sex is the outcome of social processes whereby
patrilocal lineages begin to exercise control over the labour
and reproductive power of in-marrying wives.* (1986, pp. 39-
41)

I am not persuaded that violence does need to be invoked at all.
Such an assumption flies in the face of common sense, which can
accept that whereas there always have been a range of positive
benefits evident to women from the regulation of sexuality, this is
much less the case for men. The argument would be that women
have a more direct stake in the community and its moral economy,
and in finding arrangements which increase the positive contribution
of men to it and reduce their nuisance value at the same time.
Consequently they have a lot to gain from marriage systems which
tie men to them as helper-providers; they are better placed to
conceptualize the benefits of such systems in advance, and also to
discipline themselves and each other not to be distracted from these
by the short-term pleasures of personal freedom. I think that it is

these sorts of considerations, incidentally, rather than any wish to lump women together with cows and other breeding stock, which is in most people's minds when they refer to motherhood or women as being "more natural" than manhood. What it means is that women's interests coincide more naturally with those of the group.

The point can of course be conceptualized in biological terms, with men's relative lack of need for care and security, until senile if they get that far, and their drive to spread their maker's image as widely as they can, counterposed against the greater reproductive investment which a particular child represents for a woman, and her correspondingly greater interest in security (Ridley, 1992 & Fisher 1993). In the end both levels of analysis come down to very much the same thing, though, with social rules representing instruments for maximizing an individual's security, and as such overlapping with female interests more fully than male.

Men for their part certainly benefit from marriage, both through the status and privileges imparted to them, and also less visibly through the meaningful existence which family commitments afford. It is good news for them. But, all the same, the equation is less clear for them than women, and many may have mixed feelings about it, so we should hesitate before assuming with Freud either that men could anticipate these advantages from a state of nature, or even that once a marriage system exists they can keep to its rules without a lot of assistance. Left just to their own urges, and without being pulled strongly into patriarchal dependency chains, many men might incline towards a pattern of sexual arrangements in which loose and volatile associations gravitated around short-term or shared access to mainly younger women; a sort of groping towards the Playboy Club.

### The drones club

Where men are allowed to enjoy the benefits of society without having women and children personally dependent on their labors, they often drift in this sort of direction. Barbara Wootton's autobiography gives a fascinating insight into this. As one of the first cohort of life peers in 1958, she was both very busily and profitably employed, and not dependent in any sense; so her husband George retained many of his original frog features.

*George and I had lived together in a civilized way for twenty-one years: yet neither of us perhaps was well adapted to monogamous marriage, though for different reasons in each case. On my side I am too much occupied with my own affairs, and too reluctant to modify my way of life, to make an easy marriage partner. George, on the other hand, was clearly a natural polygamist. From the earliest days of our marriage he had always found it necessary to have what I can only call a secondary wife round the corner. ...*

*This experience taught me more vividly than any anthropological studies that even from a woman's point of view polygamy is a perfectly possible way of life. It has, of course, its problems in an officially monogamous society, and these problems would be aggravated if there were any children. But George, who hated to be tied in any way, set his face resolutely against our having a child; and I, who would greatly have liked a family, had to realize that the price of insistence would be too high. ...*

*In spite of his polygamous tendencies he had, moreover, a deep-seated loyalty to myself; ... Only an unkind fate which failed to endow him with a sufficient dose of self-discipline prevented him realizing his capacities to the full and accomplishing even more than he did.* (Wootton, 1967, pp 138-140)

Not only fate, perhaps. For men this is a common inheritance. Perhaps having a wife who was not dependent on him, but supported him instead, and did not adopt his name, had some bearing on his behavior. However we should not feel sorry for George. He had a ball. He lived as many men would wish to if only they had the chance. If the equal opportunities lobby achieves its goals there will be many more Georges.

If such male impulses as these are capable of generating a social structure, which I very much doubt, then it might well be something along the lines hinted at by Firestone (1970), in which the sexually most desirable women would spend their youth satisfying (multiple) male lust, and their later years as Queens producing daughters to carry on the service. This is the sort of pattern which starts to emerge in male-dominated frontier situations, or among military camp followers. But I think that it is unlikely that any such system could survive in isolation for very long, without drawing in new people from more conventional groups elsewhere, since it would be difficult to sustain within it the sort of personalized, long-term commitments between individuals needed for raising and looking after new generations. Fidelity of attachment does not seem a powerful male feature. Hogamus, higamus, man is polygamous.

Anyone who thinks otherwise should take a look at the photograph in the *Evening Standard* a while ago (7th October 1992) showing Jerry Hall standing next to a crestfallen and repentant Mick Jagger, who had gone back to her after a bout of womanizing. *"He will grow out of it one day,"* she was explaining; *"It's hard for him because girls throw themselves at his feet like flies."* The picture showed a man - with those big eyes a veritable emperor among frogs - who looked as if he felt that he was gradually being dragged into the system. Even though he presumably understood that he would be happier and live longer if he submitted - well, live longer at any rate - he was nevertheless struggling against it. You sometimes get what you need. But you can't always go on getting what you want.

Failure by feminists to give sufficient attention to this side of men renders their doctrinaire insistence that patriarchal marriage arises out of men's desire for power or control ludicrous. Surely it is the other way around. If the community is going to pull men out of self-indulgence and get them involved in useful activities then it has to *create* male privileges within the social system, to make it worth their while.

## Paternity and obligation

For this reason, feminist efforts to reconstruct the origins of patriarchy score very badly on credibility; like many of the big bang myths they refer to, they seem to illuminate contemporary anxieties and discontents rather than historical processes. Rosalind Miles' account (1986) is a good example of this. In this book, which draws together an impressive number of sources, she comes very close several times to producing a plausible model, only to throw it away when it starts to conflict with the article-of-faith premise of male authorship of patriarchy - and even though this leaves her with highly contradictory propositions.

Miles argues cogently that throughout most of prehistory women were probably doing things largely by themselves - feeding and caring for themselves, their children and the infirm, making technological breakthroughs, generally developing languages and cultures, that sort of thing - while men pottered on the margins and perhaps contributed a bit as casual helpers, or joined with women *(sic)* in communal hunting parties.

> *Dawn woman, with her mother and grandmother, her sisters and her aunts, and even a little help from her hunting man, managed to accomplish almost everything that subsequently made "homo" think himself "sapiens."* (p. 17)

Excellent, I thought reading it; I can take more of this. But when Miles comes to explain the apparent rise of patriarchal religions and cultures from around 1500 BC she suddenly brings in male will and agency. Replacement of mother-goddess cult objects by the phallic sort, she states, indicates that physiological paternity had now been discovered (p. 38). Men now realized their importance, and they were using it to take revenge for their long exclusion by making women worship a male god and by forging clever new legal conceptions of women which rendered them men's property. Knowledge about the facts of reproduction had led to the transformation of gender relations and social life generally. Paternity unleashed male power. Phallic thought reversed everything: *"Woman was no longer the vessel of nature, creating man. Now man created woman as a vessel for himself."*(p. 46) *"From the unknown moment in history when the secret of birth became known, women were doomed to decline from their goddess-like eminence."* (p. 66) They were downgraded to not much more than animals. *"No longer sacred, women became expendable."* (p. 48)

Suddenly the whole argument began to look a bit shaky, and I realized that the book was after all part of that massive mythical tradition of blaming men for evil, compared to which the Fall in Genesis is a very modest retaliation. Surely, I thought, men cannot have been elevated from offstage helper into the starring role of villain just by an idea? If the drive to power was so insistent there must have been plenty of other pretexts that men could have come

up with during the 40,000 plus year period that Miles is considering.
Nor is the idea itself such a big deal. One man can fertilize
thousands of women. You don't actually need them all. So
awareness of the part played by the male seed is hardly going to
make women lie down, as it were, to men as a whole; nor is it
guaranteed to enable men, pottering in their semi-domesticated state
on the edge of culture, to find gripping common cause to unite them
against their sisters. It did not add up.

There was worse to come; much worse. Miles, in her eager rush
to show that women knew it all and did it all, eventually trips
herself up. For later in the book, at a point when many readers may
have started to turn the pages more rapidly, she discusses early
contraceptive techniques likely to have been developed by
prehistoric women, and she remarks almost casually that of course
women must have used such devices from time immemorial. Birth
control would have been essential for them in organizing their lives.

> *Notions of the cervical and penile barrier, cap or sheath, had*
> *been around for as long as humanity.* (p. 214)

Oh, really? So what did she have in mind earlier when she proposed
that the most important event in the history of gender relations, the
poisonous thing which destroyed the female Eden just a few
thousand years ago, was the discovery of paternity? What, exactly,
did women before then think that those devices were protecting
them *from*? Or is it that women understood about paternity but men
had not made the connection? Or, if we were to accept the
impossible and agree that perhaps women did manage to keep a
secret for thirty thousand years or so, give or take a bit, why did
they then decide to let men find out?

The only possible answer to these questions is that the central
proposition is wrong and knowledge of paternity itself cannot have
been the crucial factor leading to the establishment of patriarchy. It
might have played a part. And the most plausible and obvious
suggestion is that it would support the imputation of male
responsibility. The idea of male power and creativity and so on is,
I believe, essentially a lever for getting men to commit themselves
to more help in looking after their own offspring, and committing
themselves to the mothers. Patriarchal marriage means in effect that

men become tied to particular women and children. If paternity did become more salient, the reason, I feel sure, was basically to do with turning men from jobbing extras into obligated and dependable providers.

## Early sexual divisions

This suggestion is of crucial relevance to Miles' key issues, which are about why women have allowed men to subjugate them. And it is interesting to note that although, throughout the main body of the book, she takes very formal indicators of male supremacy as critical, such as legal status, in her preface she makes it clear that the essential inequality with which women are actually concerned is unequal sharing of the primary work of reproduction. Men are only too glad to share in the fun bits of this, but then leave the rest to women (1986, p. xiii). "Subjugation of women" means not helping them out. We are back at the New Man question.

Curiously, or maybe not, Miles avoids the issue of how far men did their share of domestic labor before patriarchy, and lets us assume implicitly that it is the social institutions of patriarchy itself which are to blame for the situation since their emergence. This is a weakness which features in many of the reconstructions of the big bang variety (e.g., Eisler, 1988).

When the matter does get addressed, as by Liebowitz (1986), the craziness of these models turns out to be quite staggering. Liebowitz's thesis is that the sexual division of labor is not rooted in prehistory or nature, because before the introduction of political and economic exchanges between groups, the moment of Fall in her analysis, males and females both performed the same productive tasks. However, her definitions and formulation beg some very large questions, and I am sure that she ought to be seen as having let the cat out of the bag; for when she says that males and females played the same roles in production, what she actually *means* is that women did the same things as men and all of the child care in addition.

*The common sense explanation of the origin of the division of labour by sex is that it is related to size and strength differences between early hominid males and females and to the lengthened biological dependency of the young. This implies that the sexual division is protocultural, and therefore "natural." This notion does not, however, bear up under close inspection. In this paper I will try to show that early hominids of both sexes, despite their differences in size after reaching sexual maturity, engaged in the same kinds of productive activities. Adult females simply combined these productive activities with bearing and nursing the young. The sexual division of labour developed in conjunction with certain specific* cultural *innovations.* (Liebowitz, 1986, p. 43)

I don't see anything simple about fitting in domestic labor, and wonder whether Liebowitz appreciates the complex effects having children has on both opportunity and motivation to engage in what she calls production. However, it is good Marxism to leave out domestic labor from the definition of division of labor - although undoubtedly misleading for other feminists who may well assume that child care is in fact what it is all about, and draw entirely wrong inferences if they only read Liebowitz' stirring conclusion that:

*The (model outlined above) proposes that production for distribution is fundamental to the human condition. It says that production not only precedes the sexual division of labour, but also precedes incest taboos, marriage and kinship systems. ... The idea that women are and always have been subordinated to men is not expressed in the model just presented. I do not subscribe to the view that the subordination of women is a "basic" part of our heritage.* (Ibid., pp. 74-75)

In the last analysis, this trick is very like that of Miles. Prehistoric child care is made unproblematic by being excluded from key aspects of the argument. But it obviously played an overwhelming role in the life of pre-patriarchal woman herself. Consider some of the comments made by Liebowitz about the performance by men and women of their similar productive tasks, *before* a sexual division of labor became established.

*The remains in the ancient sites and evidence from contemporary human foragers and other primate groups suggest that these males and females engaged in several kinds of foraging activities. These rarely involve distinctions between what males and females (or young or old) are called upon to do. They include: 1) individual foraging for small game and vegetables; 2) group hunting (of either the surround or drive type, or of the "chase and exhaust" variety) focusing on small animals; and 3) killing or scavenging large animals that are, somehow, incapacitated. These foraging activities could have been accomplished with simple tools by the physically similar young foragers and the few sex differentiated adults who, if female, were not necessarily encumbered by either pregnancy or an infant. These activities - undifferentiated along sex lines - whether individual or cooperative, when rewarded by more than could be consumed on the spot become production if the surplus is distributed for later consumption. Production proves to be advantageous for all the actors involved. (Ibid., p. 60)*

There is an extremely naïve assumption here that male and female behavior will be the same, and that because men *can* contribute equally to a community by sharing their "surplus" with it, then they *will* do so, and that the balance between individual and group interests will weigh equally regardless of sex. In reality there must have been tremendous differences between what fancy-free, wandering males and tied-down females could do. Socio-biologists generally agree that males serve their own genes best by multiplying the number of females helping to reproduce them, rather than by worrying too much about the well-being of particular partners. Liebowitz herself indirectly acknowledges this by showing that difference in body size (governed by access to food) between the sexes, i.e., "dimorphism," seems to have been markedly greater *before* sexual divisions of "productive" labor emerged under patriarchy. That is, though she does not spell this out, until tied down themselves by obligations to help provide for particular women and children, men would have behaved even more selfishly than after, using their freedom from domestic labor to spend more time searching out the best life-style for themselves.

> *If a male who wanders widely grows big enough to avoid or intimidate predators and survives, he is obviously in a position to bump into a female (or two or three)... A male who is not as active as he, and/or fails to survive the trip, obviously has fewer mating opportunities. ... Having big males serves the species well. It allows the males, who are engaging in the same kind of food-getting activities as the females, to get more food by going abroad for it. This removes some of the pressure on females. Note here that their sexual dimorphism, far from reflecting even a casual or pragmatic division of labour by sex, allows both males and females to engage in the* same *foraging activities, only in different geographical ranges.* (Ibid., pp. 54-55)

What we have here is a setting in which males wandered freely, fending and foraging mainly for themselves, and sometimes bumping into fresh females. A truly idyllic *pastorale* to set before sisters as an illustration of the cultural basis of sexual divisions of labor. Dawn frog!

Surely, in these circumstances, if they ever did exist, women - the feminists among them at any rate - would have seen that the burden of child rearing placed on them by Mother Nature could be best lifted by making personal deals with men whereby sex and submission were rationed and traded in return for some services, such as a share, not necessarily very large, of the food foraged from further away by the less tied-down male, plus perhaps some work seeing off other wide-ranging males who might be encroaching on nearby forage. (Liebowitz fails to notice that one woman's abroad is likely to be another's backyard). During childbearing periods, at least, even a relatively small amount of help would be significant (Ridley, 1992).

In fact, common sense cries out that women *would* have seen all this since the dawn of history and would have made sexual contracts with men to this end. If there has been any movement towards patriarchal religion and families, which is not clearly proven, then it all makes most sense as a means of refining the idea of male responsibility for their offspring, in order to tighten the screw on them, and get more support, including a larger transfer of food to women - reducing sexual dimorphism - and increasing the volume of production and property. Such a process could have involved some ceding of power to men, but this will have been regarded as the price for achieving mens' fuller domestication. It may also have involved cultivating new needs and social interests in men of which they would not have been aware in advance, and which could not have motivated them beforehand. The more that men are given positions in the community whereby high status hangs on proper performance of family roles, and which multiply the benefits that they can hope to get via women, then the greater women's control becomes over *them*. So women are extremely likely to have been instigators and principle actors in devising marriage. Insofar as it is now officially a man's world, we must not forget that it was probably created, and may still be kept as such, mainly by women, in the endless (and I am sure frequently thankless) quest to make men better and more useful people.

## THE SEXUAL CONTRACT

*The creation of the public domain is a creation of men in order to wrest power from women in the private domain.*
(Hearn, 1992, p. 21)

*The crucial process of civilisation is the subordination of male sexual impulses and psychology to long-term horizons of female biology. ... It is male behaviour that must be changed to create a civilised order. ... This is the ultimate and growing source of female power in the modern world. Women domesticate and civilise male nature. They can destroy civilised male identity merely by giving up that role.*
(Gilder, 1973, p. 23)

I doubt very much that patriarchy represents the outcome of conquest or male snatching of power or bullying; though I can see that portraying it in this way has the beneficial effect, up to a point, of stirring men's guilt and enabling women to get a better deal out of them. What seems altogether more plausible, and worthy of fuller investigation than it has been given in recent years, is the more traditional idea that men are continuously being drawn into social groupings basically regulated by and organized around women, partly as providers of some food and protection but also of those services least consistent with full and harmonious membership of the moral community, and typically as nominal "heads." In return for some flattery and sex they would do morally dangerous work which mothers would be glad not to have to tackle themselves. And as the more visible actors they could serve as scapegoats for divisive tendencies with the community itself. Displays of wholesome outrage in condemning male sexual predation draw eyes away from the ways in which female sexuality comes between women.

This sort of account of the forces sustaining fatherhood and patriarchy is much more consistent with protection of the mother-daughter and sister-sister axes at the heart of community life; and it does not require any sudden historical jump from "horde" existence to civilized society. As more subtle patriarchal illusions are devised, and the increasing complexity of social organization allows the emphasis to shift away from just sex to other social benefits, men become more reliably hooked and controlled. We may be going through just such a process of re-adjustment, although more convoluted than usual, at the moment.

The original social contract dealing with reciprocal back-up in caring activities takes place between women. And the basic sexual contract, bringing men in too, has to be seen as being between women, the primordial community, and men who see potential benefits in it for themselves. The power of women in this will have been to formulate the ground rules and offer them to men; the power of men would lie, and still does, in whether or not to accept the offer. The terms of entry would presumably have revolved around a trading by women of submission to the idea of dependency on men in return for male commitment and fidelity. Here are credible incentives both for women to agree to male fronting of public activities and control of a "public realm," and for men to accept restraints on their freedom, as in conventions of sexual exclusivity. For by endorsing group morality, and becoming helpers and instruments for women's objectives and evaluations, men are enabled to become gatekeepers of society and obtain advantages over other men. Or perhaps they are better regarded as poachers adopting the profession of gamekeeper. Either way, men's passion and competitiveness, which keep them apart in a state of nature, become converted into ambition, which would channel their energy into the regulatory systems of society. As Greek myths would suggest, the first thoroughgoing princes were probably priests.

## Patriarchy and female solidarity

Advantages arise for a number of interest groups from this. The most obvious beneficiaries will have been groups adopting the new regime; and the changes in food-production techniques and increases in productivity which are often shown as accompanying the transition to patriarchy are possibly indications of the value of this development in man-management (e.g. Leacock, 1981). Also men themselves, while losing the freedom to range alone and compete in a world relatively free from morality, would gain security or place and purpose, and some social privileges. But it does need to be stressed that there are also advantages in patriarchal marriage to women specifically, both individually and collectively. These cluster mainly around the ways in which involvement of men relates to the enhancement of solidarity between women.

Firstly, and very obviously, marriage has an egalitarian potential which can give women greater assurance of sexual satisfaction and male attention, and reduce contests between them which might interfere with the smooth running of the moral economy. Given the long period of dependency of human children, it is advantageous for women to have long-term attachments to particular men, to assure them of support. A conventional, pre-feminist interpretation of monogamous exclusivity is that it requires female mutual restraint to help tie men down; and the root of the hostility directed towards prostitutes and *demimondaines* may lie in their challenge to this. Men and women can both find the idea of independent women threatening. But whereas to men it evokes that aspect of collective female consciousness which is hostile to men and would like to oust them and take over everything, to women it seems to stand for competitive individualists who refuse to perform their collective duty of taming a particular man and making him useful, and instead devise temptations to steal their sisters' partners.

Susie Orbach has shown how the woman who truly believes in sisterhood will eat well to get fat to show others that she cannot do them any harm (1989). In a strict Muslim society a veil or chador goes a long way to protect equality and sororal tranquillity. And even the tendency towards a co-ordination of menstrual cycles within face-to-face female groups is thought by many biologists to be a natural mechanism for limiting sexual conflicts (Knight, 1991).

Female solidarity is also assisted by having men in positions of formal leadership and responsibility. Sanday (1981) among others has suggested that where men are ostensibly in power this greatly increases opportunities for steering them in directions desired by women. I am sure that this is true. It also allows women to avoid accepting blame in each other's eyes for aspects of community regulation and organization which are too irksome or divisive. For example male leadership helps them to stay out of hierarchical relationships with each other. Women don't like inequality and are often very uncomfortable when required to exercise authority over others, or when they are visibly more successful than them (Coward, 1992; Gunew, 1991; Ramazanoglu, 1989). The moral economy operates most efficiently when calling for reciprocity between equals, as exchange rates are then simpler to measure, and the assertion of individual rights, which threaten cohesion, is not called for.

Male leaders can serve as figureheads and scapegoats. Their more withdrawn position is valuable here, and lends itself to leadership. As comparative outsiders to the community, or even archetypal Simmelian "strangers," who are in addition usually thought of as less sensitive and more aggressive beings, they are well suited to carrying the stress and hostility attached to a leading role. It is alright for women to gossip critically about each other in private; this is the stock exchange of the moral economy. But when it comes to publicly upholding the law then it is good to have a man to do it. It was the king who was expected to get the princess to keep her word. In real life this may not happen much; but firm fathering is generally approved of, and "discipline" is listed as one of the main benefits of having men around. This is man's work.

## Honor and possession

The regulation of sexual behavior is particularly important here, as Freud realized, since it entails self-regulation by men. But the need for control does not, I think, arise because men's passions are inherently violent and destructive. It is more that a key part of the job of helping women to look after their children lies in upholding a pattern of sexual relations which enables women to secure long term support from men, and this is usually felt to require exclusivity. Accordingly, one of the most important roles given to the patriarch is to promote this, as guardian of women's honor, chastity, fidelity and so forth. It is men who are publicly regarded as jealously possessive of their women's good behavior. But this public designation does not mean that men's actions are in reality prompted by rampaging male libido. Women's feelings have a crucial influence too. How many women, while perhaps decrying male possessiveness, would be deeply hurt if their men did not feel it or at least conform to it? Very often, I believe, it is a case whereby men, as the instruments of women's objectives, are the ones who execute, by injecting force and passion, moral work which has been desired and designed by women. Cultures responsive to women's needs may serve to plant feelings in men which - *pace* Freud - are not deep-seated and never become very deeply rooted.

> *(In the past), the worst possible insult for an Italian man has been to call him* cornuto - *it means a man with horns on his head like those of the devil. The longer his wife is unfaithful to him, the longer they grow. Some Italian Catholics even believe that the* cornuto *has been punished by God for failing to follow one of His commandments - God created man to be lord and master of woman. Fail to make it seem as if your woman belongs to you, and you're worse than a Marxist. ...*
>
> *(But now)... Only when people start to talk too much and too publicly about a wife's indiscretions does her Italian husband rediscover his sense of possession and his belief in* vendetta. *Once that happens, many of the* cornuti *become Othello-like in their ferocity - if they don't, they risk losing face.* (Della Torre, 1993)

Men are far more possessive in those cultures where they are expected by their women to display such sentiments, and where they would be accused of lack of attention if they did not, and punished by shame and other group sanctions. Some of the sanctions arise materially, too, through patriarchal obligations. The cuckold is mocked not simply because he has failed to control or satisfy his wife, but because there is possibly a cuckoo in his nest - a mouth to feed which he has not himself created. Fear of such burdens is a sharp spur to possessiveness.

The Muslim institution of purdah is almost universally attributed to male jealousy. But we have to recognize that it also serves the interests of women, especially older women. Family values which require men to protect exclusive rights in their women and which, as Moore points out (1988, pp. 106-7), make their own status in the community hang on that of their women, have the effect of getting men to police each other on behalf of rules in which the female community itself has a major stake. But obviously this works better if kept discreet; and one of the reasons why the film *Bhaji on the Beach* has offended some in the British Asian community is that it shows, perhaps too crudely, how it may take the tongue of an angry mother to get her sons to concern themselves actively (and in the event violently) to persuade a westernized, runaway daughter-in-law to return to the fold. The veil of patriarchy is drawn back too far, too revealingly.

Most cultures prefer to identify women as agents or guardians of culture, with men as its architects. This convention has benefits for everyone. It allows women to get on with the work of daily disciplining, which they experience a greater practical need to do and which men, in spite of alleged attachment to the rules, often seem disinclined to bother with; and it enables them to do it without carrying major blame for it, and without men catching on that they are not really in control.

All this is however extremely difficult to probe. One of the disadvantages of having left female anthropologists to deal with family matters is that when we try to unpick the workings of these institutions we find that our understanding of the processes is filtered through female sensitivities. Reading Mary Douglas recently, on the Walbiri, where male dominance is "accepted as a central principle of social organisation," I received a strong impression of men being wound up to police each other in forceful defense of their wives' honor, while women themselves quietly got on with their lives under this umbrella of sexual security (Douglas, 1966). If we put on one side a culture's internal presentation of what is happening, and just try to see who benefits from it, then *Izzat*, proscriptions on adultery, purdah and so on all stand out as customs or concepts which, when upheld and implemented by men or in the name of men, allow mothers and daughters to remain on much better terms with each other than if the mothers themselves had to enforce and justify them. They seem unlikely just to have been imposed on women by imperious males.

## Asymmetry and interdependence

The lasting basis of the sex war is the asymmetry of sexual contracts, and the consequent difficulties in measuring and balancing exchanges between men and women. Innumerable feminist commentaries have picked over how much more domestic labor (including child care) is put in by women; and here again the New Man principle has figured as a potent aspiration for, and condemnation of existing men. But accounts of this ilk will not I suspect carry much weight with men as they fail to allow for the greater loss of male personal freedom involved. The equation cannot be symmetrical as men's and women's desires are not identical.

This underlying asymmetry does probably make some degree of gender conflict unavoidable, but it does at the same time help to limit tensions and make them resolvable. This is because the pursuit of parity will always seem so pointless to many women that periods of intense conflict are bound to spark off almost immediately some re-awakenings of ideas about difference, interdependence and complementarity, which eventually restore some mutual toleration. Homeostasis is inherent in the gender zone. I will take this point further in the final chapter.

The backlash which has been gathering pace for the last few years represents a growing recognition that men and women do not have the same needs and interests; and this is leading to a revival of awareness that there is more than one way of interpreting the division of labor at the heart of the contract. This used to be a commonplace:

> *Schoolteachers, social workers and others who have contact with Bethnal Green families nearly always agree that the real head of the family is the mother, but a few stress the importance of the man as the final authority. The disagreement seems to be based on a sharp division of labour between men and women and a difference of opinion as to*

*which role is to be regarded as the more important.* (Robb, 1954, p. 60)

There is, I believe, a very flexible interpenetration of perspectives available within the general notion of sexual interdependence, which is now in process of being rediscovered. Feminists have chosen to adopt a "male" view, of the private realm as *serving* the public realm, and as secondary to it. I will discuss this in chapter seven. But there is also a very strong model, which was embedded in traditional women's worldviews and folklore like the frog prince story which sees things the other way around, whereby the public realm is the instrument for ends and designs conceived within the private domain. In this men are never more than lords of ways and means, while it is women who set the goals for them to pursue.

Thus the struggles between men and women, public and private, formal and informal, are open to alternative evaluations which can assign priority and greater influence to either. The constructive ambiguity in these competing views is perhaps what keeps sexual contracts on the road. But this entails a balance of anxieties as well as of confidence in the sexual political arena. One gender's hope is another's fear. Myths about the banishing of goddesses serve both to reassure women that female power is possible, while encapsulating their suspicions that men have destroyed a matriarchal Eden and have contrived to steal a march on them. For men these same traditions can be taken as confirmation that men are now in charge. But, contrarily, they can also serve as a focus for questions about whether male power may not itself be an illusion, and whether perhaps the *real* force in society belongs to women, who may have even increased their influence by making it invisible. This last question has been given rather short shrift in feminist commentaries, and deserves more attention.

# 6

# FEMALE MAGIC

## CHURCH AND STATE

*Conventional male power (is an) ideological myth. It is designed to induce the majority of men to accept a bondage to the machine and the marketplace, to a large extent in the service of women and in the interests of civilisation. ... Women control not the economy of the marketplace but the economy of Eros; the life force in our society and our lives. What happens in the inner realm of women finally shapes what happens on our social surfaces, determining the level of happiness, energy, creativity and solidarity in the nation.* (Gilder, 1973, pp. 24-5)

The most obvious message in the fairy story is that through marriage men can achieve patriarchal splendor, and this carries an implication for women that their relative status is somewhat diminished. But there are compensations for women in the deeper structure of the tale. For this suggests that while it is men who are given status and hold the highest office, the potent forces governing society, and which move everything along, are more in their hands.

In real life men are repeatedly confronted with evidence of women's importance and influence; but because it is not manifest in formal social structures it is often invested by them with a mysterious, secret character - the feminine mystique. Women's power is not visible. When men get their way it is usually evident how they do it, by exploiting some public principle or position, or by using material force, or very evidently running away from responsibilities. There is little subtlety in it. Women on the other hand more often exert influence by conjuring up suitable motivations for others, by persuading them of their best interests, praising or criticizing their behavior, playing moral cards and so on. Frequently women's power is effective without its objects being fully aware of it. And so it has a magical quality. The spirits who cast spells in folktales, fairies or witches according to their effect on the protagonists' fate, are almost invariably female (Opie & Opie, 1982 p. 186). Power plus invisibility equals magic.

Men's fascination with this phenomenon, which they may regard as challenging patriarchal models of the universe, sometimes verges on torment. According to the Elaine Feinstein biography (1993), D.H. Lawrence's obsession with sexual domination arose out of his childhood puzzlement at the discrepancy between the fact that women did everything and knew everything, and the orthodoxy that God was a man. In his struggle to understand and resolve this he felt himself becoming ever more fascinated and trapped by the power which women seemed to hold. He knew that he was supposed to be the master. But he was also painfully conscious that this was always eluding him.

## Intimations of matriarchy

It is tempting to see the same sort of angst underlying the pre-occupation with matriarchy which gripped late nineteenth- and early twentieth-century men. During the height of Victorian patriarchy a sizeable academic industry grew up, to be carried on through the first half of this century by antiquarians like Robert Graves, which collected and sifted and analysed the evidence relating to possible matriarchal societies - mainly the pre-Hellenic peoples of the heroic age. Not enough solid material was unearthed to show that there had ever been social systems in which women held formal power over men, although enough fragments did emerge to whet the appetites of later feminists. What is more difficult to understand though is how it should have been of such interest to men at this time.

I suspect that it was largely because it afforded a means of dealing intellectually with the manifold inadequacies of the prevailing model of male omnipotence, very pervasive during this period, and yet which men conspicuously fail to match up to in all societies. The practicalities of female centrality and competence are constantly breaking through the shallow illusions of men's supremacy; and the concept of matriarchy, safely projected to another place and time, is a contrary model, maybe only embryonic and half-articulated, though perhaps nearing the status of a subcultural alternative among some groups, which helps to explain these awkward and irreverent phenomena.

For men in the street with little time or inclination to explore the issue thoroughly, the same feelings are normally dealt with through a tendency towards idealizing women, and romanticizing their power as female virtue. There is no harm in this, so long as it makes them behave better towards women. Lawrence, who was not a classical scholar, apparently did the cooking and washing up while Frieda stayed in bed until lunchtime. However when men entertain these ideas I think that they are frequently confusing women with the strength and moral force of the community itself, and attributing to women as individuals features or characteristics which they really only possess or share as members of the group.

Two things are important to recognize here, I believe. The first is that women, the primary carers, have much more direct experience of the moral community than do men, whose own position is mediated by a few key relationships to women. Men's experience of community is as sons and lovers, so to speak. It is their mothers and wives who consequently appear to embody the virtues (and unwelcome demands) which community life entails. This is not all though. Not only are women closer to the heart of the caring community, but the web of mutual obligations and services which make it up are predominantly between women, and are concerned with activities largely confined to women. So the community does itself have a distinctly female character.

This quality is essentially a collective rather than individual feature. Women have their own personal interests, which have been amplified by feminism and do not always identify with community values and judgments. But virtually all women, no less within feminism, feel great moral strength in solidarity - more so than men, I am sure, who find political strength in numbers but moral certainty in solitude and mystic union with impersonal or abstract forces - so that for women relatedness, caring and mutuality is the basis of their influence on the world and security in it. They have a much greater stake in community.

Female power seems magical to men because it is not vested in individuals but arises - with the usual and significant exception of the harlot's - out of collective support and moral cohesion. This is the antithesis of life in the forest where everything relates to survival of self and time spans are very short. The essence of community is mutual care between members, with no time limits, and highly pragmatic prioritization of actual people and relationships over abstract principles. This is what gives it its strength, durability and spiritual cohesion, and this is why it may seem so mysterious, even clandestine, to men.

But whether he understands it or not, or on what level, a man cannot ignore the values which operate within the community. Whatever slogans political leaders may dress themselves up in, they ultimately derive most of their own influence by calling on particularistic values in daily use by the community - that is reciprocity, loyalty, personal respect and commitment. The prince is secular head. But he has to rule over his subjects in a way which is acceptable to them. This means listening to spiritual voices of the church - that is, the virtuous public opinion which underwrites legitimate authority. Women score heavily here. As the backbone of the community and experts in mutual care and support, women are the chief authors of relevant practical opinion, and experienced auditors of the moral economy. It is they who make up the living body of the church; and this puts them morally above men. Men run the state; they are Kshatriyas. But the Brahmans, to whom the state must defer on moral questions and issues of deepest policy, are women. Men have control of force. But women have the capacity to sanctify it or not. It was Les Tricotreuses who licensed the guillotine with their nods - while, some might want to add, keeping their own hands clean.

This comes back to the ways in which a sexual division of labor does allow for a pluralistic balance of power. The strength of women is not incompatible with patriarchy because the puffed up public realm can be seen as licensed by the "female church," giving a separation of powers between the formal, physical and visible where men are dominant, and the spiritual, informal and invisible in which women hold a collective advantage.

## Community and religion

But feminists have become so blinded by the glory of men's privileges that they have persuaded each other to believe that only individual freedom and formal position is worth having. This lies behind the assault lately on patriarchal religions; and my representation of women's moral power as a church would no doubt prompt many to point out that specific churches worship male deities, are headed by male priests, and therefore serve male interests. This is a popular line at the moment.

*What have the churches, with their male hierarchies, got to offer women? ... God (Dr. Hampson says of the transcendent monarch so often prescribed) is up there, out there, ... all powerful, self-sufficient, able to assert His will - many a man's wildest dream fulfilled. What would women's dream of religion look like? ... It would be about relatedness, connectedness, healing, power and spirit woven together in a new way, with a vision of God ... as a dimension of all that is.* (Furlong, 1991)

No one could dispute that Christian theology is androcentric and church hierarchies are male. But the rider about serving male interests simply does not follow. On the contrary, I would argue that male officiation and leadership is essential if these churches are going to stand successfully for community values which for most men have a female orientation. The male priest is not necessarily an oppressor of women, nor a symbol of male domination. What he *can* do better than any woman is to give male confirmation to virtues which many men feel do not belong to them and were not made by them. For, surely, what religion is mostly about, as Durkheim persuasively insisted, is not abstract schemas but the representation and celebration of people's social relations and participation in an ongoing stream of group consciousness. It is above all a symbolic statement about membership of family and community.

The bulk of work in any living church focuses on giving expression to people's sense of relatedness (as Furlong notes) and in particular on regulating kinship duties and organizing the rites of passage which mark significant changes in family obligations. Real churches are not about theology but about weddings, funerals and baptisms, and also nurseries, youth clubs, and local activities which endorse the family at the same time as extending the spirit of belonging together outwards from kinship groupings to other members of the congregation and local community.

So the concerns of churches and the traditional domain of women overlap greatly. In some religions like Islam the concern is ritualized and abstract. But the central business of a Christian church is the orderly promotion not just of a set of values but also practical activities to secure family welfare and destinies within the parish. The chief realm of women's activities revolves around implementing such values, to the benefit of a particular family (E. Roberts, 1984). Any caring community is a church in a broad sense for rationalizing and mediating support between different family groups and networks. Family ties constitute the most enduring and compelling threads running through a community; and it is by helping each other to meet their family obligations that women are able to support each other most effectively. It is precisely because they are locked into these activities at a practical level that there is, I submit, far less need for women to play key roles in the symbolic work of institutionalized churches.

There may be some religious functions that are inherently more suited to being done by men. Their penchant towards detachment and universalism may enable them, for example, to prevent a parish becoming too localized or inward-looking. But this is not very crucial; a small amount of abstract theology goes a long way. In a day-to-day sense what is important is not scriptural exegesis, but church action in securing acceptance and renewal of obligations to kin, and in a general underlining of the sacrosanct nature of the family-centered moral economy. This is the substance of church business and is what the flock expects the padre to offer. It is also why many more men "find god" through their female partners rather than vice-versa (Finney, 1992), just as historically queens have been more active in converting kings (Mount, 1982, p. 231). Induction to religion is part of men's moral apprenticeship. The importance of a male priest here is crucial and almost entirely theatrical. Because the content of routine work is female, and the sector of the community which most needs persuading to accept the rules is male, then symbolically it is much more valuable if the formal officiation is vested in a man.

## REDEEMING MEN

*Female power, therefore, comes from what the woman can offer or withhold. She can grant to a man the sexual affirmation that he needs more than she does; she can offer him progeny otherwise permanently denied him; and she can give him a way of living happily and productively in a civilised society that is otherwise oppressive to male nature. In exchange modern man can give little beyond his external achievements and his reluctant faithfulness. It is on these terms of exchange that marriage, and male socialisation, are based.* (Gilder, 1973, p. 23)

Ostensibly it is male priests who tend the souls of men. But this is an abstract convention; and in the real world it is women who determine men's fate, by mediating and channelling their membership of adult society. This is because of their strategic position between men and children, the ultimate dependants and thereby sources of legitimacy in the community. For the basic rule in a world of mutual concern is that to be a full member you must recognize some commitments and obligations to others. The language of belonging is responsibility; the sign of grace is responsiveness to the needs of others; and the first commandment is not to be independent or allow it in others.

As the frog story indicates, there are two stages in men's lives which are problematic in these terms; and in both of them they are subject to female evaluation and magic. Firstly, adolescent boys are rejected and sent off to learn to be useful; and then they may be re-admitted as family men with dependants of their own. It is possible to argue about how far the first process always needs to involve women; but the redemption of men very clearly does, as women are the source of men's immediate motivation, both as individuals who arouse and then respond to men's sexual desire, and also collectively, through their role in determining the rules for access, that is in marriage and the obligations it entails, and as general evaluators of men's performance.

Becoming a family man does marvellous things for a frog. But they are not things he could have anticipated, nor what, in his frog state, he would have wanted for himself, if he had been in a position to draw up the criteria for readmission. Commitment is not a concept which comes easily to the individualist. In many cases it is only the gross flattery of the princely imagery, overcoming the fear of entrapment, which gets the groom inside the church at all.

Many women these days would take issue with the notion that they play an important part as arbiters of male behavior, using praise and criticism to channel them in desirable directions. But their objection would be that women shouldn't have to do this, as it cramps their own life-style, rather than that it does not happen. It is however extremely valuable for the community. The two-stage process of repudiating boys and then reclaiming adult men is a very neat procedure for allowing core members of the group, predominantly women, to steer male energy into useful activities. Among many primates the adult male is little more than a drone and may even be disruptive of community life. By rejecting men and allowing them back on terms acceptable to themselves as major guardians of the general interest, women in concert act as filters for a natural resource which would otherwise at best be lost to society, and at worst pose dangers.

Pre-feminist women are conscious of this role and deliberately strive to bring out the best in men. At a very general level this means joining in the approval of "nice" men, in an attempt to raise overall standards. At the most intimate level it may involve desiring to have children by, and perpetuating the transmissible characteristics of, the man or men most admired. And between these two poles there is a good deal of space for degrees of flattery and approbation which altogether can exert tremendous influence on men. Since men's evaluations of women are more superficial and less related to their behavior their own moral influence is infinitely less.

## Steering or doing

This point is frequently misunderstood or misrepresented, and seen as excluding women from interesting activities. It is again significant, I think, that this was a central element of Betty Friedan's *Feminine Mystique* argument (1963), which was a crucially important text in launching the contemporary feminist movement, and which, equally significantly, she has subsequently repudiated (1982). What Friedan did was to assume that this evaluative or arbiter role was something that just went on in bedrooms and kitchens, that it was purely domestic. She reports with disdain a commencement address made by Adlai Stevenson in 1955 at Smith College, in which he tries to calm educated women's worldly ambitions by telling them how influential their role was as women.

> *In short, far from the vocation of marriage and motherhood leading you away from the great issues of our day, it brings you back to their very center and places upon you an infinitely deeper and more intimate responsibility than that borne by the majority of those who hit the headlines and make the news and live in such a turmoil of great issues that they end by being totally unable to distinguish which issues are really great.* (1963, p. 60)

The speech does not appear to have gone down very well, and I think deservedly. It confirmed women's suspicions that domestic life is isolating by making it look as if the male alternative was excitement and turmoil. Many women would prefer that to boredom. Also by concentrating on the big M, motherhood, it managed to convey the feeling that the only significant contribution they could expect to make was by homemaking and nurturing children. What it failed to indicate (and Betty Friedan, by selecting it, helped to obscure) was that even where some preference is given to men in frontline public positions this does not mean that women cannot participate very actively in drawing up the ground rules by which the great issues of the day are ultimately identified and resolved. This enables them to exercise very real power outside of the domestic sphere, in addition to controlling things within it, as Friedan now concedes:

> *The power of "women's sphere" in shaping political as well as personal consciousness has clearly been underestimated by feminists today.* (1982, p. 297)

There are important roles in wider society for women, both as paid workers - so long as this leaves a main breadwinner position for men - and also as moral trustees. Women can play a major part in determining the major objectives without taking away positions from men; for male officiants then have the task of trying to put these aims into operation.

Obviously there is some cost in this for women as individuals. If

they are cast as arbiters they become disqualified from taking a
leading part in the action themselves and are held back from
individual achievement in certain areas. Judges cannot also be
competitors; or in Parsonian terms you cannot combine expressivity
and instrumentality (Schwendinger & Schwendinger, 1971). Men
will do, while women set goals and motivate; and the price for
tapping male creative energy has to be some neglect of women's
own. But there are many benefits to the community, and thus to
women collectively, from unleashing and regulating male action.
The relationship between female inspiration and male performance
is recognized and highly valued in most cultures. Arthur's magic
sword, *Excalibur,* was given to him by the Lady of the Lake. And
countless women through the ages have seen their central purpose
in life as discovering, inspiring and rewarding men. Rhine gold was
all about this; and the art of great hostesses and society queens like
Alma Mahler lies in recognizing and then using their charms to
bring out the genius in men (Keegan, 1991).

Ruth Brandon (1990) has suggested that many women propping
up great men have regretted the sacrifice of their own creativity. But
in other cases it seems to be performed with every indication of
satisfaction and fulfillment and in the knowledge that other people
know how crucial and formative their support has been. Our own
Edith Londonderry, glittering hostess of the inter-war period, whose
"Ark" of men drawing inspiration from her included Churchill,
Macmillan, and MacDonald, was seen as exercising valuable
political influence; although her own case is complicated by the fact
that she also used this influence to promote the career of her
(philandering) husband. But the rule is the same. Behind every great
man, look for a great man-manager. In the contemporary world
fewer women are prepared to see themselves as rewards and
inspirations; A.A. Gill recently declared that this "Nubility" is an
endangered species, although sightings can still be made at charity
performances.

> *I watched the Nubility as (Carreras) sang. All had the same*
> *rapt, clear, thoughtless expressions on their faces. They were*
> *beautiful and placid, their long necks curved forward, their*
> *etiolated fingers alabaster steel on the tablecloth. They knew*
> *that the sad tenor voice was singing songs of loss and love*

*and death that were for and about them. The Nubility have*
*inspired troubadours and poets since before Homer. Beside*
*each of them, a fiscal prince touched a shoulder or wrist -*
*just a touch, like a pilgrim touching an icon.* (Gill, 1994)

The same sort of principles, but in a different corner of the
marketplace, lie behind groupie phenomena whereby women may
regard it as an honor to have casual sex with men they don't know
personally but whose achievements they admire. Public adulation is
an aphrodisiac. This is a valued perk for political leaders and heroes
in some societies, as in the well-attested cases of Fidel Castro, Mao
Tse-tung, Hastings Banda, Saddam Hussein and presumably
countless others, though one can never be quite sure about François
Mitterand. It is rather muted, if not ridiculed, in Anglo-Saxon
culture, as for example (unless this is just about British class
attitudes) in the old Music Hall number "I slept with a man who
slept with a women who slept with the Prince of Wales."

What I feel is not properly appreciated by advocates of fully
equal opportunities is the extent to which men and the domain
created for them rely on some such inspiration, at all levels. The
public world really only consists of an empty shell of formal
relations and rather generalized purposes which can serve as a
framework for organizing men's material activities. But except
perhaps for a few leading and powerful players it cannot generate
reasons to take part. It cannot itself motivate them. It is a world of
means and instruments. Most people work in order to get resources
to transfer to their private lives, where they do have compelling
interests and aims. Whereas women may have strong objectives
irrespective of men - because they have dependent children and
other obligations to fulfill - most *men* are not able to develop strong
and clear purposes without taking into account women and aims
originating via them. This is the kernel of Gilder's case.

*A man who is oriented toward a family he loves - or wants*
*to create - is apt to work more consistently and productively*
*than a man oriented towards his next fix, lay, day at the*
*races or drinking session with the boys ... A man who is*
*integrated into a community through a role in a family,*
*spanning generations into the past and future, will be more*

*consistently and durably tied to the social order than a man*
*responding chiefly to a charismatic leader, a demagogue, or*
*a grandiose ideology of patriotism.* (Gilder, 1973, p. 91)

Or as the poster for *Patriot Games* declares more pithily:- *"Not for*
*honor. Not for country. For his wife and child."* Thus the machine
driving the public world is both fuelled and guided by the sorts of
expectations women have of men. Men are quite good as agents; but
they need women to wind them up and discreetly point them in the
right direction. It is a partnership which is captured well in the
venerable epigram deployed by a thousand best men at weddings,
to the effect that the happy couple have agreed on an excellent
formula for dividing power; he will make all of the important
decisions, and she will decide which ones are important.

## A trustee role

This distinction between publicly doing and quietly steering is fairly
obviously relevant at informal and individual levels; but it also
applies I believe at collective levels too. Women's voices,
organized through a multitude of voluntary associations and
committees, living fragments of the female church, have tremendous
moral force to endorse or condemn public policies. Or rather they
used to have before feminism repudiated and compromised them by
representing them as Uncle Toms to patriarchal segregation and
obstacles in the march to gender integration in a desegregated public
realm. So the picture is more complex now. Traditional organs like
the Mother's Union or even the Daughters of the American
Revolution are less vocal these days. But in some ways feminism
has replaced them; and in its ability, for example, to determine
political correctness in the public arena it is currently exerting even
greater secular influence. It is wielding the traditional moral power
of the female church but in a new and particularly overt manner. I
would expect this to be self-defeating quite quickly as it tries to
monopolize influence by combining both formal and informal
power, which men will not see as equitable and be happy to play
along with for long. This may well be a signal factor contributing
to men's growing unmanageability.

Even within traditionally more discreet modes of asserting and
acting there is a great deal of innovative and creative work that

women can do in the public realm. Part of the role of guiding men in acceptable directions entails initiating new activities themselves, to show men the way. The important thing, lately disparaged, is knowing when to withdraw and allow men to take over the leadership. David Donnison recently made the following comment about this in the context of the institutionalization of new community projects.

*(These projects) tend to follow a pattern to be seen in many other movements - religious, political, industrial and military. During the early, heroic years they operate in open, informal, highly participative ways. Women often play leading parts. But hierarchies reassert themselves, formality and secrecy creep back, men take over, the organisation comes to exist increasingly for its own sake and for the benefit of the dominant groups within it.* (Donnison, 1988, p. 12)

Moving over like this surely does not need to be seen as signifying inferiority for women; though now that so little regard is paid to the moral trustee role this is how it is often interpreted. I think that it is, however, not too difficult to re-establish the idea of a separation of powers, in which women are seen to regulate men's overall social contribution, not just as family men but as leaders and champions in the public realms of market and state. These areas are not, as feminists insist, generally regarded as beyond the reach of the moral community. Many people still see them as corners of social life which for a variety of reasons women are prepared to leave mainly to men, but over which they continue to exercise broad moral control so that men operate there, as it were, under fiat. This monitoring role accords women plenty of scope for involvement in the public arena - especially in creative and critical areas, like research, rather than in frontline executive positions so valuable for constructing male career lines. It is also, in the opinion of the re-born Friedan, highly compatible with working on a part-time or voluntary basis when possible.

In a rapidly changing world there are bound to be plenty of opportunities for women to develop the trail-blazing roles mentioned by Donnison. For example the vast re-organization of material priorities which we refer to as the green movement is constantly opening up new possibilities for socially valuable inputs from women. More than enough turmoil here to go round for those who want it, and there is certainly no need for confinement to a cheerleader role. As John Vidal (1993) recently noted,

> *There is evidence of a new agenda everywhere: Britain's 250 anti-road groups - protesting about community desecration,...- are often dominated by women, if fronted by men. .... .The communities ... fighting chemical companies, incinerators, toxic dumps ... may have men up front but their impetus, time after time, has come from women resisting what they see as wrong-headed decisions.*

Radical eco-feminists have a tendency to blame men for the rape of the earth and to try to exclude them except where they identify as motherers and nurturers. But they should recognize that even men who can't compete at mothering might still be very good as executives pursuing the cause when it has become institutionalized. The British Army has an excellent conservation record.

The only essential sacrifice which is entailed for women by their redemptive role towards men is that they hold back from full-blooded competition with them for formal positions and rewards in the public domain; for this is the key to priming men as providers. This surely leaves plenty of scope, and sacrifice of self does not, I think, mean acceptance of secondary status. Properly understood, self-sacrifice is the price which we all need to pay for the sake of community, but which, I suspect, and unfortunately for women, men will not or cannot pay unless women do so first.

## ALTRUISTIC SPELLS

> *Love performs its most indispensable role in inducing males to submit to female cycles of sexuality. In a civilised society men ultimately must overcome the limited male sexual rhythms of tension and release, erection and ejaculation, and adopt a sexual mode responsive to the extended female pattern - proceeding through pregnancy, childbirth and nurture... In civilised societies, the majority of men have come to recognise that it is the female time-orientation and*

*the family that offer the highest rewards. ... Love for women
and children becomes love for the community that supports
them and faith in the future in which one's offspring will
live.* (Gilder, 1973, pp. 34-5)

Transformation of the frog by the princess's magic carries a price
for her in that she becomes his dependant. Similarly, creation of
family men calls for self-sacrifice on the part of women, because it
is their acceptance of an unequal rate of personal exchange with
men which brings them into the moral community. We are in the
presence here of what Friedan identified and repudiated as the
feminine mystique, and what Stevens called Marianismo (1973).

Referring to this sacrificial aspect of women's behavior as a
mystique tends to imply that it is just a lot of hocus pocus with no
real social value, and this is how many women have come to treat
it. But I would argue that it is a phenomenon which feminism can
ill afford to neglect as it is the key to understanding the conditions
of women's influence over men and for developing strategies which
do effectively bind men into the caring community. Some men, it is
true, do tend to idealize the whole thing a bit themselves, by
imagining that women must have enormous reserves of virtue to
draw on. They do not always appreciate just how much pressure
women are placed under to act in this way, nor the practical benefits
that follow when they do. All they know is that a frog would have
to be extremely virtuous to choose such a path voluntarily.

The circumstances of women's lives make it much easier for
them than men to take the initiative to surrender some freedom and
bargaining power. This comes down to the fact of their prior
responsibility for dependants. Having or anticipating children gives
a woman a reason for putting up with conjugal inequality which
does not in the last analysis undermine her self-respect. If she is
doing it for the sake of the children this is a boost to traditional
female self-respect and a sure source of legitimacy within the
community. Acts of self-sacrifice in which the needs of others are
placed ahead of the cost to oneself are very strong medicine. They
not only benefit others - in this case the rescued prince, as well the
children - but also ennoble the subject and many more besides.
Society as a whole benefits from man's entry; so the princess who
dutifully finds a prince also saves the kingdom, which is restored

and re-integrated by her denial of self. The acceptance of this role
may involve a realization of men's dependence on women, and
even their childishness:

> *There has always been a theme in women's folklore, at least
> in the Western world, that women know best what men need,
> that men are often childlike and incompetent, that their egos
> need bolstering because they are unsure of themselves and
> easily threatened at work, that they are vulnerable and need
> to depend on woman's strength in matters of emotion, and
> that they cannot cope with children, the home, and other
> aspects of life in the female domain.* (Epstein, 1988, p. 237)

Epstein herself treats this all as a conspiratorial myth imposed by
men. In the immortal words of Mandy Rice-Davies, she would say
that wouldn't she. I am sure that it is more pertinent to see it as
evidence that for men to be made useful does require sacrifice by
women. Skynner (1991) sees this male dependency as a powerful
factor keeping some women in unhappy relationships. *"The women
were far from being passive, fearful victims... They had married
their partners because they sensed their underlying vulnerability and
need, and felt they could heal them."* And Andrew Morton (1992)
suggests that it was this impulse which drew Diana to Prince
Charles. After seeing him during Mountbatten's funeral she said to
him *"You looked so sad when I watched it. I thought 'You are
lonely, you should be with someone to look after you.'"* Suddenly,
Morton suggests, she was overwhelmed by his enthusiastic
attentions. But as we all know there have been limits to her
subsequent denial of self; and it remains to be seen whether this
kingdom is saved.

It is hard for modern women to play this role, but Paglia has
argued that it was precisely Hillary Clinton's appreciation of the
need for it during the presidential campaign which secured victory
for her Bill.

> *There was a pivotal moment in the campaign when Hillary
> said, in response to a nasty question about being a working
> mother: "Well, listen, I could have stayed home and baked
> cookies." Many people in America, especially women, did not*

*like that at all. There was an outcry, and the campaign could have been lost at that moment. My admiration for Hillary Clinton is that she knew immediately that she had made a mis-step and she deftly adjusted. You never heard that voice of hers again. .... She knew the progressive issues that she and her husband stood for - racial harmony, women's rights, toleration of gays - would benefit more from her husband's election than from her being able to be fully herself and do her own thing. She sacrificed her own self-expression for a great good. The reality principle triumphed.* (Paglia, 1993)

She sees this as a *sexual persona* outside of the repertoire of feminism.

*Hillary was tapping into the power of the Southern woman, which she had learned after many years as the governor's wife in Arkansas. Southern women can be both earthy and glamorous. They are superb hostesses; they know how to flirt wittily with men. Down south the women are very potent. There's a way they can command men that Hillary learned when she arrived there from the north. ... I think there is a problem that the feminist establishment refuses to face: career women in the Anglo-Saxon world have desexed themselves. Latin countries still acknowledge and celebrate the sexual power of woman. There is a mystique about it which we do not have.* (Ibid.)

## Contagious magic

*All the selfish propensities, the self-worship, the unjust self-preference, which exist among mankind, have their source and root in, and derive their principal nourishment from, the present constitution of the relation between men and women.* (J.S. Mill, 1972, p. 176)

Mill and the many breast-beaters who have followed his trail are entirely wrong I think; the opposite is true. Women learn to hold themselves back, or fail, or overcome self to accept an unequal marriage for the sake of men (Mead, 1949, p. 234); but once this is done it then draws men into women's domains where, because the act brings them too into relationships with dependants, they are rendered capable of suppressing self as well. Altruism begets altruism. Just as a woman can justify dependence on a man as a gift for the sake of her children, so too a man who is given dependants can start to learn to forego his own autonomy and become readier to submit to the tyranny of a boss or patron or bureaucratic superior, in the name of his wife and children. For men equally, the responsibility of carrying the fate of other souls in their hands can call out heroic displays of self-abnegation.

Libertarian feminists commonly mock the greater willingness of family men to put up with hardship and hard work by arguing that this shows how capitalist bosses (Fordists to a man) know that they can exploit families to get more out of men. This is rubbish. It is not only capitalist bosses who do this; communities of all persuasions find family men more reliable and useful than the other sort, and this is because these men are discovering how to submerge their egos into commitment for others, and to find new dimensions of meaning through this.

It is possible to suggest that because there is a larger element of volition in men's acceptance of caring roles then it is morally superior to women's. Women are under great pressure to take it on, from the fact of the immediacy of a child's needs, and from the community around. For men more has to come from inside. The truly caring husband and father is a rare creature compared with the good mother. He deserves more praise, and often gets it. Cashmore has commented that among carers men coping alone are indeed regarded with awe, as a sort of elite:

> *Whereas women (single parents) get little pity or support and, in many cases, have to endure embarrassment and hassle, men get revered for doing the honourable thing.* (1985, p. 250)

Such behavior attracts respect in the community and builds self-respect in the actor. This elevating effect of supporting others has to be learned by men in adulthood; but for women, who know that they are unlikely to be able to avoid caring, it can become second nature much sooner. They learn from childhood onwards that community is something which exists where people derive at least part of their satisfactions in life from concerning themselves about the well-being of others, respecting those involved in caring, and in turn receiving respect for their own efforts.

This is perhaps acknowledged in the fairy tale by the manner in which the princess matures so rapidly. At the beginning of the story she is still a very young and self-centered girl, who thinks only of her golden ball. The encounter with the frog sets off a process in which she discovers what it means to be needed by someone else, and thereby to hold some power over that person. In responding to the frog's requests, and releasing him from his enchanted captivity, she evolves into an adult capable of taking responsibility for other people.

## The children factor

The dependency chains running through family life go beyond run-of-the-mill reciprocity because of the large amount of long-term asymmetry involved. Instead of limited exchanges of support and respect between equals, they entail huge self-sacrifices by older generations in return for none-too-certain returns in the distant future. Only family interdependence goes this far beyond rationally calculable mutual benefits (Zaretski, 1988); and this makes it the strongest moral thread in community life.

Although women are the conduits for this, and may have the spells attributed to them, it is children who ultimately are the main ingredient in the transformation of men. They are the focus of a group's awareness of immortality, like a constantly renewing Babushka doll, and the relations of dependency springing from them are the organic growing points, the evolving edge, of that community. Each union which takes place and produces children continually recreates the community and projects it further into the future, so that the living group is built up and sustained like a coral reef through the endless commitments and sacrifices of its members.

Sometimes feminists seem to treat any wish for personal dependants on the part of men as a grasping for domination - whereas for women it is simply seen as a normal fact of life. I accept that this view is tied up with the politics of shared parenting, which are highly fraught, as discussions elsewhere in this book note. But it is nevertheless overly partisan. Surely dependants, for men and women equally, represent the primary means of attaching to society, and of realizing a sense of fulfillment and moral worth. We are always being told by feminists that this is why many single mothers decide to have children. Why should this only apply to women? Accepting responsibility for others gives one a right to be there oneself. Women qualify very easily for this and they should not dismiss too haughtily as a drive for power the efforts of men to abandon obsessive individualism and to experience, hopefully, some release from the endlessness of desire.

For the road of self-sacrifice, once entered on, leads to some very satisfactory destinations. In the last analysis fulfillment through service to others is more likely to bring contentment than a hedonistic quest for personal excitement. Lonely pleasures are fleeting, are soon forgotten, and sometimes even difficult to believe in while they are still with us. This is not least because it is easier to perceive the happiness of other people and to promote this than it is to know whether we are content ourselves. If someone asks us if we are happy we usually say yes, not because we know that we are but because to say no is to demand their attention and sympathy. Hence we are all more likely to appear happy to others, and likewise they are to us, than to actually feel it. How do we even *know* if we are content ourselves. What does the question mean? The happiness of other people is so much simpler and more definite than our own, and this is an additional, non-collectivist reason why we treat their needs and desires as more legitimate. We know that our own are both wayward and volatile, but cannot suspect it of theirs.

So finding satisfaction by caring for others offers a surer route to contentment. Call it enlightened self-interest, or altruistic egoism (as suggested by Hans Seyle [1978]), or whatever you like. The best way of looking out for yourself is by becoming necessary to others.

Looked at this way, dependants are a lifeline, the ultimate antidote to anomie, as rich West Coast "gatherers" who collect adopted children hope to find (James, 1993). Caring for dependants keeps you sane, and being brought into support systems is the best thing that can happen to men. They make realistic and down to earth demands which pull you away from the brink of crazy and hopeless ambitions. Their needs compose an external world which can break through male solipsist reveries and humanize the dreamer. Even selfish activities like taking advantage of others in work situations become more satisfying when they are defined as "for the kids." There is a dark side to this, in that altruism may underlie the most destructive or barbaric acts; the bombers of Dresden and Hiroshima have confided that it was the future of their families that they were thinking of as they squeezed the triggers. But this is a small fraction of the total energy mobilized.

Immersion in a group helps to avoid existential angst and brings men within the magic circle of creation and communal renewal where they can learn a different type of religious experience, as belonging to an eternal stream of collective consciousness and feeling. But it is essential to remember that entry to this promised land requires highly personalized, long-term obligations. This is something which the libertarian Left, still getting it wrong after all these years, signally fails to take on board. The idea that the state can "help" families by relieving people of their personal responsibilities is just incredibly inept. The spiritual wilderness which Hillary Clinton is bemoaning is exactly the sort of human wasteland which results from inappropriate state help. How long before she discovers that too?

### New Men and alienation

Surely the most extraordinary and damning feature of contemporary feminism, and which reveals that it was largely laid down by women who had yet to become mothers, is that it attaches so little importance to individualized obligations. For these are so much more compelling and reliable and rewarding for all parties than those pooled and executed via common citizenship. The welfare state is invaluable as a fallback for people who don't have a proper family or who are on really hard times. But where it is seen as a routine provider it greatly reduces the channels for achieving self-respect and meaning in life. A man with a family mission knows that his work is important. If his dependants will be materially no worse off, or even better off, without him and living on benefits then any desire to provide for them himself soon starts to look like stubborn male vanity and pride. Better for everyone if he gives up. Abandonment itself becomes a form of sacrifice.

State providing as a matter of routine soon creates a victim culture in which all but the richest people feel that far from owing the community anything, they deserve more from it. This deprives the mass of citizens of the elementary self-respect which they need to have in order for a moral economy to operate. Men may take some time to come to understand this. I did. But it is hard to believe that so many women still fail to see it and act on it.

Any moves to reduce men's personal responsibility for children constitutes a serious attack on the essential ingredient of self-sacrifice which goes into making up a viable community. If men are left out they stay selfish and are may be more likely to become drones than to contribute much to child support as taxpayers. And if women avoid sacrificing any of their autonomy to men through marriage, then they are losing some of their own virtue and community spirit as well. Although single mothers are currently seen as heroic, coping alone for their children, there is also a strand of older community opinion, which is growing stronger again at the moment, which sees them as selfish too in putting their preference for independent living ahead of their concern for its wider implications in society. As Rousseau argued (1911), the more that women try to be like men and maximize their freedom, instead of fulfilling their family roles, then the weaker their own position in the community will become. They will lose their magic. This is not making icons of women. It is just a fact of life.

All of these dangers to society and to women are raised visibly by the feminist assault on patriarchal religion.

## DIVINE OBLIGATIONS

The main influence of women is, I believe, always likely to retain a magical quality, because it needs to stay discreet in order to be effective. This is closely bound up with the fact that it is very important for men to take upfront responsibility for things, if they are going to treat them at all seriously. Otherwise they may not identify with and properly internalize their obligations. It is easier to lead men from behind.

This, perhaps paradoxically to some, is surely the most compelling reason to have male priesthoods and divinities, which are indispensable props to men's commitment to family life. The theatre of patriarchy requires it. Men start out as marginal to family and community life, and the material sanctions that can be exerted on them to take a full part are limited. So to increase their incentives, and bolster the inversion of reality by which they appear to be in control, it is necessary to create a spiritual world which sets up male role models and a new dimension of sticks and carrots to concentrate their minds better. The idea of a male god provider - and it is interesting that all of the great patriarchal religions are monotheistic, giving symbolic emphasis to the notion of responsibilities unavoidably focused on one male figure - presiding over a heaven which is either restricted to men or which men need to strive particularly hard to attain, encompasses all of this very conveniently.

A male priesthood is no less important. The male priest, incomplete man as he may well be in the eyes of some others, does at least give men a positive lead and, insofar as the position carries high status and some influence, offers them some stake in upholding the value system. But the rules themselves are not male. The most important areas of church regulation are precisely those dealing with the place of men in the moral community, where their behavior is unreliable. The theatrical officiation of a male priest in policing rules of the family is symbolically very significant. God the Father, and man the padre, have to be an inspiration to all men.

## The Anglican disease

This is what makes the recent tomfoolery of Bishops in western churches who have been supporting the full ordination of women so extraordinary and hard to understand. Do they really not see or care that a church without a male senior priesthood loses its social relevance and is doomed to speedy decline? There are two sorts of justifications put forward within the modern church for the ordination of women. One concerns the supposed doctrinal disrespect to women of existing conventions, and the value now of asserting their equal spiritual value. But to say that this is needed is to misunderstand previous emphases and teaching of the church which, if we leave out some unpleasant and unnecessary recriminations over events in the garden of Eden which most of the faithful regard as past business, strongly follow the line that men benefit more from religion than do women, who are naturally more spiritual or adequate than men to start with.

The figure of the Virgin has traditionally been the focus of this celebration of female qualities, and has furnished a strong point of positive identification for women, for many of whom Mary is the true spirit of the church (e.g., see Turner, 1993). In fact I suspect that she has offered a whole slate of positive images of womankind which have catered for a range of tastes and orientations, both within conventional religion and a variety of subcultures. She was first of all a devoted mother who nurtured a successful son, so she is an obvious symbol of maternal sacrifice. But she can also be seen as having produced a child without being possessed by a man, which some women might like to do themselves. She served as a most effective instrument - unlike those wordy and pompous male priests - for the realization of God's Plan on earth. She managed a man into providing for a child who was not his own offspring. And so on; a long list is possible. There are many things that women can admire her for.

This inconvenient fact has been cleverly tampered with by those who can see nothing in the world but patriarchal conspiracies. Mariologists like John Spong and Ute Ranke-Heinemann can turn the Virgin's greatest virtues into weapons for the hierarchs to use against women. According to Ranke-Heinemann (1990) Mary is not a suitable model for self-respecting women. The very perfection of Mary, as *mater inviolata,* creates a dehumanized, unattainable ideal which celibate male theologians have manipulated to ensure that ordinary women feel defiled and profane (*matres violatae*). Spong argues (1992) in the same vein that Mary was fashioned by men as a symbol of docile and asexual holiness to which all women were told that they must aspire.

Spong does however at least concede that an impregnable Virgin was also easier for men, and especially celibate priests, to worship in the right spirit. So he does recognize, perhaps as he is also a man himself, that men too must suffer sometimes in pursuit of virtue and that not the whole of church business is to keep women in subjection and self-contempt. Nevertheless the main feeling to emerge from recent analyses of Mary, several of which counterpose her to the worldly and compromised figure of Mary Magdalene (e.g. Haskins, 1992), is that it is perfectly alright for men to feel inadequate when faced with the figure of Christ or the majesty of the Almighty. It does them no harm at all. But, oh dear, women are being victimized if we say anything complimentary about Mary. No need, it seems, to spare any thought for the feelings of the scum depicted in all this as violators.

The other line of reasoning to justify senior female ordination is that women are the mainstay of the congregation and so deserve more recognition. This argument seems woefully perverse. If there are relatively few male active churchgoers nowadays this may be because the activities involved appeal more to women already. Removing men's employment privileges in the hierarchy will take many more of them away, as well as signalling bad messages to the rest of society.

What these debates have ignored above all is that male priesthood is a crucial symbolic prop to fatherhood in society generally; and the most obvious effect of more and more senior female officiants will be to give colossal endorsement to the idea that men are not really needed anymore. A poignant letter to the *Guardian* on the eve of the decisive Lambeth debate illustrated this *unintentionally* but very tellingly.

> *Last week we held my mother's funeral service. For all of us it was a memorable and glorious end to her life. ... My father died when I was very young. The rest of the family, all female, just carried on, making our own decisions, going our own way. ... It was therefore so special that we saw a woman deacon committing my mother to God with the same dignity, authority and utter conviction which characterised my mother's life. (The Guardian, 10 November 1992)*

Churches offer their most valuable support to family life in general by giving authoritative expression to the idea that men should be providers; and their bedrock pastoral function is to help motivate men towards, and then harness them into, their domestic commitments. As I argued earlier most of the values embodied in patriarchal religions are anything but masculine. Morality in general is often experienced by men as imposing on them from outside and as interfering with their ability to know what they actually want (see Seidler on Kant, 1991, p 76-69); and some Christian theologians are wondering whether religious values do indeed spring out of male consciousness (e.g., Hughes, 1989).

Religion gives men supernatural, and sometimes abstract, pretexts for doing things that women want for more pragmatic reasons. They are admittedly addressed to men. But they are geared towards male responsibility to women rather than male power over them. If anything, the church is asserting power over men; and this is conceptualized most tangibly for men in the ideas of chastity and fidelity within marriage, which have played such a central part in all patriarchal religions and have cast shadows over many men's lives. There is no mileage in arguing that this fell more heavily on women because there is a double standard of sexual morality. Most men didn't learn about any double standard until the sixties when it was declared dead.

Rosalind Miles rather gleefully calls religious teachings on chastity a patriarchal own goal - as if early male theologians became so intoxicated by the scriptures that they forgot which end they were defending. But the truth I suspect is much simpler, and it is that the desires of ordinary men have played very little part in determining the content of these religions, which are responding more to the needs of women in the community. This is not to deny that male theologians can get carried away by abstract concepts to the neglect of pastoral implications, as is clearly the case in *Veritatis Splendor* and many of its predecessors. The Church of Rome's bureaucratic pre-occupation with maintaining God's ultimate right to determine whether or not conception takes place seriously interferes with individual men's capacity to exercise proper responsibility by only fathering children for whom they can provide. The churches which broke away during the Reformation have been better geared to these pastoral considerations - until recently at any rate, when they have surrendered to feminism.

## God the provider

The central pastoral concern running through patriarchal religions has been a spiritual endorsement of the male provider role. The message implicit in the image of male god creators is that men have to accept obligations towards the children they father. Forget about orgiastic worshipping of mother-goddesses. That party is over and the new idea is about men taking some responsibility for a change. They can't go on leaving it all for women to do.

Within the Christian tradition this message is marked above all by the birth of Christ himself. Throughout the old testament paternity is given a good airing, and lines of male descent are heavily emphasized as organizing and obligating principles. Then Christ materializes within this idiom to express some full divine commitment. The male creative-dreamer, otiose god-spirit, steps by substantiation into a real world of screaming babies, and lends a hand. The universalist frog-knight has finally chosen his particular people and transforms into their carer. What a sacrifice. And what a potent example. The redeemer first has redeemed himself.

The cosmology produced by this event is one of the clearest formulations of dependency chains that could be devised. At the top is God the responsible Father, who by virtue of causal responsibility also accepts moral accountability for his works. Small wonder that the churches mainly attract women. Such a reassuring vision of supreme male reliability; and alongside such an apt portrayal of what a woman can be like when not defiled by ordinary men. God is the ultimate caring provider; and the symbolic lines of dependency, linking Him to families of supplicants on the ground, need to be occupied by men - that is the church hierarchy, and then the actual head of the family - in order that ordinary men can reassure themselves, in trying to be good providers themselves, that they are truly made in their Maker's image.

There are naturally many subtleties and variations of interpretation available within this general pattern. For example priests, especially celibate priests, may not be seen as wholly male in a conventional sense. They wear frocks, often don't have any personal dependants, and may even consider themselves to be brides of Christ. But essentially, within the dependency idiom, males look downwards while females look up.

These meanings are all pliable though, and I suspect that the real reason why feminist theologians take exception to the model is not a psychological one - that it threatens women's self-respect - so much as the practical matter that it does not leave much space for women who are not dependent on men. The independent woman is anathema to the traditional religious mind. Ideally women should be dependent on a living man, a father then husband, as that is most useful within the living community. Failing that, they may be directly dependent on God, by taking a religious vocation; and for many women this has offered the best route for achieving some personal freedom from men.

The woman who spurns dependency altogether will be presumed

to be up to no good, perhaps in league with - and inviting dependence on? - the devil. She may then become defined as a witch who resents mortal men and their authority and who must be morally excluded; otherwise, given a chance, she may herself try to banish men, with their lust to dominate women. And then, as we know, only princesses who are willing to *sacrifice* their independence can undo such spells and restore men to their rightful place. This metaphor can become silly and offensive if taken too far. But I think that up to a point it does give a valid expression of community values, because if the idea of independent womanhood becomes too strong then the deeper, communalist paths of sacrifice in society become weakened. The woman who submits to marriage is the one whose sacrifice unleashes the latent altruism in men and integrates the community. The independent woman undermines and challenges this.

Female priests are an extension of the independent woman idea. After the Lambeth conference, Peregrine Worsthorne (1992) observed rather caustically that the women becoming priests are putting their career interests before the practice of Christian virtues; and whatever their own private lives may be like their public example certainly does little to help ordinary working-class women to find and hold onto responsible male partners. If the female priest idea becomes more than a passing fad, then I suspect that the church's magic will fade for most male communicants, and possibly for many ordinary women, and it could soon become regarded as deviant and anti-social, like those relics of pre-Christian cults which periodically revive around Europe (Guiley, 1992), which are dominated by women, devoted to relatedness and healing, and call themselves witchcraft.

The Church is abandoning its pastoral concern with sacrifice in daily life as it gravitates closer to a secular mainstream public realm which is increasingly focused on individual rights and opportunities. The latest wave of power feminists like Naomi Wolf who appear to recognize that women are not victims, are nevertheless still telling them to drop saintliness and living for others and generally to go for it. Although some older activists who are moving into middle age and feeling sexually insecure, and who see fruits of their long campaigns for equal rights being carried off by younger women, are now recanting and reclaiming the family, the message has passed down a generation and is already taken as orthodoxy by many young people, who don't know how to read the fairy tale. Girls no longer want to be dependent, even nominally; and boys are losing hope of being turned into princes. It is time to re-write the story as a *fin-de-millénium* lament, or even a horror story.

In it the princess refuses to accept the loathsome frog as a partner after all. Her power to perform good magic is thereby wasted; and the original spell of the witch, far from being broken, remains unchecked and grows in strength. Soon the princess's father, the king, abdicates and turns back into a monstrous and malevolent frog himself, and starts abusing the inhabitants of the palace. Bereft of leadership, the kingdom slips into feuding and chaos, its citizens selfish and unruly; and the forest of individual desire starts to encroach upon the formerly meticulous and orderly palace gardens. The nineteen-nineties are upon us.

# 7

# THE INDEPENDENT PRINCESS

Every generation questions to some extent the justice of current relations between men and women, which are consequently subject to numerous historical as well as personal variations. As techniques of production and patterns of work change, or as population movements and settlements occur, or when periods of political instability or crisis arise in which demands on different sectors of society fluctuate, then the balance of formal and informal power between conjugal partners is forever shifting. But these oscillations are contained by a broad consistency and continuity, at least for most social groups within European culture with which I am principally concerned here. In this men are expected to help women mainly by providing for them, while women support men mainly by giving them a home and meaning. There is an interdependence here in which each party has some genuine reason for commitment to the system, and which often results in more effective equality than may appear.

Recently the stability of this general interdependence has come under significant threat. During the last twenty to thirty years the female church has become seriously divided over the central question of how to deal with men. A faction proclaiming that the incentives and privileges created for men as providers are unfair to women, and should be dismantled and replaced by a new method of managing men, has gained ascendancy. From a minority heresy in the sixties, the idea that patriarchy is the enemy grew quickly during the seventies and eighties into a new orthodoxy subscribed to by a large number of women - among them many who would not actually describe themselves as feminists - and has become written into the articles and operations of the welfare state. A separate church has emerged with more secular power than the traditional one it is reacting against, which is more explicitly hostile and judgmental in relation to men, and which is challenging the traditional separation and balance between public and private realms.

## HERESY AND SCHISM

This adoption of a new strategy towards men was linked to a variety of social and political changes. At an ideological level it was clearly bound up with the explosion of individualism which has occurred in the aftermath of the Second World War. The principle of the sovereignty of the individual has been influential in Europe for at least two centuries; but it has probably achieved its most widespread impact since the new post-war global hegemony of the United States was rationalized around a very radical interpretation of it, and barriers to individual freedom became widely discredited and dismantled in most countries under U.S. influence. This was a major factor in helping to produce a generation of young women in the West who, from the middle fifties onwards, were starting to feel that they had as much right as men, and should enjoy as great an opportunity, to follow a career rather than to become confined to being housewives. Tenets of the female church which enjoined women to sacrifice themselves in order to tame a man into useful provisioning fell on increasingly unreceptive ears. No way.

However, the crucial factor in changing sexual relations was the pill, which for the first time enabled women to exercise personal and reliable control over their fertility. They could now enjoy sex without anxiety, and plan and limit their childbearing to fit in with the requirements of a career. It was the pill which unleashed the sixties revolution, because it meant that girls were now able to plunge wholeheartedly into the sexual license and self-expression which formerly had only been safe for boys. Before the pill it was only disreputable girls, not afraid of losing credit in the moral community, who would spurn church values and enter the forest to have sex outside of the controls of marriage. But in the sixties they flocked along in masses. This revolution was one undertaken by young women, often against their mother's wishes. The novelty in mobbing Elvis and in the crowds screaming at the Beatles lay in that it was *girls* who were letting it all out, and that what they were uninhibitedly expressing included raw sexual desire, with men as objects for a change (Ehrenreich *et al.*, 1987). Femininity was *passé,* and the scream, which is usually a female reflex to summon help or express solidarity within the community, became a youthful call celebrating collective escape from conventional sexual restraints, and the headlong rush into an orgy of pre-coital anticipation and fantasy.

## The great leap backwards

All of this was marvellous in itself as a flowering of self-expression and realization. But it carried tremendous dangers for the stability of relations with the community if handled in the wrong way, which is I believe precisely what many women then proceeded to do.

The fundamental mistake which girls made then, and which feminism has perpetuated, was to take patriarchal conventions at face value both as an account of what men themselves want, and as the primary source of male power. Patriarchy was seen as the "system" or prison from which women were being liberated; and girls freed by the pill to take control of their own fertility saw themselves as escaping from male domination, and as becoming empowered by this to use their bodies to overcome traditional gender hierarchies. Bel Mooney has written (1993) that for teenage girls the Profumo affair confirmed a new sense of revolutionary strength.

> *Sex was a great leveller; a cabinet minister was no different from me. The trial was a source of entertainment - even (I confess) some inspiration. Christine Keeler and Mandy Rice-Davies were no better than they should be, but to a 17-year-old girl they seemed glamorous, independent women who epitomised energy and freedom. They used their sexuality, they toppled men of power, they were cheeky in court... The truth was that, with my nose deep in Middlemarch, I nevertheless wanted to be like those girls - to cock a snook at respectable middle England.*

Young girls intoxicated by their newfound and unexpected sexual autonomy were disinclined to hear their mothers telling them what men were actually like. Their second mistake was to engage in wishful thinking by submitting to the utopian idea that once oppressive patriarchal culture (the snake which had entered and contaminated the pre-historical Eden) had been swept away, then the underlying similarities and common interests of men and women would be revealed, and the sexes could then renegotiate in harmony, as equals with the same needs, a new system that would banish sexual inequalities for ever. Many put their faith firmly into notions of symmetrical emotional dependence and mutual caring, which departed radically from prevailing sexual contracts (Clark, 1991).

What was summarily banished in this new dawn was the understanding, which did not itself form part of patriarchy, but which underpinned traditional women's acceptance of it, that men's and women's needs, especially in the early stages of relationships before men have been pulled into the caring community, are very far from being the same. Although sex was acquiring more intrinsic value for girls because it no longer carried such a risk of pregnancy, most still reckoned that one day they would choose to have children, and already saw sexual relations partly as a vehicle to achieve this. Most also, because patriarchy told them so, assumed that men felt the same way. However for many men, by contrast, sex itself was not just an overwhelming consideration, but the only one, which they were reluctant to think beyond. Family position and responsibilities were not ends in themselves, but the names in which sex had to be pursued, and the means of securing a regular supply of it. If they found that they could get sex without taking on family obligations, they would gladly abandon patriarchal privileges, and it would be Christmas all through the year.

Sixties girls refused to hear their mothers when they were cautioned that if they allowed boys to know that women too enjoyed sex that its trading value in extracting wider exchanges and securing longer-term commitments would be reduced or lost. Freed by their reproductive autonomy from the assumption of automatic dependency on the moral economy and its rules, and carried away by the exhilaration of their sexual power, which is concentrated so heavily in young women's hands, sixties girls were able to turn their backs on the underlying tendency of men to avoid taking on responsibilities for their offspring if they can get away with it. For a while some even interpreted the enthusiastic welcome given by men to free sex, in the sense of requiring no additional reciprocation, as a sign that the world was indeed changing and changing fast.

And so it was. But as Neil Lyndon has shown, perhaps unwittingly, in his discussion of this phenomenon, what was happening was hardly progress. Lyndon's own commentary on this is an illuminating piece of period ethnography - apart from his rather idiosyncratic dating of the pill, which many were using from 1961 onwards.

> *Like our ancestors, we began our teenage years at the beginning of the sixties with identical prospects. .... We looked forward to adulthood with resigned desperation, knowing that we should, infallibly, reproduce the grim, toiling and sexless lives of our fathers, that the way to the straitness of that prison gate was fixed and undeviating. No wonder that we counted ourselves as blessed, presented with the keys to pig-heaven, when - in the mid-course of that progress, right on the dot of our twenties - the girls got the Pill and the way was cleared to every nipple and beyond every stocking top (within a matter of moments, by the summer of 1967, they had discarded stockings and bras altogether).*

> *It was some kind of heaven, at that moment, to be a young man and to know that this unprecedented and all-involving change must necessarily alter all the traditions and functions of manhood. If we didn't have to have babies when we had regular sex, it followed that we didn't have to get married. And if we didn't have to support families, we didn't have to have jobs or careers; and if we didn't have to have careers, .... what might we not do? Or be? A* tabula rasa *of adult masculinity had been presented to us, upon which we might (we supposed) make our marks as we pleased.* (1992, p. 96-97)

No wonder that sixties girls, when they started to think about having families, soon decided that men were pigs, and turned into seventies second-wave feminists looking for new ways to cope, with or without them. When acknowledging the influence of the pill, Lyndon refers to the power it gave women to choose the timing of their maternity leave. He appears (still) to regard motherhood as a three-month absence from work, after which a woman is back on her feet and everything becomes normal again. With liberated young men like this around, who could rely any more on finding a provider? And who would want one!

## A bitter pill

It did not take most women very long to notice that men were not after all turning into the sharing and caring partners of their dreams. They were in fact becoming even more unreliable and less committed than before, and many balked altogether at the idea of paternal responsibility. It was out of reaction to this disappointment that the current feminist movement really started to emerge - though it is not always easy to distinguish feminist from non-feminist elements in this (Decter, 1972). After an enthusiastic but short-lived period of consensual hedonism, a brief Spring of sexual equality spanning Germaine Greer's sojourn in Amsterdam and Erica Jong's *Fear of Flying,* many women started to redefine sensuality as male vice and selfishness (sometimes spiking the analysis with neo-Freudian references to infantilism), and transmuted into what Stassinopoulos, in an early and perceptive critique (1973), dubbed as the new sexual anabaptists. Mooney refers to men's refusal to do more than reciprocate sex as "exploitation."

> *The optimism almost disappeared into a drug-induced haze, and suddenly the sexual freedom women had taken for granted showed its bitter side; we were free, yes, but to be exploited by men, and we allowed it. (op. cit.)*

This idea became the mantra for the age of lost innocence, and helped to mark out the new feminist agenda. The early seventies, when sixties girls began to have children or to think about it, were marked by a surge of interest in new domestic structures, and speculation about what might henceforth be viable. For a lot of women the unfolding betrayal by men prompted speedy reversion to traditional marriage and life-styles. But where girls had seriously rejected their mothers' advice or ideas and no longer shared the values needed to participate with them in a moral economy, a gulf opened up between the generations which was to tear apart the solidarity of the female community.

There has been a tendency to play down this division, which was ideologically very challenging. Feminism found it convenient to treat as fact the patriarchal injunction that it is men who have the major stake in family institutions, and who should be most concerned to uphold them, and reacted scornfully to analyses which had suggested that these served women's needs. So it had a vested interest in concealing the extent to which the sixties revolution was carried out by girls against their mothers and their mothers' values. But Jill Tweedie has subsequently commented that she regarded her mother as a "friend of the enemy":

*We had a kind of contempt for our mothers and what they'd done. It was not just that they had been doormats but that they had betrayed their daughters by delivering us over to a male world.* (quoted by Bunting, 1993a)

Defining mothers as collaborators rather than as the prime and original sources of control perhaps kept relations a bit easier. But it failed to prevent a gulf opening between the generations. These years were hard enough for women who were entering or had recently entered conventional marriages, and who could see younger sisters having a freer time and evolving a new life-style. But it was an even more difficult time to be a mother.

The mother-daughter relationship is absolutely central to the coherence of communities (Billington, 1994). But there is ambivalence within it which under conditions of moral upheaval can produce tremendous strains. Mothers take vicarious pleasure in the achievements of daughters, so that most were delighted at the opening up of opportunities which the period offered. But at the same time many felt jealous too. Some of this jealousy was sexual. It arose partly because many girls were doing things which their mothers had missed out on, and partly because the loosening of the sexual market in the sixties had raised a danger that the mothers might lose out further in middle age. The sexual security of older women requires restraint by younger. Mothers in the sixties and early seventies feared that they might end up, as quite a few in fact did, neither having had much fun in their youth - while their daughters did - nor enjoying security later in life as the reward for their own restraint when younger - which their own mothers *had*. The middle generation was losing out both ways. The resulting feelings of bitterness were probably factors in allowing a rift to develop between many feminists and their mothers.

This rift was chiefly manifested through disagreements over what sorts of relationships were desirable with men. Feminists already embraced a number of political orientations. But common to all of them at this time was a libertarian repudiation of dependency on men, and of any intention to sacrifice oneself to a man's career. This entailed turning a deaf ear to traditional advice which was urging that women's interests should not be individualized and pursued at the expense of wider obligations to the community. Women by all means could seek to improve their standing and opportunities. But to forget about everything else was heresy. The needs of children and other dependent relatives were paramount. Men surely wouldn't take this on. And men themselves required a lot of attention, or they would make trouble.

Women's work encompassed all of these items, and was essential for keeping society together. If women decided to spend their time like men, playing, then the social contract would collapse and it would all end in tears. The idea of personal freedom was destructive of community values. It was alright for men to chase after this as ultimately they were not important. But any woman who pursued it did so at the expense of those who did not, and would be left holding the babies. "Neanderthal," the feminists replied to these counsels; and the argument fuelled the struggle between generations and further divided and weakened the female church.

## The statist way

This was the context in which some women started to make the fateful, and I would argue unsustainable, departure from tradition by deciding to stop laboring to convert men into useful providers, and to transfer any residual or transitional female dependency onto the state.

Libertarian socialist ideas common among young people in the sixties portrayed the state as the most promising vehicle in history for redressing nature; and what greater natural injustice waiting to be sorted out was there than gender inequality. The Butskellite state in Britain, encouraged by reports like that of the Plowden committee, had already promoted educational opportunities for girls, and by the late sixties was also providing many with employment. So it was a logical next step for women to co-opt the welfare state as an ally against men, by seeking from it fallback housing and welfare supports for independent women to help them resist men's refusal to change. Following the liberalization of divorce laws in the late sixties in most western countries (Haskey, 1992), a long battle over entitlements to benefits by women in their own right was fought into the seventies. The oil-crisis recession ensured that many of the more ambitious demands, such as for state wages for housework, and nursery places for all working mothers, fell at early hurdles. But enough was achieved to reduce substantially the dependence of women on male partners and on traditional reciprocity through the moral economy.

A shifting onto the state of responsibilities for the support of women and children occurred in most western countries during this period. This has given feminists the whip hand within the female church. For it replaces sexual contracts between individuals, in which reciprocal but unequal or certainly asymmetrical demands are made on each other, with one-sided relations with the state in which women may not be freed from all regulation or burdens, but *can* avoid personal demands from men. Shorter has proposed (1982) that women's cultures at the heart of the moral economy had been weakening since the twenties, as a result of improved public health provisions. This trend was then seriously boosted by the new citizenship rights acquired across the whole area of welfare and personal security. The new statist compact greatly enlarges the individual freedom of women, and its availability as a yardstick of autonomy has been a major factor promoting constant review of domestic divisions of labor, in which it is significant that sexual exchanges rarely feature, in the remaining "private" conjugal sector.

The alliance of feminists with the state succeeded in nullifying attempts by older women to retain control over younger, because it appeared to get a better deal for women by allowing them to maximize their individual freedom. Feminism is currently the dominant moral system, looked to now by most younger women for guidance on how to order their lives; and it has incorporated many traditional female concerns and reflexes, as its earnest debates on pornography, chastity and male sexuality constantly indicate. In many areas it is re-merging with the traditional female church. But on the central issue of male providing there is still a rift as deep as ever concerning the relative merits of marriage-centered and state lines of dependency and support.

# THE PROVIDER STATE

## Doing without men

Women have had manifest success over the last quarter of a century in showing that they can manage without men. This has occurred partly as a result of deliberately avoiding motherhood or otherwise minimizing domestic commitments, but mainly through the extension of employment opportunities, and through the growing individuation of citizenship rights, which now tolerates the idea that women should have full access to public support without regard to their marital status. Most single mothers are now on benefits and living in local authority houses (Burghes, 1993). Lowly this may be; but it offers autonomy and personal independence and provides a fallback position which makes it possible to aim higher.

These changes have accordingly transformed women's chances of having a career, and many more are now doing so. The Henley Centre has been forecasting for some time now that by the end of the century there will be more female than male employees in Britain; and in places this is already the case. Campaigns like *Opportunity 2000,* promoted by Business in the Community, report enthusiastically that the number of women reaching management levels is rising very fast. In the view of Geoff Mulcahy, chief executive of the Kingfisher Group, and lately knighted for public services, women are no longer a wasted asset, and the wealth of the nation is being augmented:

> *Opportunity 2000 has helped us unlock rich resources of talent among our employees, giving women opportunities and allowing us to make better economic use of our total workforce.* (Mulcahy, 1992)

The assumption that equal opportunities generates a net gain to the community needs much closer and more critical examination than it has been getting; and I shall offer a few thoughts on this in the following chapter. But what I want to emphasize at this stage is that it is a mistake anyway to look at all of this, as many proponents of equal opportunities (EO) would like us to, for obvious reasons, as an "impersonal" economic trend, as it is very clearly bound up with the conscious alliance made by feminists with the welfare state and, by extension, the political realm more generally.

Although there are many women in businesses where they are helping to produce new resources, the largest expansion in women's work has taken place in the public sector, and particularly in the social services which make up the modern welfare state. Even where the jobs held by women are not themselves actually in this sector, they often depend on the creation of support services within it. So what is really happening is that some domestic labor has simply been transferred from the family. I shall argue later that the problem with this from society's point of view is that whereas the costs were formerly borne out of the breadwinner's family wage, now that they are in the state sector the community has to pay market wage rates for it.

The nature of this development is frequently obscured by the way in which feminists refer to the enlarged welfare state, albeit sometimes I suspect with tongue in cheek, as part of the "patriarchal" state. This is done ostensibly to indicate that women and children now depend more directly on the state, and less on particular men. But its clear implication is that men are now controlling women through the state and not just within families (Eisenstein, 1986). Even a cautious theorist like Walby can write dismissively of women's new direct link to the public realm:

> *The form of patriarchy in contemporary Britain is public rather than private. Women are no longer restricted to the domestic hearth, but have the whole society in which to roam and be exploited.* (1990, p. 201)

This implication is extremely disingenuous, for it is obvious to most observers, and to most feminists themselves when not trying to score easy points, that the modern state is an increasingly feminized entity, and does not make the same amount or type of demands on women that men do as individual providers. It is inherent in the nature of any welfare state, which takes individual rights previously met within the moral economy and redefines them as part of citizenship, that the male family-provider role is to some extent usurped.

The logic of this was acknowledged forty years ago by Michael

Young (1952), himself a significant actor in the postwar elaboration
of the welfare state, in his article on the consequences of 1945
legislation on family allowances. He noted that a state provision of
welfare allowances, school meals, milk and food supplements, and
the NHS, cushioned women against male inadequacies or
derelictions of family obligations, and also served to redistribute
resources discreetly from men to women.

> *In general it is as though the taxes on tobacco and drink had
> been paid into a family income equalisation pool, from which
> had been drawn the benefits provided by the State.*

The Provider State was beginning to realize its destiny.

### A new palace?

Thirty to forty years on it is possible to see (Showstack-Sassoon,
1987) that a welfare state staffed largely by women can become a
tangible embodiment of sisterhood which for many women will
offer a more congenial and sympathetic source of support than
would a conventional marriage. The feminization of the state
launches a new offensive in the gender war. It is now an orthodoxy
that one of the primary duties of the state is to protect women's
interests against men. Anna Coote and her colleagues (1990) write
that fathers are no longer essential to the economic survival of
family units. And Polly Toynbee (1989) can calmly incite women
to forget about fatherhood and just look to the state for all the
provisions needed to enable them to have careers and operate
effectively without men.

> *Women and children will suffer needlessly until the state
> faces up to the reality of its own inability to do anything
> about the revolution in national morals. What it can do is
> shape a society that makes a place for women and children
> as family units, self-sufficient and independent.*

This commentary is a bit close to the knuckle, and appears to men
to be saying good riddance, we can manage without you. Politically
more cautious analysts have been careful to play down female
volition (nothing new here) and talk up the power of the economy

and market. Anna Coote for example pays fulsome regard to the idea that men are having a hard time adjusting to the new roles expected of them, but insists that this is all down to impersonal forces, such as the decline of manufacturing and rise of service industries, over which governments can have very little control. You can't buck the trend, or go against the grain of history. If the mighty Treasury, which has made no secret of favoring male providers, has proved impotent to influence things, across the years and through many changes of government, then how can anyone hope to intervene? We must simply be practical and ensure that the state gives women the support they evidently need to look after their families at the same time as becoming the nation's work force.

Much of this sounds reasonable at first hearing; but on reflection turns out to be thoroughly specious in a variety of ways. If you look behind an impersonal social trend you can usually detect a lot of very real people pushing and shoving, and it is not hard to find the feminist hand in this. There are after all no iron laws which declare that women only do service jobs, or that men cannot do them, although Suzanne Moore does not seem so sure (1994b). Women are concentrated in this area mainly because its growth coincided with the desire of more of them to enter full-time employment, not least because service jobs were being created within the welfare state in order to help free more women for the market. The steady increase in this sector is as much a consequence as a cause of women's growing involvement in the paid economy. It is self-fulfilling, and to some extent self-serving.

Where women have taken jobs outside of the state sector, this is itself often due to the application of pressures for equal opportunities, originating within the public sector, which make it important for employers to recruit more women in order to demonstrate compliance. Coote cannot in good conscience parade figures which show growing proportions of female employees as proof that employers, the cutting edge of market force, simply "prefer to give jobs to women." There are a lot of carrots and sticks being wielded here, which need to be brought into the picture, and which are nothing to do with impersonal historical trends. Many employers do now choose female employees. But this is partly because the way that the state operates is helping to make them more employable. Women are not expected to support an adult partner, and so are in a position to accept lower wages than men. Child care is a big problem of course, and it is significant that employers are women's main allies in pressing for increased state nursery provision. If business has seen that it can get the best deal for itself by employing the workers who have the strongest moral position in the community, then we are looking at a new political economy rather than a changing marketplace.

## Integrating the realms

Thus the economic success of women cannot be separated from other feminist ventures in breaking down the boundaries between public and private domains. This is a massive topic which I can only tickle the surface of here. But much of the apparent deterioration in relations between men and women, as in matters of domestic violence and rape, especially rape within marriage, arises from the fact that conjugal behavior has been lifted out from the private domain, where most of it was invisible, and placed firmly at the centre of public attention and regulation.

Women have succeeded in mobilizing state institutions to carry out or even take over some of the management of men which was previously pursued, discreetly, within the home; and the feminized state, as it blossoms, is revealing itself as a continuation of the moral economy by other means. The immunity of marital relations from external scrutiny, epitomized in the juridical rule that spouses could not be required (and were not expected) to give evidence against each other, has been replaced by a prioritization of individual rights, particularly of women, which defines the traditional male head of household as a possessive, exclusive little tyrant jealously guarding his property.

The merger of public and private, which perhaps is reaching its fullest expression to date in the phenomenon of political correctness, is I believe rooted in sixties popular Marxism, which created perfect conditions for the germination of statist feminism. This legacy has been repudiated by most feminists now, but its influence still lingers on deep in the fundamental assumptions of the movement, and it is not a coincidence that feminism emerged at the precise moment when a libertarian brand of Marxism was enjoying its apogee of appeal and spread most rapidly among those rootless intellectuals, Doris Lessing's people, who had made the revolutionary movement their metaphorical family.

This moral environment succored feminism because it combined an assertion of the overwhelming centrality of the public realm - which justified neglect of the traditional moral economy by women, and also highlighted their victim status - with a convenient upholding of patriarchal assumptions of male agency and volition; this enabled women, in time-honored fashion, both to blame men for their existing problems and oppression while presenting what women were now doing, in this case joining a principled assault on capitalism, as a gift to male comrades, which would oblige them to give paramount importance to women's interests in the New Jerusalem.

It was Marxist ideology which was largely responsible for spreading the idea that the central dynamic of history derives from conflicts between men in the marketplace. This turns on their heads classical models, which regard the market as an instrumental device or area wherein men seek to maximize their resources for satisfying extrinsic goals, originating and culminating in the private domain, and declares instead that society serves and is controlled by the market, and that even the state is merely its political wing. Under the influence of this theory women ceased to see the family as a magical palace in which they performed daily miracles, and re-cast it as a medieval prison from which escape was necessary, possible, and in everyone's best interests.

## The revolutionary *scenario*

Escape was deemed necessary because family life, when de-mystified, is shown not to be the focus and microcosm of wider society as previously thought, but merely a nursery for reproducing labor, outside of the social mainstream, and virtually a part of nature. The real action is monopolized by men, who are meaningfully engaged in production and in the titanic struggle between labor and capital, while women and children must huddle on the sidelines. There is a clear and direct link made in overtly Marxist feminism between the heroic participation allowed to men in the processes of production, and their provider role which gives them domestic authority over their families on behalf of capitalist overlords (Rowbotham, 1973; Barrett, 1980). The financial contribution which a male provider makes to the running of a household is represented in this model as a patrimonial fee for housework and maternity services, which excludes women from full participation in capitalism and its opportunities at the same time as turning men into feudal chieflings who, regardless of, or perhaps to compensate for, the menial position of most of them in the public realm, are thereby given some status illusions to increase their loyalty to "the system."

All of this is not just grossly unfair, but also anomalous and ripe for change, since it embodies medieval survivals of unfree labor which can have no justifiable place in the modern world. The parallels which Marxism discovered between feminism and anti-colonial movements, echoed in Yoko Ono's characterization of women as the Niggers of the World, gave a revolutionary legitimacy to their desire to escape from this domestic captivity. What is more, the model indicated that eradication of this bondage was in men's true interests, as it would simultaneously sever the ties which kept men over-dependent on their bosses. Dependency chains were not seen as growing upwards from children, and giving meaning to the lives of adults. They hung, heavily and inexorably, down from the ramparts of capital to enslave its laborers, and imprison their children as soon as they were born. In an age of decolonization the denial of patriarchy served as an important revolutionary act which could help to restructure the whole of the social order around a more socially responsive market.

This was moreover an achievable objective, because bringing women's activities and energies into the marketplace was consistent with the long term expansion of market forces and would surely increase its resources and productivity. The post-sixties feminists, who turned to Marxism to help them draw up a new way of raising children which did not entail personal dependency on men, were naturally greatly encouraged by its vision. If women were just let into the market, instead of being kept outside as feudal dependants, then they could be paid as workers, given jobs to do like men, allowed wages to care for citizens in need rather than doing it free for relatives, and perhaps could even, if they chose, be given a salary to do housework. The traditional convention that family work is done for men was soon refashioned into an ideological and tactical prop for charging the public sector (becoming defined as the patriarchal state) for more and more of the costs of the moral economy. Family work was a job just like any other.

## Working for the state

Feminism has in several ways drawn on and refashioned traditional female wiles for dealing with men; and this is certainly true of their reflex to put responsibility for things onto men. Running throughout the arguments used to shift dependency onto the state is the notion that women have always been doing things because men told them to or expected them to. In the agricultural stage of patriarchy men needed heirs and so women had to be possessed by them. Now the male market rules society and male employers need labor, so women must have children and devote their lives to rearing workers. A woman's work for men is never done, and so on; though, ironically, the accounts which I have seen make no reference to what women do actually need to perform for men (as opposed to doing in their name), and that is give them a meaningful place in society.

Making men responsible for everything in this way is patently tendentious. Of course a wife is working for a husband; but so is he for her, and for their children. But neither is just an employee of the other, deriving no personal satisfaction from the activity. A woman does not really just have children because the state or some employers or even her partner make her do so. Any of these may be a factor. But she also has children for the sake of her own parents - and this is where a lot of moral pressure is often exerted - and for the child itself or her other children, and above all for herself, as this is what gives her own life substance, direction, form and force. We are always being told now, in defense of single mothers, that having children is what in this hard modern world keeps women going. So it is not a job like any other. Female subjectivity cannot be denied so easily.

So there is a good deal of bad faith around generally, concerning whose will created the existing world, and who is doing what for whom. Some of this goes back to Simone de Beauvoir, who not only did much herself to devalue child rearing by designating this (as a good Marxist should) as a "pre-social activity" - surely a most extravagant absurdity, every bit as much an inversion as the most crass pretensions of patriarchy - but also helped formulate current victim strategies by portraying the victim as heroine. Asserting male responsibility is an old stance, and lies at the heart of patriarchy. But it is taken to an altogether higher plane in the distinctive feminist strategy of transferring male commitment to the public realm, where it becomes a collective and abstract rather than an individual responsibility. Here it is reduced almost completely to an empty ideology of public service. It is, I admit, an ideology which women very much need to believe in; and it would not be overstating the case too much to suggest that it is the need of feminists for socialism which has kept the Left going for the last decade or longer. For as a theory of how society works it is surely discredited now. Economic systems which give so little prominence to individual incentives and responsibilities are not competitive. They are now surviving in the world through political pressure and force, in the form of military strength at the international level, and internally by dint of political correctness, which treats attempts to unravel the social accounting of welfare as tantamount to the rape of defenseless women.

But looking the other way will not prevent the current welfare state system from collapsing as a result of its own contradictions. Feminists have built their new palace on sand.

## FIGHTING FOR THE CROWN

Before pursuing this last point further I will look at another aspect of the drive to autonomy by women which is having a great influence on gender relations and the position of men in the community. In a traditional chain of interpersonal dependency, both men and women have access to the legitimacy in the community which derives from recognizing obligations to others. The efforts by women to free themselves from dependency on men are now dislodging men from their positions of responsibility for children - the ultimate subjects in the domestic kingdom. In spite of the rhetoric from a few concerning the equal sharing of parenting, most women in practice want to exercise main control over this traditional female domain (e.g., Banks, 1981; Epstein 1988). Fewer feminists would now agree with the argument (Barrett & McIntosh, 1982) that children are used by men to push women back into the private domain; more of them are trying to bring children into a feminized public realm. As Hacker has pointed out (1991, p. 69), women now count the rights to reproduce, and to receive help in this, as part of their basic citizenship package. It is this which feeds the anxiety of those men still clinging to the prescriptions of patriarchy (before abandoning it perhaps in favor of a life of irresponsibility) that when feminists ask to be equal partners what they are really seeking is overall domination. They appear to want a monopoly of legitimacy.

There are mixed messages flying around here, which have to be interpreted with caution. For example, the prospectus issued by Anna Coote and others at the IPPR (1990) urges that equal partnerships are needed in which men are loving companions and responsible fathers rather than (mere) providers. But this idyll is soon polluted by the throwing in of a number of reservations and qualifications such as that, of course, mothers should stay in control "for the protection of children" from male abuse, etc, and that families must be organized always around strong and self-reliant women. If fathers can be responsible, then it is clearly only under female supervision and license.

All except the most devoted and idealistic of New Men must be aware by now that the deal is spurious and that their actual position in any non-patriarchal household will be as mother's little helper. The idea of equal parenting is a dodo. It is no use women saying that men have to show that they can be trusted. That is all humbug. Women are finding ever new ways to exploit the fact that children are the most reliable source of moral power in the community; and it was interesting to see that a few days after the publication of Neil Lyndon's sixties-style book, declaring his undying commitment to "joint parenting," his (estranged) wife, who cares for their child, wrote a piece in the *Daily Mail* (22 September 1992) accusing him of wanting to "strip women of motherhood."

Feminists certainly seem to be holding onto children more firmly as the gender war deepens and spreads. Many men have reacted to women's withdrawal of tolerance in the ways most readily open to them, that is negatively and often destructively. Abdication and flight have always been the chief male weapons; and since the sixties the popularity of the homosexual way, in which the term gay, although originally an acronym, also effectively stands for a life free from major responsibilities, represents the expansion of one such direction of flight. But this time women have not come running after men to beg them to return; not yet anyway. Instead they are using the feminized state apparatus to help keep their distance and consolidate their position on the high moral ground where they have their main advantage, that is their closeness to children.

Whereas sixties and even much of seventies feminism was muted on the importance of children, they are now central again to women's lives, and even equal opportunities hardliners are increasingly referring to the needs of children, to bolster women's claims to better treatment in the public realm. The feeling that it is possible to raise children without any help from men is ascendant and spreading out from the tabernacles to all corners of society; and a 1993 survey by NOP showed that nearly half of the British population now think (48 per cent compared with 30 per cent in 1987) that fathers are not really needed, and that a single mother can bring up her child as well as a married couple (reported in *Education Guardian,* 11 January 1994). More men are responding to this by trying to exercise direct control of children themselves, and the number of abductions carried out by absent fathers is causing alarm in some circles. The old domestic contract has finally been torn up; and the mother and father of all sexual battles is brewing.

## The virgin mother strategy

Struggle over parental rights is inherent in the feminist confrontation. For most of the seventies and early eighties, as official concern grew over the numbers of children born outside marriage, there was a lively campaign to prevent men being given new rights in respect of their illegitimate offspring, and vice-versa. Several parliamentarians, notably Leo Abse, were keen to improve the inheritance and general status rights of the escalating numbers of children born outside of marriage; and this was held to require that the father's name should be entered on a birth certificate. Many single mothers, whose cause was promoted by the legal pressure group Rights for Women, objected that this entailed involuntary submission to father-right and that for once women's own rights should be given priority. But in the end communities usually define parents as vessels or instruments serving children; and legislation in the eighties eventually increased children's rights in and access to all their natural relatives. If you want to wind up a feminist, talk about children's rights.

A new twist has now been given to this saga by the development of the Virgin Mother strategy, which greatly increases female reproductive autonomy. If a known father has to be disclosed and given access, then it is better not to know who the father is. In March 1991 the British Pregnancy Service was heavily censured in some quarters for providing unnamed semen to lesbians who neither wanted to have sex nor to retain any contact with the father of their child. Traditionalists denounced these lesbian families as selfish - although it is noteworthy that this was phrased mainly in relation to the interests of the children, and made little mention of the loss of role to a potential father. The drone is now taken for granted.

Several commentators, however, thought that the whole lark was a good lesson for men generally, who deserved the collective snub. The ubiquitous Bishop of Durham noted urbanely that:

> *Men have made a mess of it and women have revolted. ... Because men have been so dominant over the years...There's no harm in men feeling left out and jealous for a change.* (Rumbold, 1991)

Sheila Kitzinger was delighted too.

> *The unpenetrated woman has not been possessed. A woman has proved that all she needs is access to semen, and it's hitting men where it hurts.* (Ibid.)

Perhaps the Bishop, like the many other progressive churchmen who have responded sympathetically to the much more common situation in which women know their children's fathers but prefer to bring them up by themselves, or like Michelle Pfieffer choosing to adopt a child so as to avoid having some man hanging around the house (Gordon, 1993), was being influenced by the idea that the first lady of the Christian church was a single mother, and a virgin to boot. And if this is the case, it is further evidence of the failure of the contemporary church to understand its pastoral role.

Doctrinal insistence on the virginity of Christ's mother has not been seen in the past as supporting the implication that women can manage without men. Nor is it, I think, as Rosalind Miles and some others wallowing in self-pity have complained, a matter of men finding women's bodies too disgusting to contemplate, so that they require a de-sexualized portrayal of divine substantiation. Far from it. My own understanding of the imagery has been that the virgin birth concept has helped to stop men thinking about the bodies of women and concentrate more seriously on the non-corporeal element of paternal responsibility, which is the divine spirit with which they are invited to identify and of which they should become the worldly realization.

This interpretation is consistent with the way that physiological paternity is often played down in matrilineal societies where men support their sisters' children as much as or more than their own offspring. This is frequently misunderstood. Malinowski for instance (and a very influential example, at that) was fascinated by the way in which Trobriand Islanders appeared to be ignorant of the facts of life, and instead explained conception to him in terms of women having dreams about child spirits coming to them from their brothers (1929). Volumes of Freudian speculation, including Malinowski's own, have spun intricate theories about incest and sexual taboo around these observations. But a simpler explanation of it all is that Malinowski did not perhaps sufficiently allow that Trobriand culture, in which sexual activity was relatively unrestrained and continuous, took it for granted that the necessary physical conditions for reproduction were being fulfilled, and saved attention for the more important and problematic issues of what other elements were needed and the implications of these for social identities and obligations. The spiritual dimension was essential in defining men's roles.

It is precisely this dimension which is absent in modern virgin mother strategies, and in single mothering generally. The birth of Jesus to an unmarried women cannot, as well-meaning clerics writing letters to newspapers are currently prone to suggest, be seen as a rejection of patriarchy. In its religious context it is actually a celebration of it. The reason why many older people (to the intense irritation of more progressive minds) still regard single motherhood, where chosen freely, as "selfish," is that it is a denial of spiritual development to men, who are largely dependent on women for access to responsible fatherhood. The sin of the single mother lies in leaving a man in the forest, where he is likely to remain a beast.

## Rights for fathers

Not all men are however turning the other cheek with the Bishop. A number have realized that the true source of magic in society is not women *per se*, but the children who are normally kept out of men's direct control by the mother's mediation. It is children who are the treasure and investment of the community, and who are also the chief means whereby most adults find involvement in community affairs. Children open all doors; stop all traffic. They jump you to the front of public housing queues; and it is through their schooling that parents become caught up in local activities. Even beggars look the other way when children are with you, as they recognize instinctively a higher claim. The dependency of children is the most legitimate of all calls for support, and whomever they are dependent on has a secure place around the communal hearth.

Some men are now muscling in directly on this legitimacy, by asserting their own right to a parenting role (see Clatterbaugh, 1990, p. 90). Lone fatherhood has been in vogue for a number of years now, but in reality the masculinist movement is still extremely small, and in the British case is more concerned with access than full custody. Since the mid seventies the group Families Need Fathers has been helping men to mount legal cases against sole custody orders, where they are evidently up against great odds. The legal system is geared to protecting the mother-child unit, as illustrated by this letter from the vice-chairman of FNF explaining one of the reasons why violence against men is under-reported:

> *If a wife seeks a solicitor's advice on domestic violence she will be advised to pursue divorce. The consequences, she will be told, will result in her husband being expelled from the home, being forced to sign over all property to her, being required to support her financially and having future contact with their children dependent upon her discretion. By contrast, a husband who is the victim of domestic violence and pursues divorce will be expelled from his home, required to sign over his property (even that owned before marriage) to his violent wife, support her financially and have future contact with their children dependent upon the violent wife's discretion.* (*The Times*, 28 September 1992)

These fathers know that they need their families. But they are not making much impact, and at the level of general principles, in the public arena, the overwhelming mood, blending feminist and traditional sentiments, is that if women want to exclude men they should be allowed to. The view that a child belongs primarily to the mother is more likely to come under attack because of civil libertarian difficulties arising out of new possibilities of genetic control, than in the name of the right of men to be fathers.

Feminism and femininity form an invincible alliance here. Women are the main carers and need to be able to face their children daily without too much anguish which might be occasioned by interfering fathers. Even though the rules give women the chance to manipulate men emotionally over access, and even to withdraw altogether the gift of parenthood made to them when the relationship was viable this is generally, and probably correctly, seen by the community as a price which may need to be paid for the sake of children themselves. Children's rights come before men's as well.

Not all movement is in the direction of polarization though. Recent legislation has attempted to steer a way around the battleground by introducing, in the name of children's needs, an initial presumption of joint custody for children when a home is broken. This concept is embodied in the Children's Act which came into effect in the autumn of 1991. It creates a sort of parallel parenting, whereby both partners, regardless of who is actively caring for a child, should have a say in the parenting process, under the supervision of a social worker. This may help to ease the life of children while their parents are at war, although the general principle is far from acceptable to many women:

*Joint custody as a political symbol for peaceful equality in the sphere of child care should not become a means whereby women who have to deal with severe manifestations of power and oppression become legally powerless.* (Sevenhuijsen, 1986)

The concept does nothing to resolve the conflict. It may help to reduce the number of casualties.

However the fact that feminism itself seems to be failing to propagate viable new concepts of parenthood, and is just feeding gender divisions here, rather confirms that it is not evolving into a proper church capable of handling men and organizing social life in a new and superior way. The small number of much vaunted New Men, practiced in loving companionship and sharing in all things, no longer shine out as the forerunners of a new priesthood. Instead of leading us into a fertile promised land of amity and mutual respect, feminists are drawing us a long way from the old palace before it is clear that there is anywhere else for us to go. And it is starting to get dark.

# 8

# COLLAPSING REALMS

There may be a better way to manage men and bring them into active service for the community than by defining them as family providers. Looking for a one is a worthwhile project, to which we should give more time. But I would be very surprised if the strategies which have been crafted by contemporary feminism are leading us in a productive direction. So far they just seem to be weakening the slender thread of motivation which has kept men useful in the past, without replacing it with an alternative dynamic. This issue is avoided by most feminists who, when identifying "backlash" against themselves, set up other objections which can easily be disposed of. Susan Faludi's tome for example (1992) keeps reasserting that women *are* able to meet the demands of the jobs which they are moving into, and to enjoy doing them, that it is possible to be a successful worker and good mother at the same time, including as a single parent, and that none of all this causes harm or suffering to children. The bottom line is that women do *not* have to feel guilty about living for themselves.

But evidently, since they constantly need to be told not to, many women do go on feeling this. I believe that the roots of this continuing guilt lie in considerations which the rejoinders to backlash prefer to skate over, as they do not have adequate answers to them. Many women seem well aware of the limitations of feminist analyses. They know that men are socially fragile, and that to take away their formalized advantages may seriously undermine their capacity not just to cope with paid work but also, and as a result of this, to pull their weight in family life too. They can see that many of those anti-social tendencies of men which feminists eagerly fasten on to justify withdrawal of trust from them are in part the consequences of male displacement which has already started. They can also see that although feminism promotes the interests of women as individual actors in the public arena, it does so by placing an increasing burden on those who are left holding what remains of the moral economy. Gains which they have made as individuals have a community cost which women collectively have to bear. *That is why they feel guilty.*

These concerns are not fashionable, and are easily brushed aside by women transported by the excitement of the gender war. They do however deserve more attention; and I believe they are beginning to get this as the shortcomings of feminist models further manifest themselves. Merging the private and public realms is arguably leading towards the collapse of much more than the boundary between them, and perhaps is about to show us just how reliant the whole social fabric still may be on gendered social divisions. Feminists canards may soon be coming home to roost.

## A PLAGUE OF FROGS

*One evening two female academics were strolling home somewhere in that swathe of North London lying between the Tavistock Institute and the Manor Gardens Women's Centre. Going past a semi-basement garden they were surprised to hear a croaking and, on looking down, to see a frog. As they stood there, the frog said to them, "If you kiss me and take me home I will turn into a handsome stud for you." One of the women went down the steps, picked up the frog, and put it into her pocket. The other said, with mixed feelings, "Aren't you going to kiss it, then?" And the first replied "Oh no. Handsome studs are ten-a-penny. But talking frogs ... !"* (London joke circulating Autumn 1992)

*The danger in modern society ... is that the unsocialised man will become culturally dominant and it will be the civilised ones who have to resist the pressures of the society at large.* (Gilder, 1973, p. 41)

Most gender relations theories fail to look at the whole process of women's movement into the public realm, which is not just a matter of managing without men, but also entails consciously leaving the management of men to men themselves or, if they cannot cope, then to the state. What this partiality refuses to countenance is that men are not as strongly placed as they seem, and may actually need protection from direct competition from women if they are to remain useful.

I have argued that men operate more successfully in the public arena if they have a position as family provider which gives them extra rewards and also a reason beyond self to keep going and overcome difficulties. When women take this away from them then they can often displace men in competitive situations. Men are more overtly oriented to competition than women. However this is not because their position in the community is stronger, but precisely because it is fundamentally weaker, so that they have to struggle just to join it. Take away their advantages and the greater risk of losing will stop many from bothering to compete at all. Spurn the prince idea, and what you will be left with is a swarm of feckless frogs; as faced with the realities of the declining importance to others of their work, those men whose only job would be dull and low status see far less point in bothering.

If feminists do face up to this situation at all it is usually in the scornful language of emasculation. Men deprived of breadwinner status, they will say with mock sympathy, feel emasculated. (Poor things; but really that is not our problem, their smiles will add.) This is not however a situation which deserves such easy displays of hauteur. It is something which arises out of the relative positions of men and women in dependency chains, and is a matter of dehumanization rather than emasculation. To adapt the original cliché, if women didn't have children, they would be no better than men are now. We are not different species. It may not be fair on women that men need extra incentives; but the consequences of depriving them of their position may be very grave.

*Middle-and lower-middle class men value their families deeply. If asked why they work, they will show you a picture of the wife and kids. For these men, work is "meaningful" almost exclusively because it sustains their role as provider and affords an arena of masculine associations. The higher purposes are of little relevance. If the world of work becomes a realm of women, many of these men will leave it and their families as well.* (Gilder, *op. cit.* p. 187)

## Men under competition

Equal opportunities agendas are based on the diametrically opposed assumption that competition from women at work is good for men. I think this is entirely wrong and fails to see the advantages that women have in direct competitions with men, as a result of the more immediate and compelling bond which children have with them, and which few seem eager to relinquish. As Ann Oakley has remarked (1987), motherhood may be the source of many problems for women, but it is paradoxically also a great strength. Knowing that you are working for others as well as yourself provides a valuable spur to keep you going during difficult patches, and bolsters your self-respect. This also - because your paid work is less of your life anyway, and may be defined more instrumentally - makes it possible to be more practical and realistic, and to settle for a humbler job than you really deserve, leaving ambition until later. You can meet the demands of dependants on you without being successful in a universalist sense; and although this can hamper motivation at higher levels, it makes routine work more satisfying. Women workers understand this as a matter of course, and male providers can experience it too. A man emasculated by having no dependants is no match for either of them.

Working women may even have some edge over men who are valued providers. There are many practical difficulties they face fitting in domestic duties; but there is a sense in which it is very hard for them to fail. They have a firmer base to fall back on in the moral economy than men, regardless of what happens in the market, and they enjoy many more possibilities of community and state support. Women are less on their own in this way and compete from a position of relative security. Also because they are not expected to support men they can accept lower wages and hence undercut men if the going gets really tough.

The entry of women into the marketplace during the last generation as direct competitors has challenged this but does not affect all classes of men equally, or in the same ways. Basically it does not hurt middle-class men very much, and this is probably why most active feminists may not have had close contact with its human consequences. The consort of any successful woman, unless he is a failure himself, can take pride in her exploits and his own ability to cope. Denis Thatcher apparently loves everyone to say how confident he must be to survive life with Margaret. It is perhaps unfortunate for the Labour Party that its policies are so influenced at present by professional women whose experience of marriage is similarly atypical, but who publicize themselves as models for ordinary people. Bill Birtles, for example, the husband of Patricia Hewitt, is clearly quite a catch:

> *He became her second husband in 1981 and sounds like a model New Man. "He is a very, very involved father," says Hewitt, without irony. He took paternity leave, got up in the night, changed nappies and, these days, being a barrister, often works at home and picks the kids up from school. This is what the new book is about: flexibility in the family, part-time working by choice, what women really want.* (Langdon, 1993)

Barbara Wootton must be looking down now very wistfully. But Bill already had a fulfilling job himself before meeting Patricia - so for him a successful partner could be an added adornment to life, a trophy some would say, and not in his case a reproach to his own uselessness. It is not an ordinary situation.

More generally, men whose work is interesting and prestigious can be expected to respond positively to competition from women by working harder, because their job carries intrinsic rewards or social legitimacy. Apparently a new breed of superman workaholics is evolving in Scandinavia to fend off the growing female challenge (Dahlborn-Hall and Hord, 1993). Also the latest figures on U.K. degree results suggest that male students are starting to work much harder as they take female rivals more seriously. They are now nearly twice as likely to get firsts as women, including in arts subjects where women have traditionally done well (Hymas, 1993). At lower levels however, that is GCSE, and especially in technical and vocational subjects, boys continue to be overtaken by girls (Bates, 1992; Hymas, 1992). So elite and high interest jobs may still be mobilizing boys, though in the end women might be able to elbow out even such heroes as these.

Working-class men have fared less well. The changes in western economies have not helped, with old industrial heartlands declining, and any compensating growth mainly confined to service sectors where women have concentrated. But the restructuring of work opportunities can only be a partial explanation for their problems.

With appropriate incentives, many redundant men could have moved into expanding service industries, as in non-western economies like Japan. But this has not happened, because in the West this is where the additional women workers have been coming into the market. So it is men in the working class who have seen their chances reduced through the feminization of labor. This is where unrealized princes remain trapped inside uncouth yobs, and why many working-class girls, seduced by middle-class media images of female independence which they personally are not qualified to pursue, are being drawn into over-dependence on the provider state.

## Back to the forest

The standard feminist line on equal opportunities is that competition from women in the workplace will motivate men to try that much harder to be good fathers and providers. In reality the outcomes at both ends of the job market seem to be bad for the community, as in each case it makes it easier for men to avoid their moral responsibilities. This is why it is a priority to mount new research ventures exploring the detailed connections between men's sense of economic responsibility for others, and their wider sensitivity to dependants' needs. Morris (1991), and Pahl (1984) among many others have looked at the way in which unemployment may be associated with male withdrawal from domestic activities; but less has been done to explore how being materially responsible helps men to become positively involved and caring, across a range of employment situations. I would guess that many middle-class workaholics fending off female competition are too busy to be actively caring fathers, while working class benefit-drones on the other hand are too demoralized and dehumanized to be much use even though they have time on their hands. Equal opportunities has helped to let both categories off the hook and both are learning to survive outside patriarchy. Radical feminists then come along and use them as manifest justifications for writing men even further out of their script for the future. A self-perpetuating vilification of men is in process.

From this perspective, the new art of publicly bad-mouthing men seems in very dubious taste. Many men are now caught in a classic vicious circle of degradation and exclusion. They neither receive any respect from anyone but their closest buddies, nor do they have any real chance to win it. The things which they then do to help keep up their pecker, like fighting to show that they are men, or emulating Sid the Sexist in clumsy attempts at romantic conquest, just count further against them. For the circle to be broken they need women to flatter them a bit, and turn down the volume on equal opportunities so that they can believe there is some chance of becoming a prince one day.

But more women seem to be doing the exact opposite. A segment of those employed in the welfare state, the fully-paid-up members of the Marietta Higgs Tendency, spend their time diligently amassing evidence that men are abusers (a term which is much abused itself, and which, while always pronounced as if indicating sexual interference, sometimes refers to nothing more than an exercise of verbal firmness which in a different age would have been applauded as paternal discipline) or harassers (likewise "attentive"). Some men are guilty of these offenses of course, and I think that it is pointless to argue alongside David Thomas (1993) that women are as bad. But the generous margins of amplification and innuendo speed the self-fulfillment and tighten the vicious circle. Most men still do not feel under too much attack. But at the bottom of society there is a growing lump, Bea Campbell's "lawless masculinity" incarnate (1993), who are unemployed and probably unemployable, unfulfilled, have no self-respect because they know that they are despised, and who have little incentive to be nice to anyone, even or especially women. Men are very aware of the constant assessment by women. When they feel a reasonable chance of approval, their motivation to behave themselves increases by leaps. But when judgments against them seem unrelenting, many lose heart and stop even trying.

There may be gender differences involved here. Within a framework of close personal relations, criticisms are usually felt as constructive, because they are part of ongoing negotiations about a relationship. But to a universalist, which most men are until or unless fully locked into paternal responsibilities, criticism indicates failure. So instead of responding positively they drift instead into negativism and self-pity.

It is hardly surprising therefore that social problems involving men are spiralling at the moment. Feminism may not be directly responsible for this. But a non-feminist generation of women would have done far more to prevent and contain them; and in their absence the state is increasingly called on to tackle them punitively. George Gilder predicted over twenty years ago that the state which takes on child care, and detaches men from their role as fathers, will find that *"society's underclass of males will steadily expand, and policing it will become the chief concern of the state"* (*op. cit.* p. 187).

A fast growing library of studies, starting with Murray's development of Gilder's ideas (1984), and progressing in the United Kingdom through Field (1993), Anderson (1991), Dennis and Erdos (1992 & 1993) have all identified a core of irresponsible and purposeless men at the centre of our current social malaise. The culture of sex and violence (Greenstein, 1993), a rising tide of male early mortality and suicide (Hacker, 1991; Thomas, 1993), high long-term male unemployment rates, the deterioration in academic performance of boys even in science subjects, possibly some of the loss of business confidence at the heart of the recession, and arguably the formation of right-wing nationalist movements across Europe giving a sense of belonging to otherwise unattached and unlovable young men, have all been linked in some way to the erosion of the male breadwinner vocation.

Many of these arguments are undoubtedly overblown and over-simplified. The literature on absent fatherhood and crime, for example, shows that the situation is very complex (Murray, 1993; Hewitt, 1993c; Burghes, 1993). In particular there is a need to recognize that in a mass communications society where families are less sealed off from outside influences the effects of people's behavior extend beyond close relatives and explanatory models need to be more ecological. So it is not surprising, and quite right, that two people out of three questioned in a NOP study should say that they did not accept a direct link between one-parent families and criminality (*Sunday Times*, 14th November 1993). But at least, after years of stifled silence, the issues are being widely and openly discussed.

### Unemployment and flight from fatherhood

But equally predictably, most commentators still seem hugely reluctant to link this collapse of men openly to the rise of feminism. For example Campbell's recent analysis (1993) of the flight of young men from order into mindless violence observes usefully that contemporary lawlessness cannot be explained in terms of maternal neglect or single parenting, and constitutes a form of male rejection of domesticity and fatherhood. Fine. But then she puts it all down to "endemic unemployment," as if this was not a widespread problem in the thirties, when there was far less disintegration of law and order.

There is a difference now which needs to be explained; and surely an essential part of this is that until recently men still had a valued role as providers to look forward to, which pulled them through hard times and gave them a stake in the system. That is all but gone now. Young men have not rejected fatherhood; or not, at any rate, in a vacuum. Women who would prefer to have paid jobs or live on welfare than to prioritize work for a male partner have done much to render it a less than serious ambition.

This is a nettle which few seem willing to grasp, or even allow others to. William Julius Wilson has cleverly contrived to dull the sharpness of Charles Murray's analysis of the cycle of male marginalization in the United States, which did try to tackle it. Wilson, himself black, disarmingly declares that Murray's thesis that female independence, backed up by welfare generosity, is a major cause of black family disintegration and promotes joblessness among young men, contains much "psychological truth."

> *the logic of the association between welfare and family/work disincentives is intuitively compelling and appears largely consistent with aggregate trends in social welfare spending and changes in family structure over time.* (1987, p 93)

This proves however to be only a token nod before knocking the position down, to off-stage cheers from white libertarian statists coast-to-coast, by deploying massed financial statistics to show that female-headed households are in fact slightly worse off living on welfare than if they had working partners. *Ergo,* he concludes, it is joblessness among men, and the associated low *Male Marriageable Pool Index,* rather than the availability of welfare itself, which has caused the severe rise in numbers of one-parent families living on welfare.

His conclusion is not acceptable. By concentrating heavily on highly empirical indicators, hard data, Wilson neatly sidesteps the motivational factors crucial to understanding the process under examination and the *meaning* of the figures. It may well be that women on welfare are not better off financially. But they may still prefer it and seek it because it gives them more personal autonomy and fulfillment; and the autonomy may even enable them to eke out the slightly smaller income more efficiently. If Wilson listened to women talking about male heads of household and looked at how income is distributed within families he would surely see that benefit levels could fall even lower before they ceased to offer an attractive alternative to conjugality for some women.

Male marginality is far more than an economic phenomenon, and involves an interplay between a variety of cultural, personal and material factors. Above all it is necessary to explore the effect of rising female employment on male motivation and aspiration, as this may be *why* male joblessness is rising and men are not moving around looking for work as they did in the last great recession. It is clear from what Gilder had to say about this in 1973, at a time when most black men still did have jobs, that the sequence of events may well have been that male providers were undermined *before* recession got underway, so that these men just surrendered to it. We were warned!

> *Sociologists are rather casual when they report that the earnings of black women are about 80 percent of black male income, while white women earn only about 58 percent as much as white men. Yet when the impact of welfare is added - and the earnings of married black males are subtracted - it becomes clear that in the ghetto the male role as chief provider has as much evaporated, and that the unmarried ghetto male is too poor in relation to women to be needed by them.* (1973, p. 116; see also Gilder 1981, pp. 132-9)

William Julius Wilson's policy recommendations arising out of his analysis, which argue for a shift towards prioritizing job creation over welfare, are basically sound but are flawed by the suggestion that this should include more programs for unemployed single mothers too. This is pouring oil on the fire. He should learn to listen to his intuition, which is probably closely linked to his own motivation and success. He remarks in his preface, when dedicating the book to his wife, that *"her enthusiasm for my work has had a rejuvenating effect that allowed me to overcome periods of fatigue during the latter stages of writing ..."* Where would *he* be now if he had a partner who saw her own work as more important than servicing a man's ambition?

## Fall of the black prince

I have recently done some research myself on the very similarly placed African-Caribbean community in Britain (Dench, 1992), and this clearly presents a cautionary illustration of the direction which the West appears to be moving in more generally. Among this group the erosion of responsible male roles, and the virtual institutionalization of female independence, has proceeded alongside a massive collapse in community integrity and morale. Family culture is not the sole cause of this, but it seems to play a very important part.

There is a long but regularly misinterpreted tradition of female independence and single parenting in African-Caribbean cultures. In the aftermath of slavery, a whole spectrum of family and household types emerged, ranging from survival units consisting of just mothers and children, through a variety of extended family networks carrying childhood relations into adult life in which men played intermittent roles as fathers and uncles, to conventional Christian marriages, which people adopted when they achieved economic security and to which most people aspired (Clarke, 1957; Gonzales, 1984; Henriques, 1953; R. T. Smith, 1956, 1973, 1988, for example). Obviously there were many nuances and local variations within such an array of alternatives; but on balance it seems fair to say that single mothering was tolerated, and indeed respected as doing the best that one could, rather than being in any sense a preferred life-style. It was at no time an available option for the society as a whole, only for the lower classes, and the various other family forms can be seen as mechanisms for helping people to claw their way up from the lower depths towards the ideal of settled marriage.

The migrants who came to Britain in the fifties and sixties sprang from a range of social backgrounds, and included many married people and children of married parents, as well as some who were hoping to be able to climb permanently out of poverty and low status. But they had not reckoned with feminism. Most men in the migrant generation had jobs arranged before they arrived or found them soon after arrival, and were generally involved in stable domestic relations, albeit not always formalized. Nevertheless the community contained a fair number of independent women who combined working with mothering; and these were quickly seized on and lionized towards the end of the sixties when feminists started to look for alternative models of domestic life. The single-parent family was soon being celebrated as a viable rival to conventional patriarchy; and feminists manipulated liberal colonial guilt which was widespread among the professional classes at the time to shoot down as racist or imperialist anyone who objected to the suggestion that this was a genuine cultural preference. Even younger, locally educated African-Caribbeans were encouraged to taunt as stooges any elders who spoke out of line; and soon African-Caribbean women were collaborating with feminists in building support networks and pressing for the expansion of welfare provisions to assist female independence (Bryan *et al.*, 1982). Eventually the idea that parenting without men was the African-Caribbean norm percolated into commonsense worldviews of the educated classes in Britain, and even a meticulous scholar like Janet Finch could write with confidence that:

> ... *the model of the family which informs social policy not only is out of line with the reality of many people's lives, but also can be seen to be ethnocentric, since a mother-headed household is a cultural norm for people of Caribbean or African origin, where it can be seen as a sign of a strong family life rather than an undesirable modification.* (1989, p. 126)

This inference is not merely incorrect but has I believe done great damage to the community, by making men feel superfluous, and undermining their incentives to struggle against the difficulties they face in this country. Men subject to discrimination need stronger, not weaker family demands on them, to help them know that what they are doing with their lives does matter to other people. At first sight it may not be very obvious that any harm has been done to the group, because African-Caribbean women have been so successful here. They have achieved high educational attainments and rates of employment, and are wheeled out periodically (e.g. Mike Phillips, 1993) to show that single mothers with long-term jobs need not be heavily dependent on welfare.

But the relative success of black women has been partly at the expense of black men, who have become ever more demotivated, demoralized and degraded as black women have demonstrated how well they can manage without them. Male unemployment has risen faster in this group than in other racial and cultural minorities with broadly similar market positions. The number of single male households is large and getting larger, and rates of ill-health, drug abuse, mortality including suicide, crime and general disorganization are all climbing. Deprived of the feeling of being useful and needed, many men are losing their purpose in life, and finding it ever harder to struggle against the discrimination they encounter.

Unfortunately there is a real conflict of interest between men and women here. The more that men crumble and fade into the scenery, the easier it becomes for women to succeed. They are the ones piling up a monopoly of virtue, and as one of Phillips' informants points out, the responsibility of being a lone parent may call out the best in people.

> *Far from thinking about themselves as a problem, the characteristic response of black lone parents to being asked about their experience is to describe it in terms which are sometimes close to the inspirational. Claire Shepherd, for instance, lived on the Broadwater Farm estate, north London, through the 1980's while her son was a growing adolescent. "It's not a burden, it's a gift," she insists. "I don't have any regrets and I didn't think it was a big deal. Having him kind of inspired me: we went through the educational system together. We were doing our degrees at the same time, but I got my MA first."*

But the piling up of virtue and inspiration in both domains by women is creating tremendous disequilibrium within the community, between men and women, between generations, between individual and group interests; and this now arguably outweighs the personal benefits to women. Men demotivated from useful activity in the public domain are becoming a moral drain on the rest of the group, and potentially a financial problem too as the welfare state begins to fray at the edges. The crisis of the African-Caribbean man is turning into a crisis for the group as a whole, prompting those who are able to leave it to do so. Bernie Grant's elderly repatriation fodder are in part escaping from broken dreams of founding family dynasties here: and the racism they blame for their disappointments includes the attribution to their community of a fundamentally different set of family values than the rest of the British population. Many of the more successful younger women are choosing to marry out of the community if they do so at all. The group is turning its back on itself. A time has arrived of *sauve-qui-peut*.

There is a history waiting to be written here of the disservice done by white middle-class women, in helping to promote absent fatherhood, to an economically hard-pressed group which collectively desired and certainly needed stronger families if it was going to establish itself properly in this country (Dench, 1993). Instead it is now the scene of massive demoralization. The fate of the black prince is a serious warning to the rest of us.

## ECONOMY UNDER SIEGE

The storming of the public realm by women is informed by a very flimsy quasi-Marxist theory in which, as I outlined earlier, the feudal pockets of women's unfree labor are to be made more productive by being brought into the free market system. After a few temporary perturbations, we are reassured, creating a single labor market will make everyone much better off.

### The shift of personal servicing

My own prediction would be rather different. Allowing women to become genuine competitors with men has to be seen as entailing the withdrawal of large amounts of women's energy from the moral economy, and some of the services previously performed within it, and their relocation in the market. This would be alright if women's energy removed from the private realm was being replaced by men's, and if there was a clear idea of which parts of the moral economy could and could not easily be shunted in this way. Overall equilibrium would then be preserved. But, mainly because of the convention that the public realm is a "great out-there" which can absorb the moral economy easily, several times over if necessary, and maybe also because there is still a belief that men will eventually see the light and start taking their personal obligations seriously, most feminists seem to think that it is fine to push for total integration as quickly as possible. It is however rapidly becoming evident that this is wrong, and that serious imbalances are building up.

Firstly, as indicated in the previous chapter, it is important to recognize that much of the growth in women's employment consists of paying them for activities which were formerly done freely. Within the welfare state, professional carers, who are predominantly women, are paid a salary for performing services for other women's children or sick or elderly relatives, which they do less of for their own because someone else is probably being paid by the community to do that as well. All this is bound to be inflationary insofar as paid carers are remunerated at rates in excess of what could have been subsumed within a man's family wage, for this means that the proportion of community resources allocated to personal servicing is continually rising.

The relocation of personal dependency away from the family and into a welfare system as public dependency can only go so far before hitting some very real limiting factors. Paying separate salaries for services formerly subsumed within the family wage concept both increases tremendously the total share of available resources devoted to them and stimulates a vast additional demand. Before this shift the family was the first point of call for someone needing help or support, and the public purse was used only as a last resort. Under that regime people mostly did what they could to manage within their private means. But once that all citizens, not just the most indigent, are encouraged to reverse this precept and to expect the state to provide for their needs, or to pay *them* where they are providing for other people's, then the position becomes untenable. Potential claims are virtually limitless. So too are grievances, for any categories of the needy or their carers who do not receive entitlements which universalistic reasoning might lead them to expect will become extremely bitter. The cost of operating the system fairly would soon far exceed the public resources on call, and operating it unfairly helps inflame the victim mentality which escalates demands even further.

## Half for the price of two

This leads into another, less self-evident area, where equal opportunities accounting also must be explored and probably reworked. The costs of transferring what was previously women's work into the welfare state are in theory calculable, because the activities involved are visible and can be listed. What is much less easy to estimate is the cost of reduced work motivation among men who are no longer called on to be the main breadwinners. How many marriages break down or don't take place, and how many men work less hard, or less efficiently, or not at all, because there is no one depending on them? How much, too, does the state lose through lower tax revenues, or higher unemployment payouts? Single-parent families are known to cost a lot in terms of direct benefits; and the British government has not only set up the Child Support Agency to recover some of this expenditure from absent fathers, but is frequently hinting that it cannot continue to carry this burden much longer. Mother-headed families increased in Britain from 1 percent of all families in 1971 to 18 percent in 1991 (*General Household Survey*, OPCS), and with a growing proportion of these living on welfare, as the fashion spread down from professional career women to working-class girls. In 1992, 885,000 single parents were claiming lone parent benefit, and 985,000 income support, at a total cost of £66 million per week (*The Guardian*, 10 November 1993). No wonder Peter Lilley looks like a trapped animal.

However, the hidden costs of weakening the male provider role may make the overall bill to taxpayers much greater than this, as changes in family arrangements which result from it may add a variety of expenses, from demotivated men working less efficiently, drawing more unemployment benefits and taking up additional subsidized housing, or drifting into crime and becoming expensively pursued and then detained at Her Majesty's pleasure.

So just when calls on the state for welfare expenditure are being multiplied by women's flight from domesticity into work, the productive and taxable base from which this expenditure is met is becoming progressively narrower, and subjected to additional new calls elsewhere, and all for the same basic reason. We may have now gone beyond the point where as Charles Murray predicts this contraction is accelerating, for how many men will labor willingly in boring jobs to support a wife and children if the state is prepared to take that responsibility away from them?

Thus there is a false accounting at the heart of the equal opportunities case. Apart from the right of women to develop themselves, the economic argument in favor of EO is that a country cannot afford to waste female talent, so that almost any expenditure which frees women for work is bound to repay itself - through increased incentives, efficiency and commitment of the work force. As Joshi and Davies recently, and very reassuringly, calculated in relation to childcare:

*For a woman who changes her labour force participation as a result of the availability of childcare, the resources generated exceed the resource cost of the childcare, and the revenue gain to the exchequer may exceed the costs of a 100 percent subsidy.* (NIESR, November 1993)

But the motivation and commitment of male workers is either ignored as an issue or just assumed to be a constant. When the question is pressed, the answer comes back that a little competition from women at work might make men pull out their fingers and raise their own levels of productivity. Researchers at the Thomas Coram unit have even cheerfully proposed that if the state helps women to be more independent, this will stimulate men, who are fearful of losing their place, to be better fathers.

*The end of the notion of the breadwinner might open the doors for negotiating a new, more equal partnership. It would make men work harder inside the family. They would have to learn how to earn their keep.* (McRobbie, 1990)

The confident message is that public welfare does not necessarily weaken kinship obligations and incentives. In short, we will all be better off.

This case blithely ignores the possibility that workplace

competition may drastically reduce rather than enhance male effort and outputs. This neglect occurs perhaps because women, the main architects of the policy, simply do not understand how weak men's incentives may become if they are displaced as breadwinners. Women are very keen workers given the chance, because as mothers or potential mothers they have the expectation of dependency on them. A newly liberated generation of such workers will be especially enthusiastic and stimulated; so, as in eastern Europe between the wars, women today in the west are exceptionally good value as employees.

But their gain and that of their employers may be society's loss, if the result is to turn men into drones. By encouraging women to work, often only part-time, while paying unemployment benefits to men who don't, the modern state may not be getting two workers for the price of one, as equal opportunities activists have promised, but only one or even half for the price of two. As the marriage rate dips, female employment rises, and proportions of mother-headed households increase, more boys will remain frogs for longer and engage in more of that loutish and rough behavior which confirms the derogatory stereotypes women hold of them, and stiffens female resolve to stay independent. If opening up the public realm to women is in fact multiplying their chances of being exploited, as Walby proposes, this may be largely because its feminization is reducing severely the productive contribution which men are making to it.

## Undercutting men

In spite of the Marxist credentials of much EO theory, the cushion of public support for women helps them in practice to collaborate with employers in a double act which puts more of the costs of production onto the state while displacing men from work. The increase in jobs for women in the United Kingom over the last two decades (2 million) nearly matches the number lost by men (2.8 million); and in nine counties in England and Wales, and two in Scotland, women employees now outnumber men (*Sunday Times,* 9 May 1993). Yet when suffering arises out of all this, it is held to be because men are not responding and joining in with the right spirit. Germaine Greer in a characteristically intemperate piece (1992) blames gender inequalities in pay for the growing impoverishment of women's lives.

> *The men rant and rave that women have stolen their jobs; the truth is that, because they were too mean and too dumb to give women equal pay, the employers now use women because they are cheaper... It was trade unionists themselves who institutionalised the differences in the valuation of jobs done by men and jobs done by women, on the eve of a radical restructuring of the job market, and left themselves outside the factory gates. Unemployed men bash women and children, but their brutality should not be excused as "backlash" ... they had the power and they brought it on themselves.*
>
> *The myth of backlash then represents another attempt by men to pass the buck for their own failures and to justify their own tyrannical behaviour. As long as women pretend to believe it, they will be simply humouring the troublesome male, in order to get on with the tasks of every day, which are heavier and more demanding than they ever were.*

Hang on there! This argument simply does not set the events in a wide enough context. Of course men are pricing themselves out of a market when they insist on a family provider wage in competition with women who will accept less. But this is not because they are being stupid so much as that they are continuing to believe in a role for themselves which women, with state backing, are more and more rejecting. After all, it is not pay differentials, but the drive to equal job opportunities, which is the new factor in the equation.

When men ask for higher wages, or for preferential access to employment, what they are looking for is not simply a payment for the work that they do, nor even simply enough money to support a family as well as themselves, but also some encouragement to take on responsibilities in the wider community. In a sense, a fair wage for men is one that includes a reward for performing, and a realistic incentive to accept, the roles of husband and father and general family man. As they are more removed than women from the dependency of children, and can more easily avoid it altogether, they arguably need this bonus in order to take it seriously. Or even to do it at all. This is not a matter of inherent character differences,

but of different placement in dependency chains, which, as I have
indicated earlier, I guess that patriarchal privileges were devised,
probably largely by women, to address.

Unless this is confronted it is impossible to predict the
consequences of tinkering with the sexual division of labor. The
marketplace, as a principally male preserve, routinely offered high
rewards for labor, and operated as a crucial primary mechanism for
co-opting men to society by giving them something of value to take
into the private realm, where they would otherwise be worth very
little. That is it compensated men for their essential marginality in
society by inflating the importance of what they do and establishing
a gradient in rewards. Overall, women labor longer and harder than
men. But until recently they have done this mainly within the
private realm where it is not paid for in wages but repaid in kind
through reciprocation. Men do altogether less but get more generous
rewards for it, in the form of wages in their privileged public
domain. This effect is clearly being lost as women start to enter the
market in large numbers as free competitors.

## Breaching male enclaves

This I believe is the underlying reason for the paradox that equal
opportunities policies seem to be accompanied by growing female
poverty, and women's dreams of financial independence via the
market are turning to dust. Early proponents of EO saw themselves
as leading an escape attempt from what seemed a small and
oppressed corner of society, an internal colony, into the great wide
marketplace where they would be free to sell their labor for its true
price and sweep away unfair male advantages. But this model was
faulty on at least two major counts. Firstly, labor in the market is in
fact rewarded at a grossly exaggerated rate; and this is only possible
if most social activities or services are carried out freely or for
reciprocation in kind. The larger the proportion of total services
which are organized through the market, the lower the artificial
bonus is bound to drop, and the wage rate with it. Secondly the
market is not actually the main and dominant part of society but a
rather small male enclave or haven within it, and it would be at risk
of serious flooding if the protective restrictions around it were
broken down.

So any effort to integrate the two economies is bound to cause tremendous problems. Even bringing a small fraction of the interpersonal services carried out in the moral economy into the public domain, for example by creating state nurseries to free women for paid work in the market, is liable to reduce wage levels. If in addition it is assumed that the community will pay for this work via the welfare state, then this places a heavy burden on the market's productive taxable base. For the market value of the work done in the moral economy must be truly colossal.

Most of the really essential and demanding social functions are carried out in the moral economy, which as well as being larger is more reliable, and has no eight-hour working days, or strikes, or holiday entitlements, or sickness benefits. The hardest work is caring for other people; and looking after small children for example is infinitely more wearing than any "real" job, as well as carrying very great responsibility. All efforts to cost such work in terms of prevailing market wage rates inevitably lead to absurdities. Thus Arnold Toynbee, in conversation with Daisaku Ikeda (1989), declared heartfelt support for the idea of the state paying women to bring up children, and went on to consider some possible equivalent occupations.

> *....insofar as, and for so long as, she serves society as a mother, I feel sure that a woman ought to be given the high status and big salary that the key profession of motherhood deserves. Her status ought to be at least as high as, say, a professor's or a magistrate's or a pilot's, and her salary ought to be of a corresponding size.* (1989, p. 118)

A sophomore could tell you that although such a proposal might seem highly equitable, there is absolutely no point in pursuing it. For if all mothers deserve to be paid three times the average wage, albeit just for a period of five, ten or sometimes fifteen years, then the state would be required to impose a levy on the marketplace equivalent to around three-quarters of its existing turnover, before it could begin to summon up adequate resources. No market system could bear that. If you took the idea to its logical conclusion and also paid wives for their work in looking after their husbands ( and vice-versa?), and middle-aged people for looking after the aged, and able-bodied for looking after the disabled and handicapped, then you

would obviously consume the entire GNP several times over before
you even started to think about paying for the services already
performed by the state, such as education, specialist medical care,
housing and general public administration and infrastructure, not to
mention defense of the realm. It is just not on.

## Burdening women further

> *The grim economic facts show that while some women earn*
> *more, women as a group are poorer than they have ever*
> *been in relation to men, and when women are poor, so are*
> *their children.* (Polly Toynbee, 1993)

The market as we know it only makes sense if most personal
services, most of women's labors, are kept out of it. If they now
insist on defining the private domain as a captivity from which they
must escape and target the state and market as a common birthright
in which they must have equal rights then I would imagine that the
effect will not be to raise their rewards to the levels once enjoyed
by men but rather to reduce progressively those enjoyed by
everyone.

Men, as their protected enclaves are invaded, are not able to
survive female competition, and increasing numbers are drifting
further to the margins of society, where they will place growing
burdens both on public agencies like the police, and on private
households, in that more families will be fatherless or have men as
additional and probably expensive dependants. Liberated women
who move into the jobs vacated by men will find that real wage
levels are collapsing as ever-expanding welfare and policing
demands are made on the state and the ratio of servicing
occupations rises. There would also soon be conflict between those
women who do receive proper wages for their work, like paid social
workers, and those who remain in the moral economy as unpaid
carers, where there is ever more to be done but even fewer non-
working adults both free and suitably motivated to take it on.

In the end, or even sooner, as the process may be well underway,
the welfare side of the state would fall away, leaving well paid work
only in those productive areas which had once been mainly the
domain of men but which by now, very possibly, had been
feminized too. The pursuit of equal rewards is not helping women,

but will divide them and drive many into greater poverty while letting men escape back towards a state of nature.

So an experiment in merging domains is unlikely to continue for much longer. Weakening of the welfare state might lead quite rapidly to a re-invention of the division between private and public work, and probably go hand in hand with restoration of wage differentials and rediscovery of male providers. There would be powerful political incentives to do this as societies which over an extended period do not utilize their male members efficiently will find themselves open to colonization by others less wasteful. Norman Macrae reminds us that the fast-growing oriental economies are thoroughly patriarchal and anti welfare state:

> *To feminist annoyance, most of these marvellously educated young women stay at home in their child-rearing years. With the world's most skilled motherhood, plus stable family fatherhood, the next generation of teenage Japanese (and of imitating South Koreans) pile up all evidence of beating their Western contemporaries hollower yet.* (Macrae, 1993)

He quotes Lee Kuan Yew on the crucial importance in this of personal responsibility for children:

> *The West has then taken the worst possible course by substituting the state for the family. "If you bring a child into the world in the West, the state cares for him. If you bring a child into Asia, that's your personal responsibility."* (Ibid)

Pursuing equal opportunities is an expensive exercise, and it is noteworthy that feminists working in the field of international development are now becoming perplexed at the way that economies of western-oriented client states, in which efforts have been made to give women more of a role in economic processes, are not performing nearly up to the standard of more patriarchal competitors like China, where *"...male bias has been intensified ... even though peasants may have better housing and more consumer goods"* (Elson, 1991, p. 17). The standard of living of women and children in these countries is leaving behind that of third-world sisters in states where feminists have been helping to make the plans. The problem seems to be all those under-employed men hanging around. It is not only the boundaries which collapse when the domains are merged. Time to go back to the drawing board perhaps?

## ABANDONING THE PALACE

More than economic prosperity may be endangered by the mission to abolish sexual divisions of labor. I would be very surprised if a large-scale transfer of women's energy into the marketplace was not also weakening the moral cohesion of the community, by removing their labor from the web of interpersonal servicing which makes up the basic fabric of social life. The palace of orderly social relations requires a solid foundation of commitment to mutual care and responsibility. If enough women decide that participation in this is optional then the whole edifice could start to crumble.

Modern women's preference for paid work is often justified by the argument that, quite apart from considerations of economic necessity, and the personal independence it permits, a job in the market boosts self-respect because it is of higher status than work done domestically or voluntarily; the pay is a measure of social value. The effect of this judgment is to devalue the private realm, which comes to be seen as a waste of time and talent. Many feminists are themselves unhappy about this; and some try to argue that historical forces beyond their control, the inner motors of capitalism, or even currents of ideology springing from the Enlightenment, are really to blame. But their own analyses commonly deny value to the private domain even more ruthlessly than do other peoples,' and must have been a powerful influence in their own right.

It would be a mistake to suppose that sixties feminists were dragged by intellectual fashion against their will into the value systems which have now had the effect of weakening the private realm. This is to yield too easily to the women-as-victims-never-agents mentality. They have chosen this path. Young women in the sixties were keen to get "out there" and create more choice in their lives, and the doctrines of Marxism served this end. There was moreover a two-way trade-off, as I believe that it was in large part the fact that many younger women put shoulders to the great socialist wheel which imbued that system with its popular legitimacy, which was greater in the sixties than it had been hitherto in the West. Feminists have not only, as I proposed earlier, helped the New Left to survive during the last decade, but actually gave it a very significant boost at the outset. It is also their continuing involvement, and use of the movement to help fend off the demands of the traditional female community, which has sustained such a level of confusion within the Left generally, concerning the moral value of the family and whether it is a selfish or collectivist institution.

## Family and reciprocity

From time to time voices on the Left claim affinity with the family, and propose rather sententiously that the values of socialism are based on the family or are even identical with it, only writ larger. This qualification is however significant, because in practice the effective operation of families and socialist institutions or states could hardly be more different, and to suggest that it is all just a matter of different levels at which principles are applied shows that the Left is still resisting the point. Families are unique groupings forged out of enduring, interpersonal relations, and entail observance of mutual rights and obligations. Socialism on the other hand has little use for individual ties and enjoins even-handed loyalty to as large a segment of humanity as is possible, certainly not less than the citizenry of a state in which some of its principles are embodied or can be enacted.

As a result, whatever metaphorical value may be given to families, or to an abstract principle of siblingship, any real bonds between actual kin are quite definitely suspected by the Left of being "selfish." Most left-wing activists still agree with Barrett and McIntosh that *"caring, sharing and loving would be more widespread if the family did not claim them for its own"* (1982, p. 79). Recent opinion polls give evidence of strong public endorsement for the principle of parental responsibility for the support of children (e.g. the NOP findings reported in the *Sunday Times,* 21 November 1993); similarly the British Social Attitudes surveys indicate that (in 1991) ninety per cent of men and ninety-five per cent of women believed that fathers should continue to support their children after divorce (Jowell, 1992). But Labour thinkers still tend to equate the "family" with the interests of children as virtually isolated units or even autonomous citizens and to urge that *"children are not appendages of their parents, but people in their own right"* (Leach & Hewitt, 1993).

Within socialist thought, in its western forms at any rate, parents are trusted most when operating under public scrutiny as agents for the community; and the wider, universalized relations are the ones given priority every time. The essence of the distinction lies in the quality and strength of reciprocity. Networks of family relationships are steeped in the spirit of mutuality whereby, in the last analysis, every individual involved is expected to give as well as take. What makes family the heart of the moral community is that this is not something which can be entered into voluntarily, but which happens by virtue of one's very existence, and which can never really be broken, only disregarded at peril of not being able to call on support when needed.

A child spends the first years of its life receiving care from others so that before it has even come to understand what family and community are all about it has already accumulated a large set of debts. By the time people reach an age when they can fend for themselves they can generally look forward to paying these back for most of the rest of their life - not just to the elders who have cared in the past but, through a process of passing on deficits to the future, to their own children in turn. This cascade of delayed moral credits gives family relationships their eternal, and in a sense often timeless quality, which pulls past and future generations into a moral unity, a corporate spiritual entity, which in all cultures is a powerful focus of religious feeling and fundamental social cohesion. Childrearing, by virtue of the need to organize long-term relations around it, is what makes society possible: or as Virginia Bottomley put it (quoted in the *Guardian,* 9 November 1993) *"without families, individuals are like a frantic whirl of atoms, attached to no one, responsible to nothing, creating a vaporous society, not a solid one."*

I have argued throughout this book that women are much more receptive to the claims emanating from others within their framework of relationships, and more punctilious about repayments. This is because their roles or anticipated roles as mothers mean that they are much more likely than men to need continual support

during adult life. They put more in so that they can take more out
as they know that unless they honor debts and obligations other
people will not be willing to help them, whereas men see less need
and may well never pay back properly the debts incurred in
childhood, or rely on their wives to do it for them. This is part of
the problem of men. Nevertheless most men do pay something back,
even if at a patriarchal discount and, as in the situation of child care
and support, they may compound and confuse it with payments to
women for current personal services. Insofar as they become active
members of the community, the rules apply to them too.

## Attenuated mutuality

All of this is utterly different from relations between citizens in the
public realm. A mass-family just does not operate in the same way,
not at any rate in the class-structured western societies where the
welfare aspects of the state have developed furthest - or, to put it
more pertinently, where the public sector has been taken furthest in
absorbing personal services from the moral economy. For within a
state the idea of reciprocity is highly abstracted, and also becomes
mediated by bureaucracy, so that sentiments of obligation towards
other citizens may be extremely attenuated. Original "insurance
principle" protocols about everyone putting resources into a common
pot from which each can draw in situations of need slide all too
easily into a qualitatively contrary notion of the state as a sovereign
body dispensing benefits to its members, who are passive recipients
rather than participants in an exchange.

Family relations are a far more compelling vehicle for reciprocity.
Debts and obligations between individuals in face-to-face contact are
much harder to walk away from, as all sorts of emotional sanctions
and restrictions can be brought into play. Loyalty to the state cannot
compete with this.

Socialist ideas about the state as a capitalist plaything, which
feminists greatly helped to disseminate and popularize in the sixties
and seventies, have done very much to erode the idea that public
benefits are moral debts, and have weakened the sense of civic
mutuality. If the state is used by stinking rich businessmen to
protect their evil profits, then morally it owes its workers and their
families whatever they can get out of it. So the moral cohesion of
citizens which informed earlier visions becomes transmuted by this

ideology into a solidarity of the claimants' union, standing shoulder
to shoulder to insist on their entitlements from the massively
wealthy puppet masters behind the scenes. The state becomes the
friend of the enemy.

This is the fat, cigar-smoking idea of the patriarchal state that
sixties feminists helped to conjure up as the alternative to individual
male providers. Although they affect to despise it they also love it
because unlike the guy getting under your feet in the kitchen or a
censorious mother it cannot morally demand much in return.
Capitalism has already taken enough during its history, so its
offerings now don't need to be reciprocated. Its gifts are pure.
Whatever can be wheedled out of it is a net gain. Not only is
anything available from the state virtually certain to be greater than
could be afforded by relatives, but it also has the very significant
and liberating virtue of not putting recipients under any personal
obligations.

## The wrong kind of socialism

So the supposed socialist antidote to selfishness actually makes the
condition much worse. It is bad medicine. By aiming to promote a
far higher group interest than family, what the expanding concept of
state provision effectively does is to end up serving and sanctifying
a lower interest, that of the individual, who is now the unit of
entitlement and consumption, unhampered by any tedious
obligations or sense of mutuality which could set a boundary for
both aspiration and disappointment. Feminism is thus heavily
implicated in the creation of what Dennis and Erdos (1992) have
labelled "egotistical socialism," the practice whereby citizens grab
benefits for themselves with no regard for the common good. There
can be little doubt that this phenomenon is a major factor underlying
the present moral crisis in the West.

What is puzzling, perhaps, is that it should be regarded as a
"wrong kind" of socialism, and this betrays survival on the Left of
an astonishing naïveté concerning what the outcomes and
implications of welfarism are generally likely to be. Amongst better
off families living comfortably above the threshold for qualifying for
many state benefits it is certainly possible to treat welfare as a
fallback support system to be called on only when really needed, as
a proper last resort. So civic self-respect and family relations can

both remain more or less intact. But for most other people, and the more insistently and insidiously the lower we go economically, welfarism sooner or later bids to become regarded as the call of *first* resort, and proves destructive of interpersonal relations and commitments which seem less worth maintaining, and is liable to lead claimants into traps of dependency where the state is the only possible source of support. Family networks of reciprocity, the base of the moral economy, have atrophied as the welfare state has bloomed. That is exactly what many feminists wanted. But it is a short-term gain, which is impoverishing the lives of whole sectors of the population, and turning households into hostile aggregations of competing egos.

The establishment of welfarism in the West has been a major factor behind that explosion of selfishness which statist gurus are now at pains to denounce and to blame onto their political opponents. Centralization in the state of responsibility for support of the needy tends over time towards the moral polarization of citizens into two strata. At the top there are saints who ask for little but give much - even though it may be other people's - taxpayers' - resources that they mainly deploy. This is the ethical side of socialism. At the other end there are the dependent, receiving classes, who practice egotistical socialism. Both aspects are inherent in the system, and no one should really be surprised by what has come to pass. If the actual drafters of the welfare state did not anticipate this they are perhaps not guilty themselves of hypocrisy - but most definitely of very shoddy thinking and truly monumental optimism, approaching criminal magnitude, regarding human nature. For the doctrines of libertarian socialism, which feminists eagerly snatched as a means of breaking away from traditional controls and morality, are so obviously perfect as instruments for the concealment of true interests, and for translating unacceptable motives into unimpeachable missions.

### A charter for hypocrisy

It cannot have been an accident that it was during the sixties, when the realities of individual freedom were being grasped for the first time by young women, that a great fog of woolly collectivist ideas was summoned up in the West, which made it much harder for anyone to focus clearly on what was actually happening. Declaring commitment to a higher cause is always a good way of repudiating a lesser. We should listen to Weber and heed the distinction between the purposes which movements formally declare themselves to be pursuing, and the real interests which we suspect that they encourage or license.

Eighties materialism, often blamed for so many of our current woes, is not, as socialist luminaries keep chanting, the antithesis of sixties idealism and collectivism; it is actually their bastard child, still unrecognized by its parents and their tutors, and forced to carry alone the burden of their sins. Even if the spirit of the sixties was innocent of what it would itself beget, there is no excuse now for not seeing that it was itself a highly selfish era, very closely formed by the partisan preferences of young people, who mocked almost without hesitation the values of older people, regardless of their content, just because of who held them, and in order to deny the right of anyone to tell them what they should do.

This sixties libertarianism was the individualism of childhood or innocence and survived well into the seventies still believing narcissistically in its own perfection and marvelling at its remarkable conception. But when its own progeny later emerged, the individualism of greed in the eighties, followed by that of despair in the nineties, it did not want to know, and is still piously washing its hands of them and trying to convince everyone else that really these overtly selfish creatures must have been sired by Tory city yobs.

> *(Disintegration of the fabric of British society) has to do with the breakdown of the reciprocity between individuals, with the diminution of the possibility of evoking any responsibility that we might have for one another. There is only one political and moral force that has been in business over the past 14 years, which has eaten away at the cement of social reciprocity, and that is the Thatcherite project.* (Hall, 1993)

But the Left is surely wrong here, all down the line, and a few *mea culpa*s would not go amiss. It was wrong in the sixties not to see, or take into adequate account, the obviously shallow and tactical nature of the current enthusiasm for community. It has been wrong all the time to fail to see the greater importance of personalized obligations, rather than rights, in maintaining genuine concern for others, and to neglect the crucial role played by personal demands by actual kin on each other in underpinning the civic virtues valued by socialism. It is also wrong now to label the Right as the source of modern individualism, in a pejorative sense, when what it is really doing is to emphasize the personal and family obligations which are such a feature of most non-western societies celebrated by socialists for their sturdy collectivism. The true germinators of corrosive individualism in the West are those welfare systems which, beneath cloaks of sentimental communitarianism, are in practice geared almost entirely to individual *rights*. And a major reason why this deceit has been so successful is that it has coincided with the interests of the women driving towards independence.

Men are always prone to selfishness and are mainly held back from wholly surrendering to it by the ability of women to pull them into longer-term commitments. If women refuse to do this, and instead sanction egotism and give female endorsement to philosophies elevating self above group, then there is little to stop men from going the whole hog. The sixties alliance of feminism with the state is finally beginning to bear unholy fruit in a big way. For what seems to be happening now that women are moving strongly into the public realm is that traditional interpersonal networks for organizing the moral economy, like the family, are being supplanted by depersonalized, abstract processes in the public domain. The phenomenon of political correctness is an aspect of this, as it involves traditional female evaluation of men, but channels its judgments through public institutions, especially the media, backed up by the police, rather than using them to inform and control particular personal ties.

### Public charity and private egotism

This is what is fuelling Dennis and Erdos' egotism, as it removes the personal sanctions capable of enforcing morality discreetly and effectively, and spreads the message that private citizens do not need to uphold values because this is now the responsibility of the state and market, which can provide for all of our needs. In Elliott Currie's "market society," interpersonal exchanges and services have become commodities. Parents do not need to teach their children about right and wrong. That is what schools are now for, and *Sesame Street* and *Blue Peter*. Personal and sexual relationships are now often taught in terms of militant anti-family values (Amiel, 1993), and the hearth is only the moral centre of society if that is where the television happens to stand, and Big Sisters appear on its pulpit with bite-size morsels of life instruction.

As for churches, gone are the days when these were where key personal relationships and responsibilities were sanctified and, in particular, men were inducted into the mysteries of family and community life through identifying with the ultimate authority and principal celebrants. Now they are just becoming another sector of the communications industry, where women may expect to prove just as successful in finding proper salaried jobs as they have been in the media generally, and in the process drive down further the self-respect of women who are merely mothers. Stern moralists like Peregrine Worsthorne consider this a very poor exchange:

> ...*what the Church of England will gain, English motherhood will lose. ... All that the encouragement of women to go out to work has done is to deprive homes of their civilising influence, where it really worked, without in any way improving the quality of life in the professions where their civilising influence has proved a pitiful chimera. ... That ambitious women should find family life less than wholly fulfilling is easy enough to understand... But... we are talking about Christian women, holy women, and that they should want to be full-time priests, rather than full-time mothers, is less easy to understand. Least easy to understand of all is why the Church should encourage them in this anti-social preference.* (Worsthorne, 1992)

This attrition of the moral economy as it is dragged into the public arena and universalized may not have dire consequences immediately, as changes take their time to work through, and there are still many non-feminists around with old-fashioned views. But we are now in the middle of what some sociologists would sneeringly refer to as a moral panic about the family taking shape in British society, with some horrific violence among children in recent months fanning public anxieties about the dissolution of family values.

Western society is still generally a good place to live. So why, it may be asked, all the fuss? Because, surely, the pattern which is emerging is already unsustainable, merely a stage in a greater slide. We are now probably well into borrowed time. The women taking jobs as priests are not themselves daughters of the marketplace, and did not get their religious convictions watching Channel Four - though that is possibly how they discovered their present vocation. Although they have rejected an important part of it, they grew up in and imbibed the values of a much more traditional society, powerfully held together by a strong moral economy - that deeper church built on reciprocity in kind within a largely female community, which understands that what the marketplace is for is to create a halfway station into society for harnessing men's energy and making them more productive, not to provide an escape for women from basic community work.

Not so long ago women spent much of their time in mutually supportive work - often within a framework of long-delayed reciprocity:

> *And so it goes on - the daughter's labours are in a hundred little ways shared with the older women whose days of child-bearing (but not of child-rearing) are over. When the time comes for the mother to need assistance, the daughter reciprocates, as reported elsewhere, by returning the care which she has herself received.* (Young & Willmott, 1957, p. 39)

But women are spending more time in the market and turning their backs on caring for each other. Grandmothers in their fifties have not yet retired and so cannot help their daughters much with childcare, and then when they become infirm they in turn do not receive much support from their daughters, who are still at work themselves (Finch, 1989). Moreover women who are not mothers are increasingly reluctant to help out those who are, so that children come between them much more:

> *So why isn't it possible for all the other mothers to be loving, responsible parents without making life hellish for*

*those whose existence does not revolve around child care?*
(Kogbara & Lowenthal, 1993)

As these changes of life-style pull apart the moral community, women become little better than men. Their sexual solidarity is already showing signs of weakening, with more explicit poaching of partners leading to more overt conflict and violent revenge, as in the cases of Susan Christie, Christine Dryland, and Lady Sarah Graham Moon (Driscoll, 1992). Female aggression generally seems to be on an upsurge, with the number of women carrying out crimes of violence up by 250 percent in the United Kingdom since 1973 (Burrell & Brinkworth, 1993), and films like *Thelma and Louise, Fatal Attraction* and *Dirty Weekend* at once celebrating and helping to set the trend. The fabric of the female community is starting to unravel, as more women are rejecting outmoded wholesome concepts of female modesty and restraint, and preferring to take a chance on their own in the beckoning forest of individual delights, lured by its darkness and secrecy and mysterious cries of wild beasts and the sweet tang of soft mossy banks draped around the pools. The palace meanwhile grows empty and a quiet desolation reigns.

# 9

# LOST IN THE FOREST

## WAKING UP TO THE PROBLEM

There is a pervasive atmosphere in the West at the moment of things falling apart, of modern society rotting into a spiritual wilderness. It is tempting to dismiss this as post-modern gloom or millennial despair, in which we yield collectively to cosmic rhythms outside our understanding and control, or pull out and dust off Orwellian visions of the fate that modern technology has in store for us. The great wheel rolls on ever more relentlessly and careless of the lives it crushes, etc. But I believe that these feelings are less a response to great events and impersonal forces beyond our power, to economics and international relations, than a weakening inside us all of the knowledge of interdependence within community, between individuals, generations and above all between sexes, over which we do in fact retain significant control if we choose to.

More people in modern society are living in that state of moral isolation which has in the past mainly been the province of men; we are all sliding together towards the disorders and insecurities which have always made most men's lives shorter and more brutish than women's. But we can and I think will change direction, and may already be doing so.

This cannot however be a matter of just going back to how we think society was in the past, as the world is constantly evolving and cultures need to adapt with it. Nor am I saying that it is easy to see or agree positive ways forward. There are some deep conflicts of interest involved between men and women, as it is the efforts made in the last thirty years to improve women's lives which have largely shaped the present situation. So there are some tricky dilemmas which have to be faced up to and steered around. Giving men a place in society by making them responsible for women and children is to some extent bound to limit the freedom of women to develop and express themselves. On the other hand promoting

women's independence allows men's fecklessness full rein, which
itself may place additional burdens on the female community, and
feed the creeping alienation which threatens to engulf us all.
Something must give; and this is I think the quest by women for
freedom equal to men's - since it is not on anyway.

## The wrong side of community

In any realistic appraisal the struggle of women for emancipation
needs to be treated as more than just a gender war, and as part of a
wider problem of interpersonal demands, for many of the restrictions
on women's freedom do not just arise out of a petty battle of the
sexes but occur because they are women, bound closely into a
community, and would do whether or not men were powerful in it,
or even present. At a day-to-day level it is other women who are the
sources of most personal pressure; mothers or mothers-in-law who
disapprove of the way that you bring up the kids; neighbors who are
critical of your taste or domestic standards, or who want to dump
their children at your house more often than they look after your
own; women who regard their time and effort as more valuable than
yours. These are aggravations which many women could well do
without, and they are really the dark side of community life, which
inevitably accompanies the benefits which women need to claim for
themselves. Hell is demands by other people.

Child care is a central matter here. I cannot imagine a society
which could operate successfully without what I have called the
original social contract, in which each woman is expected by others
to take primary responsibility for the wellbeing of her own
offspring. In an all-female group the range of possible alternative
arrangements for sharing and exchanging child care might open up
considerably, because most members would have an equal interest
in taking part. But the principles of prime caring would remain the
same; and there is no compelling reason to prevent new forms of
exchange from developing between women even where men are
around. I suspect that it is only the twin misperceptions that a new
species of man is about to hatch, and that until then the state can
provide an escape for women from the demands of the moral
economy, which have prevented more inventiveness and initiatives
along these lines already.

We must start to move on now, and this means giving serious

attention to the view that although patriarchy is the source of many difficulties and injustices for women, the drive to reconstruct men may be taking us back to even worse problems of male marginality and irresponsibility. The alternative which feminists have posed between dominating, patriarchal Old Man and an egalitarian new partner is a spurious one. The real options available are men who have some formal privileges, but may come to care and reciprocate more as they travel life's long journey from body to soul, and those who are not given family obligations and so remain uncommitted and unreliable. I may be wrong here, and it would be good if I am. But I feel increasingly sure that this is the true choice.

## The nature of backlash

Although these considerations are not often aired publicly, I believe that many women already treat them very seriously, and that this is the true nature of the backlash which Susan Faludi has been unearthing. She goes to great lengths (592 pages) to try to show that a backlash is being orchestrated by men to divide and demoralize women. But the feeling I get reading her amassed evidence is that although men may do a certain amount of sounding off, and perhaps, as media magnates, of promoting controversy, the main debates and divisions really do take place among women. It is convenient to throw in a few straw men as a distraction and in order to be able to portray revisionism as collaboration with the enemy. But Faludi is just playing the time-honored game of projecting blame for conflict between women onto men. The viper which intrudes in the holy sanctuary of female unity, and threatens the achievement of feminist goals, is on an errand for men.

This is a smoke screen. I think that there is a complex debate going on among women and including between feminists, involving traditionalist elements who believe that female collective interests require the preservation of a strong moral economy as the foundation of mutual support, and modernist factions who don't, either because they want to avoid female activities (especially child rearing) altogether or for as long as possible, or because they prefer to bring them into an enlarged public realm. During the last twenty years the latter faction has had the upper hand, as it has succeeded in delivering jobs and own-right state benefits into the hands of younger women who wanted them, thereby breaking the hold of older women over them. But as time passes and the damaging effects on the community of female individuation become more evident, coupled with the failure of men to emerge as surrogate women, the traditional ideas will recapture the central position.

Faludi shows that similar backlashes have wiped out earlier waves of feminism, and that they too included women who had been influential in leading the emancipatory movement in the first place. She sees these defections as a succumbing to male pressure rather than genuine doubts. But analytically it is more convincing, when we look at elders of the movement now like Betty Friedan going over to the other side and giving a reasoned explanation, to conclude that the merits of the opposing view may have played a part. I find it hard to imagine Betty Friedan succumbing to pressure male or female. As women grow older their interests and place in the community shift so that they come to take a different and probably broader view of the issues. I will explore this further in the final chapter.

Waves of feminism and backlash against it have followed a cyclical pattern, first one on top and then the other, with several rotations unearthed by Faludi's labors between the mid-nineteenth century and the present day. She insists that there is a gradual overall improvement detectable in women's rights through this period, so that feminism is the stronger force, which will eventually prevail. But her argument is specious. If your baseline for measurement is the Victorian period you would expect to find general improvement since then, as this was a period of high patriarchy in European culture.

What seems much more likely than a gradual progression of female legal personality is that we are dealing with a number of forces, locked homeostatically into long-term balance, within which both short and longer-term oscillations can take place. In all societies women are potentially interested in achieving greater personal freedom, as that is what they can see men always have more of. That is a strong motive. But collectively they also have to be concerned with maintaining the inner strength of community spirit on which vital reciprocity depends; and women in groups will eventually repudiate heresies which damage community by upholding individual rights to a point where major inequities are created between women, while allowing men even greater license.

That controlling reflex is an even stronger force. It may be slow to come into operation, and will tolerate experiments in the name of improving women's condition. But it will step in to damp down women's individualism before everything collapses. The previous backlash against feminism in the thirties took place largely among women (Pugh, 1992): and this will happen again.

## Renegotiating sexual contracts

There are signs that this is already underway, and that the balance of opinion among women is shifting. The stranglehold on progressive legitimacy which right-on sisterhood has exerted in the public realm seems to have loosened in the last year or so, and we are moving nearer to a position where more open and easy discussion can take place between men and women on contentious matters to do with the sexual contract. Provided that the premises for this take account both of the different positions and needs of men and women, and of the centrality of women in the community and their share of historic responsibility for many of the rules and pressures which as individuals they find so irksome, then men will I think gladly and sympathetically help to redraw the boundaries between public and private roles and realms to make them more satisfactory. What hinders cooperation is the presumption that everything now is men's creation and fault, coupled with the demand that the boundaries be dismantled altogether.

There is much to discuss. Conventional definitions relevant up to the sixties are clearly no longer applicable, and this would be true regardless of feminist influences and designs. Technological development has greatly reduced the physical demands of housework, although some of the savings in labor have been offset by trends toward larger living spaces and higher standards of furnishing and cleanliness. Even more crucially, with enhanced control over reproduction in an overcrowded world where childbearing has lost its automatic value, families are generally smaller, and started later in life. This creates many more chances to take on other activities, so that it is now much easier for women to integrate motherhood and a career, but at the same time family life may be rendered more socially isolating and problematic. The consequent need of women for useful occupation outside of domesticity, albeit often on part-time or short-term bases, has interacted with other factors in the job market, like the loss of industrial jobs to foreign competitors, to produce conditions in which feminist demands, seeking particular types of new deal, can seem eminently reasonable.

The altered circumstances and contingencies of women's lives can make it look as if the whole of society must be cast anew, and that gender relations, as Neil Lyndon puts it, have become *tabula rasa*. However, when you stand back to examine the great variations in form which we know about in non-western and historical societies, what I think is more likely to impress is precisely the enduring relevance of broad gender patternings.

## FINDING NEW PATHS

Most societies do offer men alternative routes out of the forest, which do not have to be mediated through the dependence (and submission) of individual women, but are achieved via institutions which allow men to make direct contributions to the life of the community as a whole. These usually take the form of military professions, merging into political roles, and religious or ritual functions. But the limiting factor here is that while these positions can suitably reward the efforts of a few honored saints and heroes, the principles cannot be extended to many in the male population, as in normal circumstances not much labor of this sort is actually needed. When serious fighting breaks out, most of it is done by men conscripted from other walks of life, and who are motivated as family men, rather than as bachelors wedded only to their country's cause. Where a society contains a large standing army, or extensive religious orders, these are often little more than licenses for men to play, and to think that they are being useful when they are not. The cost-benefit ratio is not attractive. A monastery, like a military barracks, may help to keep numbers of single men out of trouble, and possibly instill in them a sense of service to community; but both paths are essentially unproductive and parasitic on the rest of society, and create large numbers of drones.

A century ago about forty per cent of Mongolian men at any time were living as lamas in monasteries; and a modern-style economy clearly would not be viable with this sort of input-level. New Age environmentalists might willingly embrace a spartan or spiritual life-style involving much fellowship, renunciation of materialism and penance for man's (*sic*) rape of the earth, plus a little honest low-tech labor to heal the wounds. But this is science fiction in today's realities. It is not a program which would re-activate and sustain the large populations now reverting to the wild in their dense urban jungles. The only realistic way out which I can see at the moment that is compatible with our industrial economies, in which productivity is critical to both domestic and international stability, lies down some branch of the patriarchal way of co-opting men to society by rewarding them as family providers.

There are obviously dangers for women if the patriarchy idea is taken to an extreme. The Afghan mullahs who issued a fatwa a while ago declaring that girls ought not to receive education because it was the job of men to provide for all the needs of women, were being carried away by the idea. Similarly, practices such as female infanticide and suttee are obscenities which defy comprehension outside of narrow and closed mind-sets. But the fact that the idea can be taken too far does not mean that we can contemplate discarding patriarchal prescriptions altogether. Problems mainly arise for women when male rights, which should be instrumental to the performance of family obligations, come to eclipse those responsibilities. But we must recognize also that even within very extreme cases, like in some contemporary Islamic cultures, women still hold great moral power to draw attention to male duties.

Thus the account not long ago of a child custody tussle undertaken by a Saudi princess (Sasson, 1992) shows very graphically that a real-life prince can be shamed by female outrage into prioritizing his obligations and foregoing his formal rights. At the heart of the patriarchal palace a woman's moral feelings, properly articulated, are sovereign. Presumably less powerful men can be pulled into line no less easily. After all the attacks one reads on fundamentalist Islam by younger women, who inevitably feel the sharp end of constraint in a highly regulated sexual system, I would be fascinated to learn more about how it is generally evaluated by older women who have lived under it long enough to be able to assess any plusses as well. But there may be many obstacles to any truly reliable research in such a sensitive area.

## Reconstructing patriarchy

The vital element in patriarchy is the prescription that a man should feel personal responsibility for the support of a family grouping, normally but not invariably containing a child or children he has fathered. For it is this expectation which, in the absence of other motivations, is most likely to bind him usefully into the community and its future through the knowledge that he has an indispensable part to play in securing that child's well-being and success. It is this prescription and the pressures arising from it which do most to make a man's social position more like that of a woman, to maximize the real give and take between partners, and offer the most likely basis for durable commitment and caring.

The general idea can however be implemented in a great variety of ways, and many of the features of family life presently regarded as intrinsic to patriarchy are not essential and no longer have such an obviously valuable place. One of the more irritating aspects of current attacks on "family" is the assumption that this term has a specific meaning - generally a two up and two down nuclear family structure of cohabiting parents and their children - which its detractors can then triumphantly reveal is neither widely applicable anymore, which is not actually true, nor all that workable in the first place. Thank you, but we knew that. We should *not* define family in terms of particular concrete forms, which are transient, but more generally in terms of personalized obligations and rights, which may be actualized in a large number of ways.

Thus it is perfectly possible to detach the essential notion of male (paternal) responsibility from the practice of conjugality, that is living together in a common household, and from lifelong ties between parents, and even from exclusive sexual partnership rights between them while they are together. I have heard it suggested that the pill has inevitably undermined patriarchy, and challenged men, by making it harder to tie women to the fathers of their children, and that because women themselves are now able to regulate their fertility while having a number of sexual partners, marriage is irrelevant and artificially constraining on them. But this confuses issues by assuming that marriage rights necessarily embrace conjugality and sexual exclusivity, which is certainly not the case if we care to look around the world at patriarchies elsewhere. Family and marriage systems draw on a number of different elements which can be combined together in various ways; and rights and duties in children may even be regulated more strictly when the control of sex itself is left out of the equation.

Anthropologists commonly refer in this context to tribes like the Nuer of the southern Sudan, as among them patriarchal descent is very firmly upheld, and marriage, once fully consummated, is unbreakable. But precisely because it is forever, and a husband knows that legally he is automatically the father of any offspring, women are allowed considerable freedom to change their sexual and conjugal partners. Wherever a child happens to be born, it belongs to the husband's family, unless someone else claims to be the biological father and he agrees to pay the husband compensation to cover the cost of acquiring an alternative child by some other means. By defining key relationships mainly in terms of descent and property rights, personal sexual freedoms are protected.

Different arrangements can be found among other no-less patriarchal groups like the Masai, where it is not uncommon for husbands to be somewhat older than their wives, and for women to have younger lovers, whose children are then accepted by their husbands as their own. Material provisioning and companionship are linked to marriage, and sex is partly linked too but not exclusively as it remains also a matter of personal choice.

Western post-pill society has been slow to explore the variety of possibilities available here, largely I think because it has turned its back on the private realm of interpersonal relations in favor of the Provider State. But the principle of uncoupling or re-arranging different parts of patriarchy is adaptable to our culture, and could help to resolve some of its problems. The growing instability of marriage in the West is often held up as evidence of terminal breakdown of personalized lines of responsibility. But I think that this just betrays our limited vision, which is another consequence of over-eagerness to shift support systems into the public realm. If marriage is irrelevant now, then this is because state benefits have provided an easy, alternative security. Unstable unions may indicate a loss of individual commitment, but only so long as we are prisoners of the assumption that men should only provide for and have an interest in their children while they cohabit with or are married to the children's mother. If we respond instead to increasing rates of separation and divorce by insisting that these events do not justify a loosening of fathers' (as the usual non-custodians) obligations to their children, and encourage a greater variety of relationships between parents, then fewer children than at present would lose touch with their fathers. It has even been proposed (e.g. Ridley, 1993) that modern career women would find other, polygamous forms of conjugality highly compatible with their less home-based life-style.

## The enabler state

We may be starting to move in the general direction of flexibility. The Child Support Agency (CSA) which began to operate in Britain during 1993, even though inspired and moved largely by Treasury calculations of potential revenue, does endorse and strengthen a principle of parental responsibility irrespective of marital status. When this is combined with the latest Children's Act introducing joint parental custody of children regardless of domicile and daily care, we have the basic ingredients for a system which acknowledges that serial monogamy or cohabitation makes it absurd, and cruel to children, to insist on all or nothing commitments and then "clean break" separation agreements. More flexibility is achievable. We are approaching a position in which it may be possible for people to experiment, perhaps via private contract law, with a variety of forms of living arrangements and types of parental relationships, without causing unnecessary harm to children, who suffer mainly because of conflicts and recriminations rather than as a result of particular structures of relations.

The CSA itself does admittedly face a struggle to survive for at least several years because it has been artificially bred by committee and hatched into a very hostile environment where many people appear to be convinced that men are entitled to leave one set of children for the general public to bring up or subsidize while they are free to start a new family. If it is not to create massive resistance to its mission, the agency will have to tread carefully for a while, by not increasing maintenance levels to market rates in one step, by not appearing to concentrate on extracting higher payments from men who do accept some level of responsibility, while allowing an easy escape for others who ignore their obligations altogether, and, as Frank Field has argued (1993) by not squeezing men so hard that they can no longer cope as breadwinners and collapse into welfare themselves. Also, and more fundamentally, it will need to work with flexible criteria which take into account the greatly varying nature of post-divorce relationships; otherwise it will not help couples to collaborate harmoniously in looking after their children. But it is potentially an extremely significant instrument for turning around our dependence on the provider state, and replacing this with an enabling role for the state as protector of interpersonal rights in the private domain.

It would of course have been better if this role had been initiated before starting to dismantle the benefit structure of the welfare state, as this would not have made it all look like purely cost-cutting expediency, and would have reduced the support-gap which will now make many people's lives worse during the nineties, and feed opposition to the new regime. But late is better than never. Transformation of parenting, and the related shift in state policy away from substituting fathers towards ensuring at least a minimum performance by them, has all been made possible by developments in technology over the last decade or so. The old Christian trinity of chastity, monogamy and legitimacy had firm practical roots in the need to identify fathers unambiguously, so as to hold men to their responsibilities as providers. The figure of the cuckold, foolishly working himself into an early grave to bring up children he had played no part in creating, was a symbolic threat to male enterprise, and needed to be exorcised continually by reassuring images of fidelity, and by ceremonies in which oaths in the sight of God and kin bound parents morally to each other for better or worse.

But there are surely better ways to enforce responsibility now. Following developments in genetic fingerprinting, the issue of paternity can be settled with great precision whenever it may be necessary. All that we perhaps lack in this area may be adequate legal powers to get presumed fathers to undergo tests. When this testing is coupled with emerging procedures for personal identity discs, or smartcards, and computerized tracking, and electronic deduction of maintenance from salary payments, it is clear that the whole business of enforcing financial obligations to children is going through a rapid revolution which makes the cast-iron marital bonds of traditional family life, revealed by feminists as irksome for women, and which men put up with because they believed women wanted them, finally dispensable.

Procedures and techniques which alarmists have seen as heralding the dawn of terminally authoritarian state machines are more likely, in practice, to help build a state which, by increasing the probability that individual contracts and commitments will be fulfilled, while providing some last-ditch back-ups for when these fail, will permit a flowering of personal freedom and genuine responsibility. Today's main cuckold, the taxpayer supporting children of men who can't or won't contribute to this themselves, does not have to suffer much longer.

This part of my argument assumes of course that modern women do in fact want the freedom from male sexual possession which many of their complaints focus upon. But I may be wrong here. Perhaps the majority don't. Or perhaps the main point of attacking monogamy and calling for personal freedom is a matter of tactical posturing within a traditional manoeuvre of pre-emptive reciprocation. That is, women may be asserting that they have allowed men to control them so that they can then go on to propose that if men want to continue possessing them they will have to start giving more of themselves in return.

But if women are being guided by this sort of strategic consideration, then I suspect that it will not get the response they seek, as on the issue of sexual possession most men feel no less, and probably much more, trapped than women do. Men would say that it is they who are "giving" most in a relationship which requests mutual fidelity. This is partly women's own fault, as I have argued elsewhere (1994), for generally choosing to represent sex as less important to themselves. In many relationships the gift of sex by women is, after the early passion fades, soon cancelled out by the taking of male fidelity. Some feminists would bring in the idea of double standards here, and say that men don't practice fidelity anyway and so cannot ask for anything in return. But an institutionalized double standard is something which plays little part in the lives of most men, certainly in European culture, and I don't think that calling up that concept resolves much, or squares any circles.

This area is all very contentious and requires much more space than I can give to it here. But I do believe and must emphasize as crucially important that the assessment of sexual contracts and their performance has to be carried out with sensitivity to the asymmetry of men's and women's needs and interests. It is essential to get away from mechanistic formulae whereby men are seen as in debt to women simply because they don't pull their weight in household chores. It is much more complicated than this - which is why committed feminist researchers, as noted in the opening chapter, often find themselves unable to communicate with the women they are interviewing.

I think that men will not be available to take part unless these sorts of issues are now open to discussion. But one of the problems for them at the moment is that it is not at all clear exactly what feminists are seeking, nor indeed how much of womankind they represent. It may well be that most women are still prepared to carry a double load of domestic work, in return for male fidelity. If a backlash is forming, who can now speak with authority for women? Another problem, no less perplexing, is whom exactly women should be addressing themselves.

# CARRYING ON TOGETHER

## Summoning up voices

The time is ripe for a thoroughgoing reappraisal of sexual contracts in the West; but it may prove hard to get a genuine discussion started. The main problem, naturally, lies with men, who may not be capable, when it comes to it, of organizing themselves to speak with a common voice. Many feminists have said that it would be good to have a men's movement with which to engage; not necessarily anything very coherent, but at least clustering around a core of ideas and feelings to set against the broad thrust of feminism. However, it hasn't happened and may never do so. Not only does male opinion remain inchoate and amorphous, but a lot of men do not feel that they have much to say on this issue - and for deep-rooted reasons.

The basic reason is to do with the content of male sentiments. Most women are not only closely interested in gender issues, but also feel clearly entitled to speak on them. Sometimes they may hold back in public for fear of showing cracks in female solidarity. But they know what they think, and can justify their positions

morally. Men on the other hand appear much less likely to express
serious views on the subject. They do have personal interests and
opinions, but these are often kept private because they are conscious
of their amoral or even anti-social character, which renders them
useless as a basis either for practical suggestions, or for action
alongside other men.

There is also a strategic side to this. The frog side of men means
that they may remain competitors, especially in relation to women,
long after appearing to become part of the moral community. This
feeds male reticence and emotional "holding back." It is not, as so
often assumed, that men stay dumb just because they lack practice
in expressing themselves. It is commonly the other way round. As
competitors they know that expressing themselves is to give away
important personal information. They learn as members of the moral
community to control that competitiveness, but at the same time
they are aware that the predominantly selfish feelings which they
continue to harbor will not make them any friends. So they keep
them buttoned up: and when men do publicly voice opinions on
family and sexual matters, these are not always deeply felt but are
frequently part of a performance of roles they have taken on within
the patriarchal family system, which define acceptable interests for
which they can fight.

The various masculinist movements which have emerged
alongside and more recently in reaction to feminism, mainly in the
United States, have not produced useful proposals for developing
sexual contracts. Robert Bly's message is all about getting back out
into the wild. He is the pied piper of eternal male childhood, and his
meetings throw up rough sentiments which female observers find
negative, to the point of being offensive. Susan Faludi attended one
of his groups in 1988 and emerged with a bruised spirit:

> When another woman in the crowd points out the
> contradiction, he gets mad. He picks up the microphone and
> marches over to the troublemaker, a frail elderly woman
> clutching a flowered tote bag. He sticks his face in hers and
> yells into the microphone, "It's women like you who are
> turning men into yoghurt eaters." Embarrassed, the woman
> tries to appease the fuming poet; in a quavery voice, she asks
> if he has "any suggestions" about how she can improve her

*relationship with her emotionally distant husband. "Why don't you stop making demands and leave him alone," Bly shouts. "Just leave him alone." (1992, pp. 345-6)*

Other groups are more concerned with fighting for specific interests as patriarchal fathers, mainly on child custody matters, or resisting female encroachments on male privileges. Such groups are usually conscious that the tide of moral feelings in society is running against them, and speak in voices of bitterness or sullen grudge, compared with the tones of conviction and righteousness used by women. I cannot conceive of this ever becoming a popular men's movement.

Those men who do speak with conviction are the ones who are not saying things that they have worked out for themselves, but are uttering time-honored shibboleths, that is traditional family values which they take on as part of their patriarchal vestment, or notions that have been freshly planted in their minds by women, as I suspect with breast-beating articles in the *Guardian* confessing tearfully that men should cry more or compete less. These are the happy certainties of parrots, and this reflects the way that men understand that their legitimate family positions and interests are located in what is properly women's domain. In family values they defer to women, who are the real church leaders. Men can be left to do the detail, as grey politicians and managers, or to police other men on the gamekeeper principle. But formulating and approving the underlying objectives is women's work.

## Figureheads and ventriloquists

The success of male statesmen acting or speaking up in the public arena on behalf of the family hangs on the messages and responses given to them by women. Stalin is widely regarded as the architect of the Soviet new family policies of the thirties which re-introduced advantages for married couples and re-imposed penalties for divorce and illegitimacy. But these reforms implemented changes which the vast majority of women had been urging for years, as the follies of earlier Bolshevik dismantling of family obligations had unfolded (Geiger, 1968). The force of Stalin's will fell on other men, rather than on women, whose instrument he became to some degree in this matter; and he was probably quarrying into this deep source of legitimacy more than acting from great moral convictions.

Whereas the women expected to benefit both personally and collectively by gender from the reforms, and believed in their validity, Stalin's own interests were more indirect and individual, and linked to his quest for political authority.

There were payoffs in this for both parties. Stalin's grasping for political responsibility and advantage in turn helped the women to maintain their own purity as dutiful citizens. The measures were not popular with men, and to have a man identifying himself with them so explicitly was convenient for women as well as the fact that it imbued the laws with greater exemplary weight. So much so that these laws have since become incorporated within timeless Russian patriarchy, and most younger Russians are unaware that a decade of license occurred in the twenties during which men became increasingly irresponsible and unmanageable and left everything to women, and that it was women who led the call for the reinstatement of patriarchal marriage.

It is tempting here to wander off further into a discussion of how neatly the theater of patriarchy traps men by linking their public status and power over each other with the role of proclaiming and upholding sexually repressive rules, which they would look foolish, not to mention hypocritical, to then break themselves. No own goals here; but an old tradition of superbly accurate female passing I think. I will resist this and move on to the corollary, which is that men themselves may have much less capacity to influence the determination and evaluation of family values in the public arena than we conventionally assume.

In the West during most of the last fifteen to twenty years the values informing this approval have been overwhelmingly feminist, and this is why the gender policies of a very mixed bag of administrations in the United Kingdom have changed very little. A broad consensus has been achieved among prominent women on a cross-party basis, which male politicians and even Margaret Thatcher, the pro-family Conservative who was rubbished by most feminists as an honorary man, have proved unable to challenge. When Teresa Gorman sits down with Clare Short, male members can have no doubt that they are in the presence of an irresistible force. Even David Willetts, spiritual progenitor of the CSA, and pope of gamekeepers, has manfully toed the line when it comes to equal opportunities (1993), although surely against his better judgment about what actually makes men tick.

But during the last year the grip of femocrats has started to slip. Public anxieties about the deteriorating behavior of children and royalty, and the ballooning costs of welfare dependency in a very persistent recession, have prompted a groundswell of pro-family murmerings, revealing elements of anti-feminism which had formerly remained below the surface. This has misled men into thinking that it is safe now to come out and say something. Convinced by the mood of the 1993 Tory conference in Blackpool that the public now wanted them to assert some moral leadership, the prime minister has been doing just that. But are men able to determine what that morality should be? That is the basics problem.

## Basics mistakes

> *The last temptation is the greatest treason:*
> *To do the right deed for the wrong reason.*

(T.S. Eliot, *Murder in the Cathedral*)

As I write, John Major's administration is riding low in the water through the trough of its deepest unpopularity yet, and a sizeable factor in this is held to be the *Back to Basics* crusade which was launched not that long ago to a rapturous party conference. What went wrong?

Two main answers suggest themselves. Firstly it was, in the nature of things, a dangerous venture for male politicians to undertake. Secondly, it was a desperately risky moment to do it. To look at the general hazard first, it is a corollary of the mouthpiece role which men have in relation to interpersonal morality, above all over rules of sexual behavior, that they are always liable to the charge of hypocrisy. Family values are much more often broken by men. It is this fact which underscores the strategic importance of having men, particularly in a priestly role, pronouncing them, and even more so appearing to be their source. The exemplary value is tremendous, and keeps up the pressure on men by significantly blurring public perception of how much harder it is for men to succeed in being moral. But the chances of self-contradiction and perceived insincerity become very great, especially when the priests have gone soft and the buck is passed, as it were, to men of affairs.

The moral summit is heavily mined against men.

None of this is a secret, however, and our lads bravely attempting to re-capture this territory from libertarian carpetbaggers obviously allowed for this and still thought that their mission was reasonably safe. I suspect that their chief mistake was failing to see just how tricky a period we are going through. Many people are in the process of changing their minds about gender and family affairs - or perhaps are clarifying them for the first time. So everything is up in the air; and it is tempting to believe that this means that things are made easier because whatever you say, you are bound to find lots of people who agree with you. For women this may be the case. But for men it actually multiplies the dangers, since there is a whole spectrum of moral positions in orbit at the moment, any combination of which can be used to triangulate a sighting of hypocrisy. It is an open season on men.

This is especially true for public figures, against whom people are likely to bear a galaxy of personal and political grudges, waiting for their moment. So Tim Yeo for example, one of the latest casualties, was a no-hoper the moment that his illegitimate child was unearthed. Not that he seems to have realized this; and his conscience seems to have been moderately clear to start with as he felt that his behavior was within the range of what is currently acceptable, because taking personal responsibility is the most basic and sacred principle of all. Although he will have been aware that many Tory ladies across the country are still partial to a tipple of total fidelity, there were (and still are) articles every day in papers and magazines telling him how everything has changed and affairs are OK and that only dinosaurs believe that we can go right back to compulsory lifelong monogamy. He may not have realized, however, that this freedom is regarded by many as positive only when seized by women, presumably on an anti-imperialist analogy whereby women, as the underdogs, can use their sexuality to free themselves or even bring down the overlords, whereas men should not do anything which might harm women.

*While men with mistresses are condemned as a seedy, greedy lot, married women who act similarly are cast as heroines for being courageous enough to throw off the mantle of wifely martyrdom and make the pleasure principle their guiding impulse.* (Neustatter, 1993a)

So when he was thrust into front-page attention Mr. Yeo probably did believe, because he had always accepted his child and taken financial responsibility for it, that he was in the clear at least. Not exactly in the running for model new-breed Tory father-hero of the year; but no great ogre either.

Yet in the event he was heavily mauled on all quarters. Feminist and traditional women sank their differences and laid into him with equal gusto, catching him in a pincer. His constituency chairman, Patricia Fitzpatrick, and a neighboring mayor, Aldine Horrigan, focused on his betrayal of wife and marriage vows. Suzanne Moore argued that although Yeo's declared moral criterion of acknowledging paternity and providing support was clearly satisfied, this did not in her view constitute an adequate principle, and therefore he was objectively a hypocrite (1994a). Maureen Freely went even further and appeared to suggest that the whole of the cabinet were hypocritical in not bringing equal opportunities into their moral scheme.

*If you're going to look after children in sickness and health, you have to look after your own health, too. If you need two paychecks to keep a roof over their heads, you need schools and other institutions to see the two-paycheck family as normal. If you're going to make sure children outside wedlock get the best possible care, you set up a system that supports and rewards the parents who take their responsibilities seriously. Most important, you need to treat all parents as equals.* (1994)

What seems to be implicit in all this is that a moral principle enunciated by men is not equal with one formulated by women, and has to be treated with suspicion. I imagine that this is linked to the idea that men are less reliable root sources of family values, since they would be more inclined to propose things that suited them individually rather than being geared to a wider pattern of needs which would involve some real self-sacrifice. I happen to agree. I think that most men would. But it would help if this was spelled out instead of being decanted into the concept of hypocrisy, which has a more limited meaning for most purposes.

It is obvious that men stand in the wrong place to make suitable moral noises about sexual relations; this is not a terrain where they can expect any dominion. One false move and they soon end up running around clumsily, toothlessly, tripping over each other in the arc-light of hostile public scrutiny, and generally looking foolish. Not a dinosaur's place after all, more aardvark park, and the scene of numerous silly mistakes and nasty accidents.

The crucial error was by Major in setting out on this expedition so confidently, especially under a flag bearing the word "back," albeit for purposes of alliterative conference delivery, when dealing with issues where considerable adjustment to *new* circumstances is both needed, and has already been set in motion through institutions such as the CSA. Down to basics would have served as a better lens for focusing on what was currently essential, and have avoided the interpretation that they were hoping to turn the clock back to a pristine purity.

But those who load criticism onto the PM are making mistakes too I think. They should appreciate that men speaking out on family values, in the absence of unambiguous guidance from women, should not, unless they are priests, be seen as presenting themselves as models of good behavior, but simply as putting themselves forward as believers in those values whether or not they manage to live up to them in their own lives. This is not hypocrisy, but a type of sacrifice to principle, which should be respected and encouraged as a male tribute to what is right even though it doesn't come easily to them.

The whole basics thing, this season's pantomime, with politicians dressing up as bishops, has been a good illustration of how men should avoid blasting off about values which they know fit them ill. If they had pretended that proper conduct of one's personal life was easy, or that they were paragons, they would indeed be flirting with hypocrisy. But they are not. They are just trying to fill the vacuum created by the abdication of bishops and the stalemate among women. What they are doing is a brave and noble gesture. Carry On Caring, John; but do remember, in these uncertain times, to give women a more visible role in signalling the directions.

## Leading from behind

The farce of basics shows that men cannot safely take initiatives in this area; but this outcome could be positive and valuable if it now encourages women to do so themselves. In a situation of moral change and confusion, it is even more difficult than usual for men to get anything right, but by the same token it is harder for women to do anything wrong. If they prefer to operate mainly within the private domain and lead from behind in traditional female manner by gently priming men on what to think and then pushing a little and above all supporting them when they do it, then that is all in the right spirit of backlash and part and parcel of healthy historical homeostasis. Also, it is in keeping with the importance of restoring female solidarity and moral unity, which are necessary in the longer run both to give clear and simple messages to men, and to maintain the sense of equity essential for the smooth operation of the moral economy.

The politics of this solidarity are immensely complex. Although women have been very divided since the sixties, the feminist faction rather quickly reached a position of being the ones holding the mantle of unity towards men. They became the ascendant and dominant voice partly because of the close alliance with the burgeoning welfare state and services sector, which gave many women good jobs, and led to collaboration with libertarian career women on the right. The women central to this alliance have been manifestly successful for themselves, and have delivered the goods for many others besides. So their strategy inevitably carries a lot of weight, and women who don't really agree have kept quiet because they are afraid of being seen as spoilers, unable to cope with opportunity themselves, or as friends of the enemy.

Another consideration in favor of this faction has been that as they have penetrated the public realm they have carried the moral invincibility of women into it, and have consequently been able to combine both moral and secular powers into a new feminist theocracy. Political clout plus spiritual force makes you utterly correct. This is a foretaste, and perhaps also a reminder, of matriarchy in action; a lesson in having it all.

However, the appearance of female solidarity which has been created in this way is not deep-rooted. There are many easy riders. The successes of statism are mostly superficial, as it is not difficult for women to be independent in the short term if there are state resources to tap into, and if men are glad to escape from their provider obligations, which is always likely to be the case. But what may not be so easy to sustain is a society in which men have been deprived of powerful personal incentives to show any initiative or enterprise, and have little sense of their worth. As feminization of society piles ever more burdens onto the female community, and creeping alienation threatens to engulf all of us, non-activist women will start to take more seriously what is being done in their names by the femocrat elite. Backlash kicks in as they wake up to the problems being stored up and start to ask themselves whether equal opportunities enthusiasts really have thought through what they are doing.

The fear of division is being used by Faludi to stave off re-unification on non-feminist terms, and to forestall criticism from the ranks. But I doubt whether this tactic can work for long. The majority of women I meet seem to feel that the best way to get more out of men is by emphasizing individual male responsibilities. The ideas of the Left about public motivation coming from direct commitment to "community" are on the retreat everywhere. Statist feminism is the last of its great empires and will surely not survive much more of the recession which it may have helped to prolong, even if it did not create. As welfarism fades, and the bubbles of over-heated aspiration dry out and start to burst, New Men among them, a reincarnation of the male breadwinner becomes visible on the horizon. A cycle of schism and re-union, deeper than usual because of welfarism, is nearing completion.

## Rediscovering interdependence

The time has come for those women who see that feminism is taking them down the wrong road, to help rebuild communities around the sexual division of labor, and to replace the disastrous Marxist idea of solidarity as arising out of similarity with a Durkheimian recognition of the importance of difference and interdependence. There is no need for such women to feel that they have failed personally if they do come out against gender equality. For the reason that feminism is wrong is not that women "can't do it." We know that women can do it all, and do it very well. That is what rubs. Feminism fails because it removes from men the vital presumption that what they do is needed, and so turns them from tolerably useful helpers into the troublesome brutes who are such thorns in Germaine's flesh.

The case against feminism is male frailty, fecklessness and capacity for sheer obstructiveness, and, as a consequence of this, that men need not equal but additional rewards in the public realm, to compensate for their inevitably secondary place in the private domain, and as an incentive to submit to community discipline and to throw themselves into reciprocity. This is not because they are different to women, just that their situation is. If women were not the ones who had children, to pick up my opening theme again, *they* would be the ones to want, as Rosalind Miles would put it, a little extra something. It is the notion of men as protectors and above all providers which gives them the fillip they need, and in ways that make them useful; and they require it more than ever now. This has nothing to do with Anna Coote's long-term, impersonal, unbuckable trends. There aren't any. Quite simply a mistake was made which can be corrected.

Things started to go wrong in the late sixties as women reacted to the male stampede from responsibility by throwing in their lot with the already expanding welfare state, and defining public support as their future safeguard. For the implication of this, which has taken a long time to work through, is that all men are let off the hook, and the network of rights and obligations tying them into the community is unravelling. Women are now in a better position to see that what they should have done then, and can resolve to do tomorrow instead, is to tighten the screw on individual men in ways which are relevant to the post-pill society.

And so, after a therapeutic and certainly instructive carnival of misrule, in which roles were swapped and stirred around, stereotypes thrown away, and fools revered as sages, it is time to clear out all those messy frogs and for the queen, who does not appear in the old story because she wrote it and made the rules, to command the refurbishment of the palace.

# 10

# RESTORING THE PALACE

*So far no break in the family pattern has been prolonged enough to eradicate men's memories of how valuable it was.* (Mead, 1949, p. 149)

*End the benefit system, and the old reality will resurface, and with it the traditional family.* (Murray, 1993)

## CLEARING OUT HERESIES

### Now we are Queen

Support for feminist ideas may continue to spread for a while among ordinary people, but with opinion-leaders it is I think already starting to crumble as two sources of division between women take on further significance. The first of these is age. No wave of feminism seems to have lasted for much more than a generation, and this is almost certainly connected with aspects of women's life cycle, and to competition or conflict between generations.

To begin with, stage of life is a major determinant of attitudes towards moral values, with younger women far more attracted than older to feminist ideas, and with older women much more oriented towards the family (*International Social Attitudes*, 1993). This is a matter where the Labour Party, true to form, is tragically misreading the entrails of the 1992 election. Recent analysis of the voting figures has revealed a very strong link between women's age and their propensity to vote Labour. Among 18 to 24 year-olds Labour enjoyed a 13-point lead, in the 25 to 34 age group the two main parties were even, and in older groups the Conservatives had an increasing advantage, from a 9-point lead among 35-44 year olds to 15 points for women over 65 (*The Guardian*, 29 December, 1993). Labour strategists have apparently concluded from this dropping off in support by age that the party is turning women away by not doing enough for them - and that its commitment to equal opportunities and women's quotas must be reaffirmed and strengthened. They could hardly be further from the truth, which is surely that all this is precisely what older women are voting Conservative to escape from. It is uncanny how consistent the party is in reaching for the wrong medicine.

Labour seems to have enormous difficulty in recognizing the simple truth that women's lives and attitudes change as they get older, and in particular as they become mothers and grandmothers. Very recent testimony to this process has been offered in Judy Rumbold's monthly column in the *Weekend Guardian*, which is currently tracing her rejection of inner-city life-style and nostalgia for family and even some stirring of desire for reception back into the traditional female church.

> *(Sometimes) I find myself aching for the civil neighbourliness of my childhood. In a complete betrayal of the conviction I held when I was younger and childless that the rich socio-cultural mix offered by London was second to none and should be embraced by everyone, I would happily surrender any last remaining shred of street credibility in exchange for a fix of suburbia, a semi-rural high...* (Rumbold, 1994a)

> *It was inevitable that when I left home, the backlash against this furious church activity would be sweet, fulsome and enduring ... Until one act of debauchery ensured that life would never be the same again. There was, I soon discovered, nothing like a dawn-rising baby to bring to your attention the fact that Sunday is no longer a hedonistic blur,... but an interminable, gaping space crying out to be filled. ... Now I have reached that sad stage in life when I am contemplating the purchase of my first Delia Smith cookery book and I almost miss the ceaseless do-gooding that plagued the Sundays of my youth. Sometimes I even think I can feel a christening coming on. Otherwise, how else do you fill the time? Furthermore, if there are any lonely old aunts out there who are up for a visit and a spot of sponge cake, I'm your woman.* (1994b)

Changes in life stage and circumstances are constantly prompting individual defections from feminism, but this seepage has not weakened the overall movement because new recruits are always replacing them, just as leadership of the movement passes on to younger women - certainly on the American scene.

But the pattern of regeneration and renewal is unlikely to continue for much longer. As more sixties girls become grannies their perspectives will change fundamentally. This is partly because marketplace feminism thrives on young faces and this alienates older women, but it is more that as they become senior members of family groups this is where their dominant interests will be seen to lie. Backsliding often takes place among feminists as sons grow up, or perhaps fail to, and they are confronted as mothers more forcefully with their role as guardians of morality and motivation. The scene now is being set for a truly massive shift to granny power, as the "me" generation, accustomed to having its own way, cottons on to the traditional power exercised by matriarchs and decides to go for it. Younger women are unlikely to be able to deploy feminist arguments against this authority because their elders will have been through it all themselves and know the ideological limitations and will be able to argue it down. Also, and crucially, the welfare state will be decreasingly able to offer alternative supports. Extended families are poised to re-inherit a central place.

It is in any case unlikely that a generation of women brought up by feminist mothers will feel strongly drawn to the doctrine, as they will have had a good chance to see through its own little deceits and humbug. The most devout feminists I know myself are not honest with their children. Those living with men uphold a pretense of New Manhood and equal partnership in the face of manifest failure by their own partners to live up to the hype, explaining away their behavior on the grounds that they have very pressured jobs and so on. This they do consciously for their children's sake as they believe that only a generation carefully reared in feminist ideals will have the opportunity to escape properly from patriarchal culture themselves. But their children are not fooled by this sham for a moment. They are witnesses to idealistic mothers propping up unreconstructed men, just as seventies feminists can recall their own mothers sacrificing themselves to protect traditional ideas about happy families. The children are just as likely to reject it all.

Equally, those brought up by a single mother can see what hard work it is and will be attracted towards some other way.

So there is little which I can see managing to prevent a considerable shift back towards the sort of family power base which older women have not ceased to exercise in Catholic parts of Europe. This may not be able to rein in female individualism at a stroke; but it is capable of capping its excesses:

> *The genie of personal fulfilment won't go back in the bottle, but its volatility can be contained. In continental European countries with a Catholic tradition, terrifying grandmothers succeed in binding extended families together with a mixture of guilt and fear, even though there may be divorce or homosexuality or illegitimacy among the younger generations. There is continuity, even if it's the continuity of tyranny.* (Stock, 1993)

## De-falsifying consciousness

The second dimension of dividing interests is class. Feminist assault on the public realm is geared to the aspirations of women who have high status careers available to them, and for whom paid work promises to be personally more rewarding than labor in the moral economy. This is not true to anything like the same extent for unqualified working class women, who may well find child care more satisfying than factory jobs, and it is at this level of society that the doctrines of equal opportunity have wrought their most pernicious influence, depriving men of incentives to play provider roles, and women of traditional families to manage, without any compensation of wider horizons (Melanie Phillips, 1993b).

Feminism and the state policies it has informed have not acknowledged much distinction between the needs of different classes, mainly because the moral strength of women depends very much on shows of solidarity and unity, so that the force of feminist ideas has required an assumption that all women do have the same need or desire to penetrate the public realm. But they do not, and suggesting they do has been largely self-serving to feminists by bolstering the progressive legitimacy of their movement at the expense of fulfillment of working-class family destinies. George Gilder foresaw most of it:

*This prospect (of public child-care) is no triumph for women, for it releases males from the civilising constraints of female sexuality. But it is a victory for feminists, particularly the upper-class women pursuing careers. For them it means government ratification of their liberated life styles. They can imagine that their "interesting," "meaningful" careers are not what they are - special advantages of wealth and position - but "options" available to women throughout the society. While enjoying the privileges of affluence, the feminists can even fantasize they are leading an egalitarian social revolution! In effect, universal day care seems to remove from the feminists the moral burden of privilege. It exempts them from the need to see their profound dependence on capitalist prosperity. While they enjoy a uniquely advantageous position in the world economy and society, they can proclaim their identity with the oppressed.* (1973, p. 164)

The lesson to draw from this is that women who prefer to give priority to their families should not feel guilty (as Faludi wants, and as Coward, 1992, confirms many *do*) that they are letting down their sisters. Similarly women who are successful in career terms should not feel that they are being selfish unless they fight at the same time for working-class women's right to easy divorce and lonely middle age. They *should* however feel decidedly guilty at cloaking their own ambitions in a language which disrupts the lives of less well-off women.

Over the next year or two as older careerists repatriate into the moral economy in greater numbers, whether because of satiation, disappointment and frustration, or because the role of family matriarch beckons and the perceived value of that realm rises, they are quite likely to bring back with them the legitimacy to define the true focus of women's solidarity, so that this once again hovers around the family in traditional terms, rather than major long-term direct involvement in the public realm. Younger working women will inevitably feel their moral independence draining away somewhat. When this happens the sixties generation will truly have had it all for themselves - youthful rebellion, adult autonomy and excitement, and finally the restoration of generation authority and respect in time for them to end their days in comfort and dignity in the palace. The cycle of homeostasis will be completed and the family will be reinstated as the centre of social life. A fitting start to the new millennium.

## Farewell to New Men

But much needs to be done to facilitate this and to set in motion the revival of male usefulness. Little can be achieved in this area without fundamental changes in state policies and procedures which, because they have come to be geared so much to women's perceived needs, are unlikely to yield without a good deal of visible female pressure. Nor should they for obvious reasons be turned round in certain areas without some period of transition, lest people whose lives are now highly determined by them are suddenly ditched.

Firstly it is essential to explore ways of restructuring welfare benefits so that these are less in conflict with family self-reliance and, in the context of this, with the obligations of individual men as fathers. Movement in this sort of direction has begun in the United Kingdom with proposed redefinitions of homelessness paying less regard to family overcrowding and more to actually being on the streets, and in the redrawing of rules which had allowed single mothers priority in being allocated housing independently from their parents. But too often these issues are presented in terms of immediate financial savings, and this will nurture resistance to change.

Secondly there must be much stronger and more confident rejection of policies tackling poverty through welfarism and movement towards programs for creating jobs for men who can then resume breadwinner roles and a proper place in the family and community. A lot of state money has been spent during recession propping up the worst hit. But this money is circulating wrongly. Women and children first is the principle of group survival in times of dire emergency. But if it becomes institutionalized as a routine precept, the emergency conditions are likely to become prolonged and aggravated. Too much state support goes via benefits into weakening families further, rather than laying the foundations for enterprise and initiative, which traditionally have been recession's silver lining. When the long winter ends there may be only a very muted spring to follow unless more is done now to feed the buds of job creation. This means watering the roots of male motivation and incentive.

Ultimately it all hangs on giving men good reasons to take work seriously, and that almost certainly means reaffirming the male breadwinner role and enforcing related paternal obligations, and turning these again into acceptable goals which are not just seen as coded phrases implying female subordination. So it may be necessary to tackle a good deal of suspicion and resistance among women. Some of this opposition will be just plain silly, like the suggestion made by Jenni Murray of *Woman's Hour* that defining men as the main family earner turned women into legal prostitutes (Amiel, 1992). This was surely intended to provoke. Prostitution is all about one-off payments and absence of commitment, and to be fair to prostitutes as well as wives and partners that is precisely its value for many men. Long-term partnerships are quite different, and revolve not only around sex, which may not be central in some relationships, but a whole range of shared interests and activities.

Defining a man's chief input in financial terms does not reduce in any way the overall value to him of his partner. What it does on the contrary is to express the value invested by a man in the objectives being served, which is in turn the source of its meaning and satisfaction to him in helping to promote them. Women prefer men who are involved and responsive, it is claimed, but in practice men tend to acquire these attributes through being material providers as it is this which gives them the chance to give and choose where to give and feel useful and become committed. What most women are looking for really is the old Mensch. Wash your mouth out, Jenni.

## Equity not equality

Other resistance hovers around the symbolic importance to women of the idea of equal opportunities; and here the objection is not silly, but nevertheless is an obstacle to forging a workable sexual contract, as this is, I think, the source of men's existential panic and feelings of impotence and irrelevance. But it might be easier to deal with than we imagine, since there is a lot of space between the concepts of "sole" and "main" breadwinner which would repay investigation.

The key here is the word equal, indicating the removal of all male privileges and protection. If the emphasis on equality were less strict, or it were replaced by an idea of sexual equity which recognized the continuing importance of zones of priority, so that men's work still figured as a crucial contribution, I think that there would be no problem with allowing women much more scope in the market than they have enjoyed in the past. The prospect of full equality is however a serious demotivator of men, and does not I believe even correspond to what most women want. By its nature it is not likely to be objectively achieved to the satisfaction of its advocates until much of the male workforce has effectively lost heart and run away. So the sooner it can be replaced by a more ambiguous and less challenging goal, the better for us all.

Women do in any case need to remind each other that the private domain will decay unless enough of their energy is given to it, and they re-invest it again as the palace at the centre of civilized life. This realm is much more than homemaking and domestic drudgery, as it includes numerous moral trustee roles in the local community and society as a whole, which men know that they can never perform equally because of their greater distance from the sources of community values and reciprocity. A significant part of this trustee role consists in helping to transform a man or men into responsible providers, and this is surely the root of traditional hostility to voluntarily single mothers, which feminists affect to find so incomprehensible.

There seems to be no imperative to go "back" to old ideas about compulsive monogamy and captive homemakers. In those societies where most families are now having few children there is room for a lot of flexibility, provided that enough positions of main breadwinning, as a basis of fathering, are available for most men who need it. If women genuinely want it, we can surely together envisage a range of co-existent alternative models. For example, there seems no compelling reason why a woman who wants children by different men should not, as among the Nuer, create several fractional male providers instead of one; and men for their part can collect fractions. If this helps to finish off the concept of men as heads of household, then so be it. The age of vaudeville is long gone and in contemporary circumstances it would be more appropriate to portray sexual partnerships as entailing equal levels of responsibility in different realms. Within this broad division of labor it would seem reasonable that where women are particularly devoted to their careers they should be seen as justified in throwing themselves mainly into the public realm and perhaps hiring other people to do most of their private domain work for them, or even, arguably, combining with kindred spirits to run female joint-households in which domestic chores are shared between full equals. Charles Murray (1993) can envisage a wide range of options:

> *This doesn't mean that a mother must marry. If a single woman making £50,000 a year wants to have a baby and continue her career while paying for professional child care, that's her business. If a less affluent woman knows she can count on support from her parents, fine. If the local feminist support group is willing to provide her with a stipend to raise the child, fine. I am not recommending that the state forbid single women from choosing to have babies. It should simply stop subsidising that choice.*

That menu could be extended considerably as perhaps by, in the spirit of workfare, the idea that the state might offer some support by organizing grouped or shared accommodation for single mothers, so enabling them to pool some child care and make themselves more available for other work in the public realm.

Any resulting shortfall of father-provider roles is not likely to be very great so long as the bottom line governing all of these options is that women should look first to interpersonal relations rather than to generalized patriarchs-as-taxpayers for their lines of material support, and are willing to go along with a presumption that men have slightly greater moral entitlement to paid jobs than they do, and to a higher rate of remuneration as a "family wage." Women are not going to be locked up in kitchens. However, what they should not expect is equal rights in the market.

## BRINGING HOME THE BREADWINNER

I do not believe that most women want fully equal rights with men in the public realm. They want to take part in the world outside of domesticity; but they also want men to go on playing the breadwinner role which they recognize as the male route to finding family and community commitment. But many have been afraid to come out with this in case feminists attack them for weakness and sororal betrayal. There is a great gulf between activists and the bulk of women who just want some modest and practical improvements in their lives, and most of the renegades mocked or vilified by Faludi were offering variations on this point. It was, for example, the main theme of Sylvia Ann Hewlett's book *Lesser Lives,* which Faludi savages for presenting "merely anecdotal" evidence that ordinary women were not seeking full economic equality.

But Faludi's own case that equal opportunity militants reveal the true soul of women is itself only tenuously supported by the complex evidence which she parades. During her final rallying call to the troops to go out and claim their birthright, she suggests that by vigorously challenging the conventional definition of masculinity, women can allow men (thanks, Sue) to start questioning it, too.

> *After all, to a great extent so many men have clung to sole-provider status as their proof of manhood because so many women have expected it of them. (In the Yankelovich poll, it's not just men who have consistently identified the breadwinner role as the leading masculine trait; it has also consistently been women's first choice.)* (1992, p. 495)

What she seems to be letting out here, perhaps unwittingly, is that women do want and "expect" men to be providers; and the exhortation to challenge conventional definitions is actually aimed by her towards women. Thus, after 494 pages (in a main text of 498) of thundering variations on the theme that men are conspiring to force women back into the kitchen, the placards finally slip to reveal that after a full generation of feminist propaganda most women don't actually want to compete with men at work after all - certainly not once they have children. Moreover the wording in this poll refers to "sole-providing," which is more strongly exclusive of women than the main providing which most men would settle for. What more evidence could any of us ask for?

Most women, if allowed to speak freely, would agree that a sexual contract reconstructed around the idea of men as the main family providers is the best overall model available as it seems to generate the greatest sum total of inputs to community life. It does not allow most women as much freedom from interpersonal obligations as men enjoy, but this sort of symmetry of destiny is not feasible. If women go for freedom, men just take even more for themselves. The best way to get their help is to give them the status and position which will prompt them to relinquish more of their natural freedom. Broadly speaking a woman's life combines security and independence most effectively within the framework of a conjugal system in which men's membership of and standing within a community hang on their performance as dutiful partners and fathers. That is what she has had in mind throughout history when drawing up sexual contracts.

Some sacrifices by women are entailed in this. But reciprocity always requires that, and if women don't sacrifice themselves a bit then they will not be able to ask men to do the same. The nature of society is such that chains of sacrifice originate with, and are initiated by women. This is what makes society possible. While it may arise out of biological roles, it is in itself a moral and spiritual phenomenon, and cannot be reduced to them. It is not, in the jargon, an essentialist proposition. (And even if it is, then so be it.)

Over-emphasis on female independence, and rejection of sacrifice, has spawned a frog culture in which the sexes are polarizing, and men are becoming increasingly marginal as they revert to a wild state. Their objective social inferiority is potentially much greater than any secondary public status assigned to women under patriarchy, and lacks the compensation of a countervailing domain to sustain them. Is that really what women want? Not many, I think. Women want men to be responsible people like themselves. But few will be if women deny them reasonable opportunity to acquire what most people need in order to become civilized beings, and that is personal dependants - other people for whom to be responsible.

On that basis men are capable of becoming much better partners than may seem possible just at present. This is how women throughout history have transformed them into useful members of communities. I suspect that it will be by making refinements within this general system, not by any radical abandonment of sexual divisions of labor altogether, that women will carry forward the process of social evolution.

# BIBLIOGRAPHY

**Almog** Orna (1993) "Women at war" in *The LSE magazine,* August.

**Ambrose** Debbie (1990) "Freddie's enforced protocol" in *Today,* 13 November.

**Amiel** Barbara (1992) "Flat-earth woman broadcasts her woes" in *The Sunday Times,* 14 June.

———— (1993) "Sex lessons hijacked by the PC mob" in *The Sunday Times,* 31 October.

**Anderson** Digby (1991) *The unmentionable face of poverty.* London, Social Affairs Unit.

———— (1993) *The loss of virtue.* London, Social Affairs Unit.

**Anderson** Harriet (1993) *Utopian feminism.* New Haven, Yale University Press.

**Ardener** Shirley (ed.) (1993) *Defining females: the nature of women in society.* Oxford, Berg.

**Banks** Olive (1981) *Faces of feminism.* Oxford, Blackwell

**Barker** Pat (1986) *The man who wasn't there.* London, Virago.

**Barrett** Michele (1980) *Women's oppression today.* London, Verso

———— & Mary McIntosh (1982) *The anti-social family.* London, Verso/New Left Books.

**Bates** Stephen (1992) "Girls gaining on boys in GCSE maths" in *The Guardian,* 25 November.

**Bergman** Barbara R (1986) *The economic emergence of women.* New York, Basic Books.

**Bernard** Jessie (1973) *The future of marriage.* London, Souvenir Press.

**Bettelheim** Bruno (1976) *The uses of enchantment.* London, Thames & Hudson.

**Billington** Rachel (1994) *The great umbilical: mothers, daughters, mothers.* London, Hutchinson.

**Bly** Robert (1991) *Iron John.* Element Books.

**Bokun** Branko (1990) *Stress addiction.* London, Vita Books.

**Boseley** Sarah (1992) "Battle of the sexes" in *The Guardian,* 29 July.

**Bottingheimer** Ruth B (1984) *Grimm's bad girls and bold boys.* London, Yale University Press.

**Boyd** Brian (1992) *Vladimir Nabokov: The American years.* New York, Vintage.

**Bradley** Harriet (1989) *Men's work, women's work.* Cambridge, Polity.

**Bragg** Melvyn (1990) *A time to dance.* London, Hodder & Stoughton.

**Brandon** Ruth (1990) *The new women and the old men.* London, Secker.

**Brannen** Julia & Gail Wilson (eds.) (1987) *Give and take in families.* London, Allen & Unwin.

———— & Peter Moss (1990) *Managing mothers; dual-earner households after maternity leave.* London, Unwin Hyman.

**Bryan** Beverley *et al.* (1982) *The heart of the race.* London, Virago.

**Bunting** Madeleine (1993a) "The lost generation" in *The Guardian,* 7 September.

———— (1993b) "The new war on women" in *The Guardian,* 13 October.

**Burghes** Louie (1993) *Lone parenthood and family disruption.* London, Family Policy Studies Centre.

**Burrell** Ian & Lisa Brinkworth (1993) "Female gangs fight for drug trade" in *The Sunday Times,* 19 December.

**Campbell** Bea (1993) *Goliath; Britain's dangerous places.* London, Methuen.

**Cashmore** Ellis (1985) *Having to: the world of one-parent families.* London, Counterpoint.

**Chadwick** Whitney & Isabelle de Courtevron (eds.) (1993) *Significant others.* London, Thames and Hudson.

**Chevillard** Nicole & Sebastian Leconte (1986) "The dawn of lineage societies: the origin of women's oppression" (in Coontz & Henderson 1986).

**Chodorow** Nancy (1978) *The reproduction of mothering.* Berkeley, University of California Press.

**Clark** David (1991) (ed.) *Marriage, domestic life and social change.* London, Routledge.

**Clarke** Edith (1957) *My mother who fathered me.* London, Allen & Unwin.

**Clatterbaugh** Kenneth (1990) *Contemporary perspectives on masculinity.* Westview Press.

**Clay** John (1991) *Men at midlife.* London, Sidgwick & Jackson.

**Cline** Sally & Dale Spender (1987) *Reflecting men at twice their natural size.* London, Andre Deutsch.

**Coontz** Stephanie & Peta Henderson (eds) (1986) *Women's work, men's property.* London, Versa.

**Coote** Anna *et al.* (1990) *The family way.* London, IPPR.

**Cornwell** Jocelyn (1984) *Hard-earned lives.* London, Tavistock.

**Coward** Rosalind (1983) *Patriarchal precedents.* London, RKP.

———— (1990) "Second nature" in *The Guardian,* 6 September.

———— (1992) *Our treacherous hearts.* London, Faber.

**Crisp** Quentin (1990) (Interview by Jim Shelley) in *The Guardian,* 21 December.

**Dahlborn-Hall** Barbro & Berit Hord (1993) "Boys back on top" in *The Guardian Europe,* 15 April.

**Daly** Mary (1979) *Gyn/Ecology.* London, The women's press.

**Davidoff** Leonore & Catherine Hall (1986) *Family fortunes.* London, Hutchinson.

**Davis** K (1991) *The gender of power.* London, Sage.

**de Courcy** Anne (1992) *Circe.* London, Sinclair-Stevenson.

**Decter** Midge (1972) *The new chastity.* New York, Coward, McCann.

**"Della Torre** Count Paolo Filo" (1993) "Just one cornuto" in *The Sunday Times,* 30 May.

**Dench** Geoff (1986) *Minorities in the open society.* London, Routledge.

———— (1992) *From extended family to state dependency.* Middlesex University, Centre for Community Studies.

———— (1993) "Young black males" in *Daily Mail,* 23rd July.

———— (1994) *Reviewing sexual contracts.* Middlesex University, Centre for Community Studies.

**Dennis** Norman & George Erdos (1992) *Families without fatherhood.* London, Institute of Economic Affairs.

———— (1993) *Rising crime and the dismembered family.* London, Institute of Economic Affairs.

**Donnison** David (1988) "Secrets of success" in *New Society,* 29 January.

**Douglas** Mary (1966) *Purity and danger.* London, RKP.

**Driscoll** Margarette (1992) "All for love?" in *The Sunday Times,* 7 June.

**Dunn** Jane (1990) *A very close conspiracy.* London, Cape.

**Edwards** Susan (1986) *Women on trial.* Manchester, University Press.

**Ehrenreich** Barbara (1983) *The hearts of men.* London, Pluto.

———, Elizabeth Hess & Gloria Jacobs (1987) *Re-making love.* London, Fontana.

**Eichenbaum** Luise & Susie Orbach (1988) *Understanding women* London, Pelican.

**Eisenstein** Zillah R (1986) *The radical future of liberal feminism.* Boston, Northeastern University Press.

**Eisler** Riane (1988) *The chalice and the blade.* San Francisco, Harper.

**Ellis** John M (1984) *One fairy story too many.* London, University of Chicago Press.

**Elshtain** Jean (1981) *Private woman, public man.* Oxford, Robertson.

**Elson** Diane (1991) *Male bias in the development process.* Manchester, University Press.

**Engel** Stephanie (1980) "Femininity as tragedy" in *Socialist Review,* 53.

**Epstein** Cynthia Fuchs (1988) *Deceptive distinctions.* New York, Russell Sage.

**Evans** Mary (ed.) (1982) *The woman question.* London, Fontana.

——— (1992) "Family of fear" in *The Higher,* 5 June.

**Faludi** Susan (1992) *Backlash.* London, Chatto and Windus.

**Farrell** Warren (1994) *The myth of male power.* London, Fourth Estate.

**Feinstein** Elaine (1993) *Lawrence's women.* London, Harper-Collins.

**Field** Frank (1993) "Fairness for two-family fathers," in *The Guardian,* 27 October.

**Finch** Janet (1989) *Family obligations and social change.* Cambridge, Polity Press.

**Finney** Canon John (1992) *Finding faith together.* London, Bible Society.

**Firestone** Shulamith (1970) *The dialectic of sex.* London, Jonathan Cape.

**Fisher** Helen (1993) *Anatomy of love.* Simon & Schuster.

**Fletcher** David (1993) "Are lone parents on their own?" in *Search 15,* March.

**Formaini** Heather (1990) *Man, the darker continent.* London, Heinemann.

**Franzerz** Suzanne *et al.* (1989) *Staking a claim: feminism, bureaucracy and the state.* Oxford, Polity.

**Freely** Maureen (1994) "In hock to family values" in *The Guardian,* 6 January.

**French** Marilyn (1992) *The war against women.* London, Hamish Hamilton.

**French** Sean (ed.) (1993) *Fatherhood.* London, Virago.

**Freud** Sigmund (1950) *Totem and taboo.* London, Routledge & Kegan Paul.

**Friedan** Betty (1963) *The feminine mystique.* London, Gollancz.

―――― (1982) *The second stage.* London, Michael Joseph.

**Furlong** Monica (1991) "Female martyrs of the modern church" in *The Guardian,* 26th March.

**Geiger** Homer Kent (1968) *The family in Soviet Russia.* Cambridge (Mass.), Harvard University Press.

**Gilder** George (1973) *Sexual suicide.* New York, Quadrangle.

―――― (1981) *Wealth and poverty.* New York, Basic books.

**Gill** A A (1994) "Upwardly nubile" in *Sunday Times,* 27th February.

**Gilligan** Carol (1982) *In a different voice.* Cambridge (Mass.), Harvard University Press.

**Gilmore** David (1990) *Manhood in the making.* London, Yale University Press.

**Gittins** Diana (1985) *The family in question.* London, Macmillan.

**Glendinning** Victoria (1992) *Trollope.* London, Hutchinson.

**Gonzalez** Nancy (1984) "Rethinking the consanguineal household and matrifocality" in *Ethnology,* 23.

**Gordon** Nick (1993) "No man about the house" in *The Sunday Times,* 15 August.

**Grant** Linda (1993) *Sexing the millennium.* London, Harper-Collins.

**Greenstein** Ben (1993) *The fragile male.* London, Boxtree.

**Greer** Germaine (1989) *Daddy, we hardly knew you.* London, Hamish Hamilton.

——— (1992) "Two fingers to the bully" in *The Guardian,* 23 September.

——— (1993) "The hard facts of motherhood" in *The Sunday Times,* 8 August.

——— (1994) "A man lacking family values old and new" in *The Guardian,* 10 January.

**Guiley** Rosemary Ellen (1992) "Witchcraft as goddess worship" (In Carolyne Larrington [ed.] *The Feminist Companion to Mythology,* London, Pandora).

**Gunew** Sneja (ed) (1991) *A reader in feminist knowledge.* London, Routledge.

**Hacker** Andrew (1991) *Two nations.* New York, Basic Books.

**Hafner** Julian (1993) "The end of marriage" in *The Times,* 15 April.

**Hall** Stuart (1993) "Basic instinct off target" in *The Guardian,* 24 November.

**Harman** Harriet (1993a) *The century gap.* London, Vermilion.

——— (1993b) "Women surge past men to cross the century gap in *The Guardian,* 4 June.

**Haskey** J. (1992) "Patterns of marriage, divorce and cohabitation in different countries of Europe" in *Population Trends,* 69.

——— (1993) "Trends in numbers of one-parent families in Great Britain" in *Population Trends,* 71.

**Haskins** Susan (1992) *Mary Magdalene.* London, Harper-Collins.

**Hearn** Jeff (1992) *Men in the public eye.* London, Routledge.

**Heller** Zoe (1992) "Don't look back" in *The Independent on Sunday,* 22 March.

**Henriques** Fernando (1953) *Family and colour in Jamaica.* London, Eyre & Spottiswoode.

**Hewitt** Patricia (1993a) *About time: the revolution in work and family life.* London, Rivers Oram.

——— (1993b) "A flexible society that would let us work, rest and play" in *The Guardian,* 16 April.

——— (1993c) "Re-inventing families" *Mishcon Lecture,* University of London, 10 May.

**Hewlett** Sylvia Ann (1987) *A lesser life; the myth of women's liberation.* London, Michael Joseph.

**Higgins** Patricia (1985) "Women in the Islamic Republic of Iran" *Signs,* 10(3).

**Highfield** Roger & Paul Carter (1993) *The private lives of Albert Einstein.* London, Faber & Faber.

**Hubbs** Joanna (1989) *Mother Russia.* Indiana University Press.

**Hughes** Robert (1993) *Culture of complaint.* Oxford, University Press.

**Hughes** Thomas (1989) *On the manliness of Christ.* London, Deutsch.

**Hunter** Flora (1992) "1 in 2 women wants to be the breadwinner" in *The Evening Standard,* 24 March.

**Hymas** Charles (1992) "Girls outshine boys in school exams" in *The Sunday Times,* 8 November.

———— (1993) "Women fall behind in degrees of excellence" in *The Sunday Times,* 23 May.

**International Reports on Women & Society** (1986) *Daughters of the nightmare: Caribbean Women.* London, Change.

**James** Oliver (1993) "Family circles" *The Sunday Times,* 13 June.

**Jenson** J., Hagen E., & Reddy C. (1988) *Feminisation of the labour force.* Cambridge, Polity.

**Jowell** Roger *et al.* (1992) *British social attitudes: the ninth report.* Aldershot, Dartmouth Publishing Co.

**Jukes** Adam (1993) *Why men hate women.* London, Free Association Books.

**Kahn** Tim (1993) "What price more time with the children?" in *The Independent,* 20 October.

**Karlsen** Carol (1988) *The devil in the shape of a woman.* New York, Norton.

**Keegan** Suzanne (1991) *The bride of the wind: the life of Alma Mahler.* London, Secker.

**Kerr** Madeleine (1960) *The people of Ship Street.* London, RKP.

**King** Ursula (1989) *Women and spirituality.* London, Macmillan.

**Kirkup** Gill & Laurie Smith (1992) *Inventing women; science technology and gender.* Oxford, Polity.

**Knight** Chris (1991) *Blood relations.* New Haven, Yale University Press.

**Kogbara** Donu & Betty Lowenthal (1993) "Blame it on baby" in *The Guardian,* 16 October.

**Kraemer** Sebastian (1991) "The origins of fatherhood" in *Family Process,* December.

**Krauthammer** Charles (1993) "The molestation of normality" in *New Republic,* November.

**Langdon** Julia (1993) "Cause and effective" in *The Guardian,* 6 January.

**Lasch** Christopher (1977) *Haven in a heartless world.* New York, Basic Books.

**Leach** Penelope & Patricia Hewitt (1993) "Unhappy families" in *The Guardian,* 13 December.

**Leacock** Eleanor (1981) *Myths of male dominance.* New York, Monthly Review Press.

**Lee** Carol (1991) "How we hurt our sons" in *The Sunday Times,* 20 October.

**Lefkowitz** Mary (1986) *Women in Greek myth.* London, Duckworth.

**Lennon** Peter (1993) "The perils of snow business" in *The Guardian,* 30 August.

**Lerner** Gerda (1986) *The creation of patriarchy.* Oxford, University Press.

**Levin** Michael (1987) *Feminism and freedom.* New Brunswick, NJ, Transaction Publishers.

**Liebowitz** Lila (1986) "In the beginning" (in Coontz & Henderson, 1986).

**Llewellyn** Dai (1992) "In praise of younger women" in *The Evening Standard,* 30 September.

**Lurie** Alison (1990) *Don't tell the grown-ups.* London, Bloomsbury.

**Lyndon** Neil (1990) "Bad-mouthing: Why the way women talk about men is hurting all of us" in *The Sunday Times,* 9 December.

———— (1992) *No more sex war.* London, Sinclair-Stevenson.

**Macrae** Norman (1993) "Oriental puritans call the wild West's bluff" in *The Sunday Times,* 7 November.

**Magee** Bryan (1989) "Women's rights and wrongs" in *Weekend Guardian,* 11 November.

**Malinowski** Bronislaw (1929) *Sex and repression in savage society.* London, RKP.

**Mamet** David (1989) *Some freaks.* London, Faber and Faber.

**Margolis** Jonathan (1993) "Family at war" in *The Sunday Times,* 7 November.

**Marsland** David (1993) "Let's replace self-pity with self-reliance" *The Sunday Times,* 31 October.

**McRobbie** Angela (1990) "Single file" in *The Guardian,* 27 December.

**Mead** Margaret (1949) *Male and female.* New York, William Morrow.

**Miles** Rosalind (1986) *The women's history of the world.* London, Michael Joseph.

**Mill** John Stuart (1972) "The subjection of women" (reprinted in Miriam Schneir, 1972).

**Mooney** Bel (1993) "The year that sex began for me" in *The Sunday Times,* 21 March.

**Moore** Henrietta (1988) *Feminism and anthropology.* Cambridge, Polity.

**Moore** Suzanne (1993a) "Not a single issue" in *The Guardian,* 16 July.

―――― (1993b) "Looking for the reel thing" in *The Guardian,* 24 September.

―――― (1994a) "Private lives, public lies" in *The Guardian,* 7 January.

―――― (1994b) "No longer a man's man's man's world" in *The Guardian,* 18 February.

**Morgan** David (1985) *The family, politics and social theory.* London, RKP.

**Morris** Lynn (1991) *Workings of the household.* Cambridge, Polity.

**Morton** Andrew (1992) *Diana, her true story.* Michael O'Mara Books.

**Mount** Ferdinand (1982) *The subversive family.* London, Cape.

**Muir** Kate (1992) *Arms and the woman.* London, Sinclair-Stevenson.

**Mulcahy** Geoff (1992) Quoted by Tony Maguire in "Women see last barriers to the best jobs tumble" in *The Evening Standard,* 17 November.

**Mumford** K. (1989) *Women working.* London, Allen & Unwin.

**Murray** Charles (1984) *Losing ground.* New York, Basic Books.

―――― (1991) *The emerging British underclass.* London, Institute of Economic Affairs.

———— (1993) "Keep it in the family" in *The Sunday Times,* 14 November.

**National Children's Bureau** (1993) *Life at thirty-three: the fifth follow-up of the National Child Development Study.* London, NCB.

**Neustatter** Angela (1993a) "The husband, and father, his wife and her lover" in *The Guardian,* 5 April.

———— (1993b) "Boys will be misogynists" in *The Independent,* 7 July.

**Oakley** Ann (1981) *Subject women.* Oxford, Martin Robertson.

———— (1987) "The woman's place" in *New Society,* 6 March.

**Olivier** Christiane (1989) *Jocasta's children.* London, Routledge.

**OPCS** (1992) *General Household Survey.* London, HMSO.

**Opie** Iona & Peter (1982) *The classic fairy tales.* London, Oxford. University Press.

**Orbach** Susie (1989) *Fat is a feminist issue.* London, Arrow.

———— (1993) "The power of the feminine" in *Weekend Guardian,* 21 August.

**Ortner** Sherry (1974) "Is female to male as nature is to culture?" (in Michelle Rosaldo & Louise Lamphere [eds.] *Women, culture and society.* Stanford University Press).

———— & Harriet Whitehead (1981) *Sexual meanings.* Cambridge, University Press.

**Orwell** George (1949) *Down and out in Paris and London.* London, Secker & Warburg.

**Paglia** Camille (1992) *Sexual personae.* London, Penguin.

———— (1993) "A real woman" in *The Sunday Times,* 18 April.

**Pahl** Ray (1984) *Divisions of labour.* Oxford, Blackwell.

**Parkinson** Cecil (1992) (Interviewed by Victor Lewis-Smith, in *The Evening Standard,* 28 September).

**Pateman** Carole (1988) *The sexual contract.* Cambridge, Polity.

———— (1989) *The disorder of women.* Cambridge, Polity.

**Peace** Helen (1993) *The pretended family: a study of the division of labour in lesbian families.* Leicester University, Dept. of Sociology.

**Phillips** Angela (1993a) *The trouble with boys.* London, Pandora.

———— (1993b) "A male disorder" in *The Guardian,* 25 November.

**Phillips** Melanie (1993a) "A lesson in the value of relatives" in *The Sunday Times,* 3 April.

———— (1993b) "The lost generation" in *The Observer,* 17 October.

**Phillips** Mike (1993) "Another type of family value that is faring well" in *The Guardian,* 18 December.

**Pryce** Ken (1986) *Endless pressure.* Bristol, Classical Press.

**Pugh** Martin (1992) *Women and the women's movement in Britain, 1914-59.* London, Macmillan.

**Raine** Kathleen (1993) (Interviewed by Naim Attallah for *The Oldie,* March).

**Ramazanoglu** Caroline (1989) *Feminism and the contradictions of oppression.* London, Routledge.

**Ranke-Heinemann** Uta (1990) *Eunuchs for heaven: the Catholic Church and sexuality.* London, Andre Deutsch.

**Richards** Janet Radcliffe (1980) *The sceptical feminist.* London, RKP.

**Ridley** Matt (1992) *The red queen.* New York, Viking.

**Robb** James H. (1954) *Working class anti-Semite.* London, Tavistock.

**Roberts** Elizabeth (1984) *A woman's place.* Oxford, Blackwell.

**Roberts** John (1994) "Why fathers must fight back" in *The Guardian,* 11 January.

**Roberts** Margaret (1984) *Living in a man made world.* London, Routledge.

**Roiphe** Katie (1993) *The morning after: sex, fear and feminism.* London, Hamish Hamilton.

**Rossi** Alice (1977) "The biological basis of parenting" in *Daedalus,* 106.

**Rousseau** Jean-Jacques (1911) *Emile.* (Tr. G.D.H. Cole) London, Dent.

**Rowbotham** Sheila (1973) *Women's consciousness, man's world.* Harmondsworth, Penguin.

**Rumbold** Judy (1991) "Goodbye to all that" in *The Guardian,* 13 March.

———— (1994a) "Back to the grass roots" in *Weekend Guardian,* 15 January.

———— (1994b) "Talking 'bout regeneration" in *Weekend Guardian,* 19 February.

**Ryan** Sean (1993) "Death or glory beckons for polar trekkers" in *The Sunday Times,* 7 February.

**Sanday** Peggy Reeves (1981) *Female power and male dominance.* Cambridge, University Press.

**Sasson** Jean (1992) *Princess.* London, Doubleday.

**Saunders** Kate (1989) "New manacles, or what the Rhett Butler saw" in *The Sunday Times,* 1 October.

**Sayer** Janet (1991) *Mothering Psychoanalysis.* London, Hamish Hamilton.

**Schwendinger** J. & H. (1971) "Sociology's founding fathers; sexist to a man" *Journal of Marriage and the Family,* 33.

**SCPR** (1993) *International Social Attitudes.* Aldershot, Dartmouth Publishing Co.

**Segal** Lynne (1990) *Slow motion: changing masculinities, changing men.* London, Virago.

**Seidler** Victor (1991) *Recreating sexual politics.* London, Routledge.

**Sevenhuijsen** Selma (1986) "Fatherhood and the political theory of rights" in *International Journal of Sociology of Law,* 14.

**Seyle** Hans (1978) *Psychology today.* American Psychological Association.

**Shorter** Edward (1982) *A history of women's bodies.* London, Allen Lane.

**Showalter** Elaine (1991) *Sexual anarchy.* London, Bloomsbury.

**Showstack-Sassoon** Anne (ed.) (1987) *Women and the state.* London, Hutchinson.

**Siann** Gerda & Helen Wilkinson (1995) *Gender, feminism and the future.* London, Demos.

**Simpson** John (1990) "Veiled equality" in *Weekend Guardian,* 7 July.

**Skynner** Robin & John Cleese (1983) *Families and how to survive them.* London, Methuen.

——— (1991) "Tarzan and Jane's pain" in *Weekend Guardian,* 1 June.

**Smart** Carol & Selma Sevenhuijsen (1990) *Child custory and the politics of gender.* London, Routledge.

**Smith** Raymond (1956) *The Negro family in British Guiana.* London, RKP.

——— (1973) "The matrifocal family" (in Jack Goody [ed.] *The character of kinship.* Cambridge, University Press).

—— (1988) *Kinship and class in the West Indies*. Cambridge, University Press.

**Spong** John (1992) *Born of a woman*. London, Harper Collins.

**Stassinopoulos** Arianna (1973) *The female woman*. London, Davis-Poynter.

**Stevens** Evelyn (1973) "The prospects for a women's liberation movement in Latin America" in *Journal of Marriage and the Family*, May.

**Stock** Francine (1993) "The family way" in *The Guardian*, 28 October.

**Swain** Jon (1990) "Women GIs shoulder arms in equality's last war zone" in *The Sunday Times*, 30 September.

**Sweet** Corinne (1991) "Dad's the word" in *The Guardian*, 13 November.

**Tannen** Deborah (1991) *You just don't understand*. London, Virago.

**Thomas** David (1993) *Not Guilty*. London, Weidenfeld & Nicolson.

**Thwaite** Anthony (ed.) (1992) *Selected letters of Philip Larkin*. London, Faber.

**Tisdall** Simon (1990) "Military moms put on a brave face" in *The Guardian*, 31 August.

**Toynbee** Arnold & Daisaku Ikeda (1989) *Choose life*. Oxford, University Press.

**Toynbee** Polly (1989) "The worm-turned symdrome" in *The Observer*, 17 October.

—— (1993) "Is feminism a dead duck?" in *The Evening Standard*, 2 November.

**Tressell** Robert (1955) *The ragged-trousered philanthropist*. London, Lawrence & Wishart.

**Turner** Kay (1993) *I dream of Madonna*. London, Thames & Hudson.

**Tweedie** Jill (1990) "Enough! I've had a change of heart over men" in *The Guardian*, 16 April.

—— (1993) *Eating children*. London, Viking.

**Updike** John (1964) *Rabbit, run*. London, Penguin.

**Usborne** Richard (1991) *After hours with P.G.Wodehouse*. London, Hutchinson.

**Vidal** John (1993) "And the eco-feminists shall inherit the earth" in *The Guardian*, 9 August.

**Vulliamy** Ed (1989) "Wagner and the Ring of life" in *Weekend Guardian,* 23 September.

**Walby** Sylvia (1990) *Theorizing patriarchy.* Oxford, Blackwell.

**Watts** Susan (1993) "Trial haunted by images of life in the twilight zone" in *The Independent,* 20 March.

**Weldon** Fay (1993) "Shame about Jane" in *The Evening Standard,* 30 September.

**West** Jackie (1993) "Dominant and minority families; ideals, values and realities in transition" (Paper at conference: *The family, minorities and social change in Europe*; Bristol University, December).

**Wheelock** Jane (1991) *Husbands at home.* London, Routledge.

**Willard** William (1938) *The family; a dynamic interpretation.* New York.

**Willetts** David (1993) *The family.* London, W.H. Smith.

**Wilson** W.J. (1987) *The truly disadvantaged.* Chicago, University. Press.

**Wolf** Naomi (1993) *Fire with fire.* London, Chatto.

**Wootton** Barbara (1967) *In a world I never made.* London, Allen & Unwin.

**Worsthorne** Peregrine (1992) "The Church's gain is our loss" in *The Sunday Telegraph,* 15 November.

**Young** Michael (1952) "Distribution of income within the family" *British Journal of Sociology,* 111.4.

——— & Peter Willmott (1957) *Family and kinship in East London.* London, Routledge & Kegan Paul.

**Young** Toby (1993) "The old devil" in *The Sunday Times,* 12 September.

**Zaretski** Eli (1988) "The place of the family in the origin of the welfare state" (In David Held, *States and societies.* Cambridge, Polity).

**Zipes** Jack (1986) *The Brothers Grimm.* London, Routledge.

# INDEX

319641